Mentoring
Matters

Building strong Christian leaders

Avoiding burnout

Reaching the finishing line

Rick Lewis

MONARCH
BOOKS

Oxford, UK & Grand Rapids, Michigan

First published in the UK in 2009 by Monarch Books
(a publishing imprint of Lion Hudson plc),
Wilkinson House, Jordan Hill Road, Oxford OX2 8DR.
Tel: +44 (0)1865 302750 Fax: +44 (0)1865 302757
Email: monarch@lionhudson.com
www.lionhudson.com

ISBN: 978-1-85424-897-8 (UK)
ISBN: 978-0-8254-6301-3 (USA)

Distributed by:
UK: Marston Book Services Ltd, PO Box 269, Abingdon, Oxon OX14 4YN;
USA: Kregel Publications, PO Box 2607, Grand Rapids, Michigan 49501

British Library Cataloguing Data
A catalogue record for this book is available from the British Library.

Printed and bound in England by CPI Cox & Wyman.

Contents

To the people of Castle Hill Community Church
in gratitude for allowing me the time to write this book
and
To Heather, Ryan, David and Tom
who fill my life with love and joy

To find additional materials on mentoring,
to make comments or ask questions,
please go to
www.mentoringmatters.org.au

Foreword

Mentoring has become a popular subject of conversation among church leaders in recent years. Many would like to locate someone to mentor them, and many others see the need to mentor the next generation of leaders. Why such recent interest? Did we not manage perfectly well for generations without mentors? Is this just a fad that will pass, and which therefore we can afford to ignore?

There is an argument that suggests that mentoring has always existed but we just didn't give it such an elaborate title. Men and women have always acted as exemplars to boys and girls and without intending to in any deliberate sense have acted as mentors to those who were within their sphere of influence. Why then the sudden interest in mentoring as a specific discipline?

It seems fairly obvious that in recent times two things have changed. First of all, there has come enormous mobility in terms of population movement and in terms of social aspiration. Whereas in past times, boys and girls would have remained within the community in which they were born, and would have naturally learnt, from the example of others in their extended family, the basic life skills which would have equipped them to survive and thrive in their future lives, today those links are often broken by physical mobility. We no longer live for our whole lives in settled communities. We have become wanderers and even in those cases where we do not wander, enough people around us wander that the communities in which we grow up change quickly. We cannot rely on the idea that some individuals will always act as guides and examples around whom we can shape our lives.

Not only is there physical mobility, but there is a mobility related to a shift in ideas and related ideologies. Life in general, cultural life in particular is undergoing regular and dynamic change. Those who might have helped us as mentors within a static cultural framework are no longer able to offer us wisdom because, as one pop song puts it, 'constant change is here to stay'. In situations of communitarian flux and perpetual cultural change we need to locate those with wisdom who can act as guides to point us to the paths of safety within a shifting landscape.

Rick Lewis is such a guide. There are some who are naturally mentors, who do not even realize that they are mentors and there are some who have reflected deeply on the task of mentoring such that they can describe the process and train others in the discipline of mentoring. Rick is both of these. He has an intuitive grasp of what it means to build a caring relationship with those who need a mentor, and he is able to reflect intelligently on the nature of this interaction such that he can describe the steps to another and induct them into the same process.

Rick has been my personal mentor and by being such a helpful guide he has assisted me to some extent to mentor others. I believe that through the pages of this book Rick can both mentor you and instruct you in being a mentor to others.

Revd Dr Martin Robinson
Together in Mission

Introduction

Bad news travels fast in church circles. Another leader had called it quits and the church he had planted and led for fourteen years was closing. I left a message on his answering machine:

'Hi, Dave. Sorry to hear your news. Would you like to catch up for coffee?'

A few days later we sat together and I was looking at a devastated man. 'I wish I could say I don't know how this happened, but I do. I've been a fool,' he said.

Dave is a highly talented leader but also highly independent. He had been in scrapes before but had always managed to dig himself out and lead his church to even greater heights. But not this time. He is not even forty, yet he feels washed up.

Several people had offered to walk the journey with him but he had refused any kind of accountable relationship. To Dave, accountability had been a dirty word, and this was what he now saw as foolish. 'People like you have tried to tell me, but I wouldn't listen. I couldn't see it.'

Dave related the events that led to his crash: the isolation, the emotional strain, the loss of perspective, especially losing track of where God was in it all. The whole fracas might have been avoided had Dave had a mentor to help him navigate his way through the minefield of Christian leadership. Raw talent had been both his greatest asset and his Achilles heel. He hadn't seen it coming because he wouldn't listen. Unhealthy ways of operating in ministry had accumulated over the years until his leadership at last became unsustainable.

Terry has heard a few of these stories and is worried that he might be next. Although he is the greatly-admired and often-imitated senior pastor of a large church, in a recent conversation with his mentor he said, 'I can't do the rabbits thing any more.'

Puzzled, his mentor asked, 'The rabbits thing? What's that?'

Terry replied, 'In my church, I'm expected to pull a rabbit

out of a hat every Sunday. I just can't do it any more.'

Unrealistic expectations are mounting up against this leader, slowly strangling his soul. But Terry is astute and is doing something constructive. Knowing that he needs a safe relationship that can serve as an external frame of reference for his life in God, he is reaching out to a trusted mentor before his ministry, too, becomes unsustainable.

We hear a great deal these days about sustainability. Sustainable energy. Sustainable agriculture. Sustainable development. Sustainable ecosystems. In the light of so many Christian leaders struggling to find a healthy way to carry out their calling, it raises the question of whether or not there is such a thing as sustainable ministry these days. This book describes a way of mentoring that helps to make Christian leadership sustainable in the contemporary context. While this process is relevant to all followers of Jesus, my particular concern is for leaders, and especially those people who pour their energy into transformation as opposed to maintenance. Without wishing to be alarmist, I believe that the crisis facing these Christian leaders today is deeper and more extensive than most of us imagine.

Christian leadership may become unsustainable for a variety of reasons. Some leaders insist on tackling challenges for which they are not suited. They may work for years trying to fulfil an agenda that someone else set for them before they finally figure out what God has uniquely called and equipped them to do. Others go about things in an unwise fashion, damaging themselves and others along the way. They may work extraordinarily hard, expending huge amounts of mental and emotional energy, yet fail to tap into the power of God's Spirit; or they may adopt ways and means of pursuing their calling that are harder than they need to be. Still others simply lack the necessary defences for going the distance. They neglect healthy habits and fail to guard against things that make a soul sick.

To such leaders, these words of Jesus offer another way:

Are you tired? Worn out? Burned out on religion?
Come to me. Get away with me and you'll recover

your life. I'll show you how to take a real rest. Walk
with me and work with me – watch how I do it. Learn
the unforced rhythms of grace. I won't lay anything
heavy or ill-fitting on you. Keep company with me
and you'll learn to live freely and lightly.[1]

God has an agenda for Christian leaders that is truly sustainable.
His call fits each one uniquely, like a glove. His wisdom shows
leaders how to operate in ways that are effective and truly good.
His power carries the day even when a leader's weaknesses are
exposed. The renewing work of God's Spirit in leaders' lives
brings growth and strength in spirituality, character and ministry.
For those of us who have seen too many good people end up in
a mess, the question is this: How do we get Christian leaders on
to God's agenda?

The mentoring process described in this book facilitates
ministry sustainability by resolutely pursuing God's agenda in
the lives of Christian leaders. In this process, mentors act like
general practitioner doctors of the soul, working for the overall
health of mentorees.[2] In this sense, the art of mentoring is the
'cure of souls'. Other 'specialist' services may also be required
from time to time – coaches, counsellors, and so on – but the
mentor maintains relationship with the individual throughout,
helping them to integrate all the input from various sources into
a coherent approach to a healthy, sustainable lifestyle of loving
and serving God.

Most of the Christian leaders I know look like they are
doing okay. But what is really going on below the surface? Like
icebergs, the part others see is only a fraction of the total reality.
The part that can so easily cause the greatest damage is below
the waterline, and who really wants to look down there? Eugene
Peterson expresses the dilemma facing Christian leaders:

I don't know any other profession in which it is quite
as easy to fake it as in ours. Even when in occasional
fits of humility or honesty we disclaim sanctity, we
are not believed. People need to be reassured that

someone is in touch with the ultimate things. If we
provide a bare-bones outline of pretence, they take it
as the real thing and run with it, imputing to us clean
hands and pure hearts.[3]

There is a question I like to ask leaders that usually causes a
pause for thought. That question is, 'How's your soul?' Leaders
are used to being asked about their ministries, their projects or
even their families. Few people ever ask them about their soul.
Some even struggle to know what their soul is, let alone what
condition it is in. Those brave enough to attempt an answer start
to tap into what is below the surface.

Of course, Christian leaders have great moments too –
moments when they know they are in exactly the place and
condition that God wants them to be. If someone should ask
a probing question, these are the highlight moments leaders
naturally prefer to talk about. There's no need to tell lies. We
just need to be selective with the truth. Over time we can weave
all our glorious moments into a seemingly continuous narrative,
and the result is very impressive! That is exactly what some
parents do for their kids when they are trying to break into the
big time. They stand there at every game, every performance,
capturing footage of their little star. After hours of cutting and
pasting the very best clips, the version that finally makes it
into the hands of the talent scout makes the child look like a
world-beater. It's truthful to a certain extent, but it is not the
whole truth.

When Christian leaders are on top of their game, their
connection with the Lord is deep and strong, their insights into
God's agenda are highly perceptive, their interactions with other
people are pure and gracious, and their ministries are alight with
the power of the Holy Spirit. In our best moments, all of us are
good – I mean, we're *really* good. But we don't always operate
at our best. We mean well and we have good intentions, but we
drift away from our best so easily and settle for mediocrity – or
worse. But what if we could find someone to help us take the
best moments of our lives and make them more typical? What

if there was someone who would keep us honest, call us to be true to what is best in us, and remind us of what God has begun to do in our lives?

In the kind of mentoring relationships that this book describes, mentors help us remember and learn from the moments when we are at our best. Mentors help arrest the drift, pulling us back to our most noble intentions, our deepest connection with God, our most perceptive insights, our most gracious dealings with others and our most Spirit-filled service. Renewed interest in mentoring in Christian circles is not just another instance of the church following after the latest fads in the world of management. This is a biblical pattern. Just as Moses was helped by Jethro to be his best, he in turn helped Joshua to rise up in leadership. Paul, having been helped by Barnabas, reached out to assist Timothy's leadership development.

Since this book has captured your attention, the chances are that you are already acquainted with mentoring. You may have been doing it, at least informally, for years. Most mentoring that is carried out, both secular and spiritual, is informal in nature. This is perfectly normal and right. Informal mentors do things intuitively that turn out to be genuinely helpful. Thinking about the informal mentoring you have given and received over the years can help you understand some of the dynamics that may be intensified and deepened through formal mentoring. That is how I began mentoring leaders in the first place. I hope this book will help bring into focus the helpful things you may have already been doing and make them even more effective.

There are many different kinds of mentoring. What I will present in this book is a particular form and application of that process. My philosophical framework is Christian and my entire approach is informed by that perspective. The kind of mentoring I am advocating will only make sense to a disciple of Jesus. If you are only familiar with secular mentoring programmes, get ready to see mentoring in a totally different light.

Furthermore, while I believe mentoring should be a normal part of every Christian's journey of faith, this book will specifically describe mentoring for Christians in leadership roles.

I am convinced that the special situation of people in positions of Christian leadership requires a particular approach to mentoring. I will make the case that leaders in recognized roles should be mentored by people outside of their organization. Mentoring programmes within local churches, for instance, would not need to be concerned with this condition.

Finally, the approach to mentoring I describe here is formal, organized and deliberate. This is not to undervalue informal mentoring, which I hope and pray will flourish and spread throughout God's people. It is rather to plead for leaders to consider establishing, among the many informal mentoring relationships they likely already have, a special intense mentoring relationship that is pursued purposefully.

I bring my own distinctive perspective to the subject of mentoring. I have been engaged in mentoring for over twenty years as an adjunct to my ministry as a local church pastor. I conducted action research into mentoring pastors for the Bible Society in the United Kingdom and used the insights I gained to write my final project for a Doctor of Ministry degree at Fuller Theological Seminary. Since then my interest in the area has only increased as I have written and taught about mentoring in Australia and the UK, including a unit in the MA in Missional Leadership offered by the training and resource agency Together in Mission.

But do we really need another book on mentoring? Several are already in circulation and serve as texts for the growing number of theological courses on the subject. Eddie Gibbs is one prominent voice calling for more work to be done in this area:

> Mentoring is still something of a novel concept in the church. The vast majority of leaders have had little experience of such a relationship. This is very strange considering the New Testament's emphasis on mentoring relationships. Currently, we suffer from a dearth of qualified mentors. The training of mentors is a priority. We who serve as trainers and

educators need to help churches realize the strategic
importance of a mentoring ministry.[4]

In response to calls such as this, mentoring as a 'fast track'
element in training is emerging as a key leadership development
tool and is becoming popular with denominational and mission
agency chiefs. While I agree that mentoring does have the
capacity to bring on leaders at a faster rate than would otherwise
be achieved, I am a little worried about this becoming the driving
reason for getting into the process. Are we really just after some
productivity gains for either the leader's organization or, more
nobly, the kingdom of God? Obviously, these would not be bad
outcomes, but I believe they are best viewed as by-products of a
healthy mentoring process rather than its direct aims.

This hints at what I think is the distinctive angle that
makes this book worth reading. In a nutshell, this approach to
mentoring addresses *who you are before what you do*. What you
do as a Christian leader is, of course, tremendously important.
Every leader worth their salt will seek to perform to their
optimum for the sake of the kingdom, and I actively encourage
leaders to secure a coach to help them press into specific areas
of competence. However, as any experienced leader will tell
you, knowledge and skills will only get you so far. If a leader is
not in good shape in their soul, their ministry will soon end up
in frustration or disaster.

Martin Robinson writes to Christian leaders engaged in
church planting, insisting that they give more attention to the
inner life than to any other area:

> Much of the success that will come in the planting
> process will flow more from who we are as people
> than on what we do as planters. People will see our
> character long before they see the programme of the
> developing church. The spiritual life shapes who we
> are and through that lens, shapes what we do.[5]

I prioritize being over doing because who a person is has an enormous impact on their behaviour and even on their thinking. In taking this position I acknowledge that there is truth in both the behaviourist and cognitive schools of thought in psychology. Behaviourists stress the shaping influence on a person of what we do, and seek to modify behaviour as a means of solving psychological problems. Cognitive theory puts greater emphasis on the role of thinking and believing as determinants of behaviour. More recent developments in psychology have begun to explore how the spiritual and emotional dimensions of a person have the greatest impact of all, deeply influencing beliefs, reasoning and behaviour.

There was a time when 'church growth' was all the rage. In some circles this emphasis gradually became captive to a kind of 'church technology' that was almost entirely concerned with techniques that would produce numerical growth. Within this distorted emphasis, ways of achieving church growth were discovered that had little to do with the kingdom of God. It became known that it was possible to achieve significant 'growth' results from certain processes. Even though some of these processes are unhealthy and actually compromise the gospel, many church leaders employed them without question because of the lure of 'results'. A corrective to this slide into pragmatism came with a new emphasis on 'church health'. Christian Schwartz, among others, urged us to embrace an organic rather than a mechanistic theology of the church, and promoted the idea that a healthy church will, under the right environmental conditions, grow.[6]

The point here is the recognition that the ends do not justify the means. In many ways, within the kingdom of God, the means are the ends. If we are to bring this critique to bear on mentoring, we see that approaches driven by the pragmatism of results run the risk of doing damage to the participants. The more that mentoring becomes focused on fast-tracking up-and-coming leaders in order to maximize their impact – especially where this is seen within the framework of a particular organization – the greater is the likelihood of missing God's agenda in the process. The individual's capacity to add value to the organization may well be enhanced in the short term. Yet at the same time their ministry is more likely to become unhealthy and unsustainable, and to result in unintended negative consequences.

As I look around the Christian church in the West, I see an abundance of resources to help leaders get a better grip on what to do. There are books, seminars, conferences, websites, DVDs and networks dedicated to helping Christian leaders make an impact in their area of ministry. It is much harder to find resources that address the issues of who we are as leaders – resources for getting a grip on what is beneath the surface that crucially affects everything we do in leadership.

A few years ago, a friend and colleague of mine, Dr Keith Farmer, retired from his position as Principal of a ministry training college and made himself available as a mentor. Rapidly, word got around about the tremendous value of Keith's approach. He is now back in full-time ministry, serving over eighty mentorees. What has caused his mentoring to be so highly sought after? Research conducted in 2007 by a professional firm of consultants into the mentoring provided by Keith produced the following observations:

> According to the mentorees, the most common experience they and their ministry peers have had with [previous] mentoring has been based around the goal of aiding ministry 'success' through a focus on what they do in ministry. The mentor in this style of approach acts as the more experienced ministry 'practitioner' who provides advice to his/her mentoree around what s/he is doing in ministry. While there is often a personal aspect to it, the goal of the relationship is to be a more effective minister/pastor.
>
> There is a real need for Christian leaders to have a relationship with someone outside of their own personal and church networks that has no agenda other than the holistic health and well-being of the person. The leaders are looking for an avenue to deal with the uglier stuff in their lives in a safe and non-judgemental relationship. Apart from Keith's

mentoring those surveyed are not aware of any other
offering of this style of mentoring.[7]

Keith's understanding and practice of mentoring is so remarkable
that I have included an article written by him as an appendix to this
book. He and I concur that the kind of mentoring that prioritizes
matters of spirituality and character is precisely what is desired
and genuinely needed by contemporary Christian leaders. It is
the critical and often missing factor that has the capacity to make
serving God in difficult circumstances, sustainable.

Outstanding people like Keith are a wonderful gift to the
ranks of Christian leaders on the front line of mission, but they
are too few to address the vast need. It is vital that mentoring
is not shut up as the specialist skill of a highly gifted elite, but
is released as a general-purpose, reproducible tool placed in the
hand of every follower of Christ. What is needed is not just a
team of experts offering a professional service but a mentoring
movement in which ordinary people tap into the extraordinary
spiritual power of grace-filled mentoring relationships.

I have a dream that the genius of mentoring will capture
the imagination of a new generation of leaders; a dream that
the church will reclaim its heritage of generous, empowering
partnerships; a dream that promoting the work of the Holy Spirit
in the lives of others will become a normal way of living in the
kingdom of God; a dream that through mentoring, the church
and its leaders will be healthy, strong and full of life to carry on
the mission of Christ.

If you are a leader pouring your energies into Jesus'
mission, I invite you to engage mentoring as a crucial support
for your ministry. Please don't regard it as a luxury, an optional
extra. The sustainability of your leadership may well rest on
this issue. Furthermore, I encourage both leaders and those who
have a vital interest in their well-being and effectiveness to
consider offering mentoring to others along the lines presented
in this book.

If you are passionate about Christ and his mission, consider
this: Your impact for the kingdom of God may be multiplied by

investing in the lives of Christian leaders. The present generation has had difficulty locating mentors who will address who they are in God. I urge you to become part of the movement that ensures that the next generation will have no such difficulty.

Chapter 1

A Different Approach to Mentoring

Looking back, it felt a bit like a blind date. We'd had one brief conversation on the phone and had agreed to meet at a roadside café – the 'services' – between junctions 25 and 26 on the M1. I was pulling together a pilot mentoring scheme for the Bible Society in the United Kingdom. Being an Australian in a foreign country with no network of my own, I had been handed a list of likely candidates with contact numbers attached. Ken sounded dubious on the phone and he still looked that way when we finally found each other.

'I don't mean to be rude,' he said, 'but I already have quite an extensive network of people that I catch up with who help me with various things. Can you tell me what it is exactly that you're offering to do for me?'

Ken had assembled what has been called a 'constellation' of developmental relationships[8] comprised of specialists with particular skills, leaders of other churches, prayer partners, a small Bible study group, family and friends. Each person made a valuable contribution to his life, but he had many of these developmental relationships and wasn't sure he had time for another one.

Like Ken, many leaders have a set of people that they can call on for particular needs. Whenever help is needed, one of those people will be sure to come up with a suitable resource. Such a range of input is a wonderful supply of raw material, but the value of that input is only fully realized when it is sifted, evaluated and coherently integrated into life. This is the kind of thing for which a formal mentoring relationship is so helpful.

Back then, I didn't have a succinct definition, but I managed to convey to Ken that it was about promoting the work of God's

Spirit in his life and facilitating his spiritual growth, his key relationships and his vocational effectiveness.

'You mean it's about putting the whole thing together – about who I am inside, as well as about my ministry?' he asked. 'If that's it, then I'm in.'

The difficult task of defining Christian mentoring

The concept of mentoring seems at once both familiar and elusive. At an intuitive level, we may have a grasp of what it is, but expressing it in a few words proves to be a more difficult task. I have read dozens of books on this subject and every one of them has a different definition of mentoring. Since there are so many starting points for approaching this process, it should perhaps be no great surprise that there is such a wide diversity of opinion. Yet even within the Christian literature, definitions of mentoring abound.

Stanley and Clinton call mentoring, 'A relational experience in which one person empowers another by sharing God-given resources.'[9] This is no doubt true of mentoring, but it could also describe so many other forms of interaction that it is not particularly helpful as a definition. Biehl prefers, 'A lifelong relationship... in which a mentor helps a protégé reach his/her God-given potential.'[10] The difficulty here is the slightly paternalistic tone conveyed by the word 'protégé' and the idea of all mentoring being lifelong by definition.

The word chosen by an author to describe the person who receives mentoring can often tell you something crucial about the way they conceive of the process. Krallmann, for example, offers this definition of mentoring: 'Operating as a facilitator... to further the full release of the trainee's talents, [the mentor] seeks to holistically impact the latter through the totality of his/her shared life.'[11] There is much that is good about this definition, especially the reference to holistic impact, but the use of the term 'trainee' presupposes an educational model for mentoring that differs significantly from the model described in this book.

Mallison takes a more relational approach that emphasizes a spiritual goal, proposing that 'Christian mentoring is a dynamic, intentional relationship of trust in which one person enables another to maximise the grace of God in their life and service.'[12] Anderson and Reese take this a step further, defining spiritual mentoring as a 'triadic relationship between mentor, mentoree and the Holy Spirit, where the mentoree can discover, through the already present action of God, intimacy with God, ultimate identity as a child of God and a unique voice for kingdom responsibility.'[13]

These last two definitions point toward what I have come to see as the fundamental reality upon which my approach to mentoring is predicated: that God is up to something good in every person's life. I believe that the best Christian mentoring takes its cue from this divine activity in terms of both ends and means. That is, good Christian mentoring is after what God is after, and it goes after it in ways that are consistent with the character and nature of God as revealed in Jesus Christ.

In the light of so many varied approaches, I don't presume to be able to provide you with an authoritative definition of Christian mentoring. However, at the risk of further cluttering the landscape with yet another definition, here is my succinct expression of what I believe this approach to mentoring achieves:

> Within intentional, empowering, unique relationships, Christian mentoring identifies and promotes the work of God's Spirit in others' lives, assisting them to access God's resources for their growth and strength in spirituality, character and ministry.

In this chapter I intend to explore that statement one piece at a time, particularly noting its application to the task of mentoring Christian leaders, which is my present focus.

Essential characteristics

Intentional

Christian mentoring is intentional because in its primary sense it is done on purpose. Now, to be fair, there are many examples of relationships carried out in a haphazard, unintentional way that might be termed 'mentoring' in a secondary sense. These relationships are not usually called mentoring by those involved in them – they are usually simply known as friendships. Whatever functions of mentoring these friendships display, they occur incidentally and are not the principal focus of the relationship. At best, this is a relatively weak form of mentoring.

On occasion, certain outstanding individuals are also referred to as mentors who serve as models and inspire others toward Christian maturity. This is a little misleading. They are only 'mentors' in a derivative sense through the sort of pseudo-relationship we may have with someone not personally known to us but who has an impact upon us. They would be better termed 'heroes'. An intentional mentoring relationship need not necessarily be a formal one, with the structures and processes that I recommend in this book as appropriate for leaders. However, meaningful mentoring will not be achieved without a conscious, deliberate, intentional decision to pursue it with someone whom we allow to get to know us personally.

I love having stimulating conversations with leaders about the issues they face in life and in mission. It's great fun tossing around ideas and looking at things from different angles. But it is disappointing to see some leaders unwilling to go the next step and thoroughly work through the implications of these discussions personally. It seems to be something of a game to them. I notice that when it gets to a point requiring deep personal change or serious work on some issue, they pull back from pursuing it intentionally.

Chris was one such person. This young woman came to me angry about what had just happened at her church. According to Chris, the Elders had pulled someone from the worship team because they had discovered something dark about their past.

'This is typical!' she said. 'They are so afraid that a scandal might damage their precious church that they treat a person with no grace at all! This is what institutional churches do – they don't act like Jesus at all, they just screw people up.'

Clearly, several things were going off in Chris all at once; some good, some bad. It was going to take some sorting out to discover what God was up to in her life.

We had spoken previously about the difficulty she was having fitting in with a conventional church. Friends of hers were interested in talking about Jesus, but she knew for sure that there was no way they would ever relate to her church. She had read some books about alternative forms of church and sensed a stirring that might have been from God about perhaps helping to start something up. Now that she had finally severed her ties with her old church, I asked her if she would like to work together on finding a way forward.

It was a moment of truth, and she didn't grasp it. Chris had isolated conversations with several people who might have been able to turn this crisis into an opportunity for growth, but she chose not to become intentional about any of those relationships and has drifted into impotent disaffection with church and faith.

In the midst of a constellation of developmental relationships a Christian leader may have multiple mentors, both sequentially through life and concurrently at any one time. My observation is that where Christian leaders intentionalize and formalize at least one of them, they gain the maximum benefit from the personal and spiritual investment that mentoring relationships can bring.

Empowering

Feelings of powerlessness are common, especially for leaders facing the challenge not only of living their own lives effectively but also of advancing God's cause in an indifferent or hostile context. Aware of this, Paul wrote to Timothy reminding him that 'God did not give us a spirit of timidity, but a spirit of power, of love, and of self-discipline.'[14] Timothy is not the only leader ever to have struggled with timidity. Who wouldn't be a little uncertain when dealing with spiritual mysteries and seeking to lead people in ways that we are not altogether expert in ourselves? It is perfectly understandable that young leaders and mature leaders alike should have moments of hesitation, wondering if they have taken everything into account and whether or not their judgment is accurate. Lurking in the background are voices of self-doubt: 'Who am I to be leading these people?'

Empowering relationships take people from a place of inner weakness, where they feel powerless and overwhelmed, to a place of inner strength, where they feel able to respond constructively to their situation. Inner weakness is characterized by timidity, double-mindedness, anxiety, hesitancy, procrastination and self-doubt. Inner strength is characterized by confidence, endurance, patience, determination, hope and courage. A Christian mentoring relationship has the capacity to address the disempowerment experienced by leaders in two ways.

First, there is the kind of interpersonal empowerment that is familiar within many helping professions, including secular mentoring. In mentoring programmes provided by some corporations to their promising young executives, empowering relationships are offered as the main attraction. Eric Parsloe, one of the experts in this area, describes empowerment as resulting from access to such things as:

- a source of reassurance; a backup figure;
- a help in lateral thinking and achieving overview of career and organization;
- a driving force to push them if they need it;
- an alternative and detached point of guidance from immediate manager;
- an opportunity to see clearly what skills and experiences they need;
- a chance to learn organizational skills;
- a qualified sounding board for any questions or problems they encounter;
- a chance to become acquainted with someone much

higher up in the company.[15]

The power that mentorees derive from such a relationship consists mainly in gaining confidence to commit to action. With a small amount of input and judicious affirmation from someone they respect and trust, mentorees build inner strength. There is a sense in which simply having a mentor alongside to assure you that you're not completely stupid is a very empowering thing. It does instil confidence to go ahead and do the thing you had in mind when a mentor validates it with genuine affirmation. Mentors empower others by reminding them of facts they may have temporarily forgotten or may not be weighing correctly. There might be a process of questioning by the mentor, but when she leans back and says, 'Okay, that makes sense,' it can strengthen the heart of a mentoree significantly.

However, a mentoring relationship between two Christians is empowering not simply because of this human interpersonal dynamic. There is an additional capacity to address inner weakness that comes from the power of the Holy Spirit – a factor that goes beyond anything that you'll read about in secular mentoring models. I believe this is what Paul was alluding to when he wrote to Timothy. As Timothy's mentor, Paul was able to speak into his life, reminding him of a profound reality that could bring him inner strength to overcome his timidity and whatever sense of powerlessness was driving that feeling.

When two or more Christians come together in the name of Jesus, he is present with them by his Spirit. The Spirit of Jesus provides the power to first of all change the very being of the mentoree through personal transformation, bringing inner strength in a more profound way than information and affirmation could ever achieve. Beyond this, the power of the Spirit enables that inner strength to be applied in action through the operation of gifts of grace. The work of the Holy Spirit is released through a Christian mentoring relationship, and that is what makes it distinctively empowering.

Unique

When I began to research mentoring in earnest after several years of amateur dabbling, I was looking for a 'best practice' method. It seemed to me that my home-grown approach was all over the place. What I would do with one mentoree would be quite different from what I would do with another. I thought that couldn't be right. As if mentoring were like carpentry or engineering, I sought to track down the most successful techniques of the experts and distil them into a standard method that would be easier to teach others and more easily replicable by them in their own contexts.

It was not difficult to find standardized mentoring processes, especially in the secular marketplace. Management consultancy firms have them as a matter of course. They claim to tailor-make these mentoring programmes to suit each specific context, but in reality it only takes a little tweaking of the template here and there, and a comprehensive system can be rolled out in no time at all. The drawback is that these systems turn out to be cold and clinical and those involved feel like they are just going through the motions. From the feedback I gathered, it appears that these programmes only work well where someone trained as a mentor departs from the script and works with their mentoree in a non-standard, individualistic way.

This reminds me of Jesus, who was constantly departing from the script and dealing with people as individuals. Throughout the Gospels, Jesus never heals two people in exactly the same way, never steers a conversation down a path he's used before, never preaches the same sermon twice, and never becomes predictable, but is always creative and highly adaptive to each new context. His Spirit, alive and active in every Christian, is still working in this free, non-formulaic way. As a mentor, it's a challenge to keep up with the ever-fresh activity of the Holy Spirit that is unique in each case.

Since every human being is unique and no two leaders have exactly the same calling, I urge that each mentoring relationship and the activities that spring from it be devised fresh and new every time especially for that individual. There really is no effective 'one-size-fits-all' method of mentoring. I know – I've looked! Please exercise caution when employing off-the-shelf materials produced as guides for mentoring exercises and processes – and that includes anything you might find in this book! Some of the methods used in mentoring are so generally useful as to be almost universal. Examples of these are deep reading of the Bible, reflection and journalling, setting goals and action steps, and monitoring progress in these. By all means use all these methods, but employ them flexibly so that the mentoree does not feel awkward using them. There are many ways to read the Bible and keep a journal and not all of them have been discovered yet.

Not only are the methods used unique to each individual in effective mentoring, but so too is the subject matter covered. It is unhelpful for a mentor to allow published mentoring materials to set or even imply a predetermined curriculum for development. The danger is that indiscriminate use of exercises, lists of topics or other resources may lock the mentor and mentoree into an artificial pathway that may contain good – even biblical – content, but lacks appropriate timing or misses the real, vital issues altogether. By all means pick up relevant materials if they serve the agenda being set by the Holy Spirit. But adapt them to fit the specific situation you're dealing with and do not allow the way you mentor to revolve around them or be captive to them. Those resources are not essential to good mentoring.

What is essential to a good mentoring process is the foundation of a real relationship between two people that is dedicated to the Father, centred on Jesus, enlivened by the Holy Spirit, anchored in the Christian scriptures and free to adapt its forms in fresh creativity to the unique personalities of both the mentor and the mentoree. Most of all, the direction that a particular mentoring relationship takes in terms of subject matter should depend on what the Holy Spirit is doing in the life of the mentoree concerned.

Relationship

Mentoring cannot take place in a context of mere transactional contact such as you might have with your plumber or your dentist. It can only exist in a relational environment of ongoing contact that involves more than simply the mechanical elements of a mentoring process. Although it may involve a formal arrangement, it goes beyond this to become a heart-to-heart meeting of persons. In the following chapters I say much more about the tools and skills employed in mentoring, the way it is best structured and the emphases good mentors express. However, more than any techniques or any content conveyed, it is this special, holy relationship between the mentor and mentoree which gives mentoring its phenomenal capacity to assist personal transformation and effective Christian living.

I will cover this aspect of mentoring extensively in Chapter 7, but for now I will just consider the argument made by Larry Crabb in his landmark book, *Connecting*, published in 1997. As a psychotherapist himself, he reviews important research into why psychotherapy, 'the talking cure', works. The conclusion drawn from the research is that the critical feature of all successful therapy is the therapist's skilful management of the patient–therapist relationship. Note this: it has little or nothing to do with whether the therapy is Jungian, cognitive or psychoanalytical, or how well the therapists are trained in these disciplines. As Crabb comments:

> In other words, people who are good at relating are people whose words will be helpful. A case can be made that training in specific theory and technique is less important in becoming a good helper than learning to be conscientious, non-defensive and caring. Engage with [people], honour confidences, and let yourself actually care when they hurt. Believe in [people], involve yourself because you really think they could be better.[16]

Even if you feel that you have no special skills to bring to mentoring (or that your mentor is not that sharp!), you need to know this: a real relationship in which someone pays attention and truly cares in the name of Jesus is a very powerful force for good. It cannot be stressed too highly how critical the quality of the relationship is to the whole enterprise of mentoring.

There are at least four ways to be involved in mentoring relationships. The first two varieties are opposite sides of the same coin, and most of what I convey in this book will be applied to them. First, you may be in a receiving relationship, in which you, as a mentoree, connect with someone who agrees to serve and be there for you as a mentor. The mentor is generally more experienced in life, although there may be exceptions to this rule. Second, you might be in a giving relationship, in which you, as the mentor, offer to serve another person and be there for them. In both of these first two kinds of mentoring relationships, there is a clear understanding by both people that the relationship has limited mutuality. During the time set aside for mentoring, the focus is exclusively on the mentoree for their benefit.

However, there are two other varieties of mentoring relationships that do involve mutuality. The third form of mentoring is a sharing relationship, in which one connects with a peer in co-mentoring. Both partners agree to be there for each other and watch out for each other. As we shall see in the next chapter, the ancient Celtic Christians termed such a person an *anamcara* or 'soul friend'. The final form of mentoring is a corporate relationship, in which a group covenant together as co-mentors. These cohorts usually only number three or four people, but some skilled facilitators can push that number up to eight or so. Although I do not deal specifically with mutual relationships in this book, many of the principles I share are relevant and may be adapted.

Identifies and promotes

As critical as an intentional, empowering, unique relationship is to mentoring, it is not mentoring itself. The activity of mentoring takes place within the relationship, so that the relationship is to mentoring what a canvas is to an oil painting. Artists will take great care to secure a good canvas for a serious work of art but, having done that, the painting is still yet to be done. In terms of mentoring, putting a sound relationship in place sets up the opportunity for the work of mentoring to be done within that relationship. To change the metaphor, think of an effective mentor as part investigator and part farmer.

As an investigator, she teams up with the mentoree to progressively discover what God is doing in their life. She looks for clues – God's fingerprints, if you like – opening her awareness to the Holy Spirit. At the same time she is paying close attention to the mentoree, listening and observing, weighing the data, making connections. Sometimes the signs are obvious; at other times the skills of a sleuth are required. Care must be taken that this work of investigation is not unnecessarily invasive. It is not the task of mentors to act as the Grand Inquisitor, tearing the mentoree apart with scrupulous criticism.

On the other hand, with permission, mentors are right to ask the hard questions. Ted Haggard's fall from grace in late 2006 illustrated this point. While some commentators observed that Haggard's swift removal from ministry proved that his accountability structures had worked effectively, Eddie Gibbs, professor of Church Growth at Fuller Seminary, took another view. In an interview he said the accountability structure was a failure. The flaw, he said, was that it provided for intervention only when the pastor was about to crash and burn, rather than establishing a process to check on him routinely to prevent such an outcome. 'You've got to have the kind of people who will ask the awkward questions about every area of life,' Gibbs said, 'especially for a high-profile pastor in a large church.'[17]

Mentors are the kind of people that Gibbs is calling for. Without stepping over appropriate, negotiated boundaries, they work sympathetically with the mentoree to listen to the voice of the Spirit and encourage them to pray as David did: 'Search me, O God, and know my heart; test me and know my anxious thoughts. See if there is any offensive way in me, and lead me in the way everlasting.'[18]

As a farmer, a mentor works with the mentoree to raise the crop that God is looking for in the soul of the mentoree. Together they prepare the soil, pull the weeds, plant good seed, add the right nutrients, water when necessary, protect from frost and birds – whatever it takes to see good fruit produced from the mentoree's life. This is the image that Paul presents in his first letter to the Corinthians:

> I planted the seed, Apollos watered it, but God made it grow. So neither he who plants nor he who waters is anything, but only God, who makes things grow. The man who plants and the man who waters have one purpose, and each will be rewarded according to his own labour. For we are God's fellow workers; you are God's field.[19]

Keeping this perspective in mind, Christian mentors understand their role as significant and necessary, yet secondary to the role that God plays in mentoring.

The work of God's Spirit

It is crucial to note that what mentoring identifies and promotes is *already going on* in the life of the mentoree. The mentor does not seek to create something out of nothing, or introduce an agenda from outside the mentoree. The mentoree is not in a position of a standing start, waiting to begin their development toward what God has in mind for them. There is already momentum in their life because God has been, and still is, very active in their soul. As Paul writes in Philippians 1:6, God has begun and is carrying on his work in every Christian. God will use the mentor and all he or she can bring to help the mentoree, but it is the power of the Holy Spirit that will bring about transformation in the mentoree's life.

So far, I have made it clear that I believe Christian

mentoring pursues directions indicated by God's agenda for the mentoree. But there are alternative points of view about this that we wish to point out. First, there is a minority idea in circulation, yet still persistent, that mentoring is about mentors reproducing themselves – their talent, skills, knowledge and even style – in another person. This is a horrible idea. Attempts to recreate others in our own image, or shape them to accomplish goals that are ours, not theirs, is the business of people consumed with delusions of self-importance.

Second, there is another far more prevalent idea which in its own way is also misleading about the source of an adequate agenda for mentoring. That idea is that the mentoree sets the agenda according to their own desires, and asks the mentor to help them get to where they want to go. From a Christian point of view, the difficulty with this position is obvious. When we look back on the agendas we had for our lives years ago, they appear now to be self-serving, small, misguided and changeable. Mentors serve others best when they encourage them to lift their sights from their own agendas to seek after God's agenda. In fact, I believe this is a critical point for agreement at the outset when mentoring Christian leaders. A clear acknowledgment that the mentor acts on behalf of God and seeks to represent him in the relationship will get the mentoring off on the right foot.

Access God's resources

I find something lacking in approaches to mentoring which place the greatest emphasis on the personal resources that a mentor can bring to a mentoree. Howard and William Hendricks, for example, begin their list of what a mentor has to offer with these items: experience, knowledge, access to networks, money and possessions.[20] Likewise, Ted Engstrom and Norman Rohrer subtitle their book on mentoring, 'Passing on to others what God has given you', reinforcing the idea that whatever the mentoree is going to gain from a mentoring relationship is already in the possession of the mentor.[21] On the one hand, it is admirable that mentors should display a generous spirit and freely share whatever they have that might be helpful to a mentoree. On the other hand, surely it should be obvious that mentorees keen to pursue God's call on their lives are going to need far more in the way of resources than a mentor can provide.

The old saying, 'Give a man a fish and you feed him for a day; teach a man to fish and you feed him for a lifetime' is apt in this regard. While giving 'fish' to Christian leaders may be a short-term solution to help them out of a jam, as a long-term strategy it will only consolidate weakness and develop dependency. But where should Christian leaders fish for what they need to progress in the life to which God is calling them? Above everything else, the resources they most need are found in God. And what are these resources that God offers?

Actually, when all is said and done, everything that God offers us is wrapped up in himself – his real, living presence. His resources are not available apart from himself. Keeping close company with Jesus – that is what makes all the difference. But can we tease out some of what it is that his presence in the life of the mentoree produces that is so life-giving? The love of God brings inner security and a sense of value. His grace brings acceptance, forgiveness and release from guilt. The wisdom of his word and the authenticity of his being set us free from the traps of falsehood. His power gives us the capacity to do right and the confidence to attempt it. His peace calms our anxieties and develops patience. Hope in his purposes gives us the heart to persevere, and his joy is our greatest pleasure.

This is just a representative sample of what God has to offer that is far more valuable and pertinent than anything that resides in even the best mentor. Christian mentors act as ushers or doorkeepers, pointing out and opening up ways and means to receive God's resources.[22] They remind mentorees that Jesus really is actually alive – not just in some unreal, other-worldly way that is unconnected with daily reality, but really, truly present and available.

Spirituality, character and ministry

Finally, I believe mentoring is about holistic development. In saying that God's resources are what Christian leaders most need, I want to make it clear that, in my view, they are what are most needed for the *whole* of life, not just for what might be termed the *spiritual* life. With our limited human capacity to see connections and consequences, we tend to deal with things atomistically without due regard to the whole. Environmentalists remind us that this is what gets us into trouble when we upset finely balanced ecosystems. The same principle holds true when dealing with the complexities of human lives.

God does not relate to people in separate compartments but comprehensively, taking full account of how every part affects the whole. He is interested in every aspect of a mentoree's life. Wherever his Spirit is at work bringing growth and strength, the mentoring relationship will seek to identify and promote that work, so the scope for mentoring includes the whole person.

No matter what issues the mentoree first presents, if the goal of pursuing God's agenda is embraced, the processes of mentoring soon penetrate to issues of character that lie behind the mentoree's capacity to cooperate with the work of the Holy Spirit in their lives. Bound up with these are the mentoree's awareness of God, self-awareness, life-orienting values, moral convictions and their key relationships with the people closest to them. Tracing the implications of the Spirit's work in these matters naturally leads back to their performance in ministry because their life is a seamless whole.

I have observed vital connections between personal spirituality, character traits, relationship dynamics and ministry performance in hundreds of Christian leaders. My model of mentoring pays close attention to these connections, beginning at the point where God's Spirit invariably begins – in the heart.

Mentoring and other empowering processes

When I explain my approach to mentoring I sometimes have people say, 'Isn't that a bit like spiritual direction?', or 'Isn't that a bit like coaching?' Unfortunately, there is no agreed terminology pertaining to various empowering processes, which can make things rather confusing for those starting to explore mentoring, spiritual direction, coaching and the like. The best I can do is explain exactly what I mean by the term 'mentoring' and how I see other processes being distinct from that.

All of the processes discussed below can bring genuine empowerment to those who participate in them, and all may be used to good effect within a Christian context. Just what the terms mean is a matter of dispute, however. The explanations given here, while simply one perspective among many, will hopefully provide a starting point for understanding the differences between processes, no matter what they are called.

Coaching

Coaching refers to the development of a particular skill and doing something well. Different skills require different competencies. Athletes require strength, flexibility, speed, coordination and endurance, while academics require reading, comprehension, logical analysis, memory recall, and expression. The coach works with the subject to eliminate bad habits and to strengthen good ones, all for the sake of performing an activity with excellence. Mentoring does deal with skills but, in a Christian context at least, it is fundamentally concerned with the inner life as a priority over outward performance. Mentoring is concerned with who you are, how you relate and what you do. Coaching is really just concerned with what you do.

However, these terms are somewhat slippery in current usage. In recent years the term 'life coaching' has come into vogue, referring to a more all-embracing process that in some cases may be indistinguishable from mentoring. At the same time, the way the term 'mentoring' is used in secular contexts reduces it from the Homerian ideal of Telemachus' guardian to something little more than professional skills development with a little career path management thrown in. There is an argument that Christians ought to drop the term 'mentoring' and use 'life coaching' instead, in order to speak the language of the world around about us. I'm not convinced, but would not quibble as long as what is meant by these terms is clarified.

Spiritual direction

Variations on this term include 'spiritual formation' and 'spiritual guidance'. This empowering process is especially concerned with the subject's relationship with God. It may be argued that everything after that is mere detail and implementation. Even if that point is granted, yet I would insist that such implementation does not take place automatically and without concentrated effort. Mentoring goes beyond spiritual direction in that it is concerned to carry the implications of the work of the Holy Spirit through to their practical outworking in the world of human relationships and Christian ministry and mission.

Counselling

Counselling is a process that revolves around remedial care. Its point of departure is a specific presenting problem which prevents the subject from functioning normally. This issue is then explored with the goal of empowering the subject to deal with and then move on past the issue that has troubled them. Although mentoring will, from time to time, tackle problems that arise in the course of pursuing goals in line with the work of the Spirit, it is not problem-centred. Rather, it is centred on the purpose and activity of God. If debilitating problems persist, the mentor may refer the mentoree for skilled counselling.

Pastoral care

In many church contexts, pastoral care has devolved into little more than tea and sympathy – a non-directive sort of Christian companionship that comes alongside when people are troubled. For this reason it is sometimes seen as a weak and ineffective process in terms of empowerment. Yet understood from a biblical perspective, pastoral care is less about sympathy than it is about discipleship. The main function of a shepherd is to protect and nurture the growth of the sheep so they end up healthy, strong and safely part of the flock. If this is what is meant by pastoral care, there is considerable overlap with mentoring.

However, pastoral care is generally implemented reactively, whereas mentoring is proactive. Like counselling, pastoral care is problem-driven whereas mentoring is driven by God's call and agenda. Furthermore, pastoral care approaches an individual from the perspective of them being part of a community, and emphasizes positive participation within that community. Mentoring has the capacity to transcend the boundaries of particular communities and may persist while the mentoree passes through several different churches or organizations.

Discipling

From a biblical perspective, discipleship is a lifelong process of following Christ in which a person is transformed by the power of his Spirit to be like him in thinking, character and action. Facilitating this process is closely akin to what I have described as mentoring, so why don't I just use the term 'discipling' rather than 'mentoring'? The reason is that the term 'discipling' is generally not used in its far-reaching, biblical sense. Instead, discipling is commonly understood as initial faith-formation: a content-driven process of orientation provided to new Christians.

According to this understanding, discipling imparts to new believers basic Christian beliefs and trains them in practices that are regarded as 'normal' for committed Christians. The essential message of discipling is 'Here is what you need to know and do.' It is usually carried out in structured, short-term programmes. Once the subject has completed the course, they are regarded as having been 'discipled'. Distinct from this, mentoring is not driven by a particular curriculum, pays more attention to the being that lies behind the knowing and doing, and is a lifelong process.

Instruction

Those with gifts of teaching are an invaluable resource for the whole Christian community. We all need to be taught what the Bible says, what it means and how it relates to everyday life. Mentoring, on the other hand, seeks to operate within the revealed truth of the Christian scriptures, taking what is known generally and specifically about God's purpose for the mentoree and helping them to integrate that knowledge into their life. Though there may be occasions for a mentor to express what he or she has learned, it is not primarily an opportunity to exercise one's teaching gift. It is vital for the mentoree to be active within mentoring to discover and cooperate with the work of the Spirit and not simply to absorb more information.

Friendship

It is a wonderful and positively therapeutic thing to simply hang out with a Christian friend. It is not a bad thing to share the things that God is teaching you or reminisce over one's life experiences. If Christian leaders took the time to develop deep, lasting friendships, they would probably avoid many of the pitfalls into which they commonly fall. But just spending time together enjoying good company does not constitute mentoring. Friendship does offer the possibility of a basic level of watching out for one another. If it is to become a 'soul friendship', a kind of peer mentoring relationship, some kind of clear understanding or informal 'contract' will need to be agreed. Without such a negotiated agreement, the rigorous, focused, intentional accountability process within mentoring would be rude and presumptuous in the setting of a simple friendship.

Varieties of mentoring structures

In this book I will be explaining a particular mode of mentoring which is geared toward one-on-one sessions between a mentor and someone in a position of appointed Christian leadership. Much of the material I provide will be useful in other mentoring settings, although I won't be making those applications here. Other modes of mentoring are used within local churches, schools, volunteer organizations, Christian communities and mission settings and have tremendous value.

For example, as a local church pastor, I have seen the benefit of mentoring for marriage, where an older couple spend time with newlyweds or other couples experiencing turbulence in their relationship. Also, single-sex cohorts of three to six individuals may enter into a peer mentoring arrangement that has enormous capacity for effective ongoing development as a follower of Christ. I encourage the Christian leaders I mentor to get into renewal retreat groups or something similar on the understanding that apprenticeship to Jesus cannot be carried on without engaging in Christian community.

Where a whole community, such as a local church, parachurch organization or mission agency, determines to take up mentoring as a regular part of their communal life, the best approach I have seen involves peer mentoring in small group settings, accompanied by personal, one-to-one contact outside the group between a mentor and each member of the group. My only reservation about this is that I am convinced that mentoring of the appointed Christian leaders of those communities cannot, in fact, be effectively carried out from within. Perhaps this is not the case for informal leaders, or potential leaders just starting out. For reasons I will explore more fully in subsequent chapters, my contention is that, for appointed leaders at least, mentoring must transcend organizational boundaries. It is especially for these people in positions of Christian leadership that this book is written.

Chapter 2

An Ancient Art for a Post-modern Context

A new way of looking at the world has been rising in recent decades in Western culture. This new worldview is associated with post-modernism – a paradigm of thought pervasive in its influence yet notoriously slippery to describe. We may expect that generations arising now and on into the twenty-first century will be increasingly influenced by this new worldview and, because of that, we may expect that the ancient art of mentoring is likely to be warmly embraced by young Christian leaders of the emerging culture. Why should this be so?

There are several reasons that I will discuss towards the end of this chapter. One reason that bears mentioning as we begin to explore biblical examples and the history of Christian mentoring is the curious fascination post-modernism has with ancient wisdom and ways. There is a tendency for post-moderns to delve back behind the modern period to find ancient roots, a process that Gerard Kelly calls 'plundering the past to fund the future':

> The deep history and traditions of pre-modern and aboriginal people are newly and unexpectedly popular. With the future unknown and the present unreliable, the past is a storehouse of ideas to explore. In the turmoil of today, the young rummage through yesterday in search of keys to tomorrow.[23]

It should come as no surprise, therefore, to discover that the current generation of women and men seeking ways to be better prepared and resourced for Christian leadership are drawn to mentoring. They have an intuitive sense that there is something deep and rich here that is anchored in divine–human interactions that cannot be fully comprehended by modernist scientific categories. This brief review of the roots of mentoring will inform these hunches with a biblical and historical framework.

Greek origins of the word 'mentor'

Mentoring was being carried out long before we had a word for it. The first modern use of the term 'mentor' appeared in François Fénelon's *The Adventures of Telemachus* published in 1699. Fénelon, as a bright young priest, had been charged with the task of guiding the personal formation of a future king of France, the grandson of Louis XIV. His concept of what he was doing caused him to draw a parallel with a character from the ancient Greek poet, Homer. In *The Odyssey*, Homer tells the epic tale of King Odysseus who, leaving his kingdom of Ithaca to fight the Trojan War, entrusts his son Telemachus to the care of an old friend named Mentor. Homer makes the character of Mentor intriguingly complex by having the goddess Athene take on his form from time to time, bringing divine assistance to Telemachus when he needs it most.

Mentor's principal actions in relation to Telemachus were these:

- affirming his misgivings about the state of affairs in Ithaca;
- stirring up his determination to do something about it;
- travelling with him on his journey to find his father;
- helping him to understand himself;
- giving him honest feedback;
- prompting him to think about what lies ahead and how he will tackle it;
- making strategic introductions;
- assisting him to find the resources he needs;
- reminding him of his father's character and priorities.

Through careful advice, encouragement and example, Mentor prepared Telemachus for his destiny with a light touch. 'I leave the matter in your hands,' he would say. 'Think over what I have said.' Mentor was not a member of the royal family and had no experience of ruling. Yet because of his personal relationship with both the king and the prince, he was able to help Telemachus become a son of whom his father would be proud. Once Telemachus succeeded in finding Odysseus, Mentor's role diminished as father and son together returned to Ithaca to restore the kingdom.

Fénelon knew this story well, and could identify with Mentor in many ways. His difficulty, however, was that he was appalled by the example of kingship provided by Louis XIV and could not honestly encourage the young duke of Burgundy to emulate his grandfather's centralized autocracy. The *Adventures of Telemachus* contains veiled criticisms of the ideology of divine-right absolute monarchy dominant in France at that time. As a Christian leader, Fénelon was keen to point toward a better example of monarchy modelled by the King of heaven. Conceiving of his role as a 'mentor' figure, Fénelon worked for nine years to help his young charge respond to his calling from God into political leadership – a calling very different from his own.

As an historical precedent for much modern mentoring, especially in the secular arena, Homer's Mentor doesn't quite seem to fit. The apparent disconnection leads Zachary to comment that the model of Homer's Mentor is woefully incomplete for today's mentor.[24] Telemachus was not Mentor's apprentice. Mentor did not coach Telemachus in any particular skill. He was not a tutor to Telemachus in the normal sense. It was not Mentor's age, experience, connections or skills that were foundational to his role. His chief qualification was simply that he knew and was a friend of Telemachus' father, King Odysseus. He therefore knew the things that Odysseus would want to see strengthened within his son, and he had a sense of Telemachus' destiny.

In terms of understanding the roots of mentoring, the

vital thing to notice about Homer's Mentor is that he was the link between the young prince and the third principal player in the drama. Although Odysseus is unseen by his son for most of the story, it is the king's character and priorities that drive the agenda of what transpires between Mentor and Telemachus. Contemporary Christian mentors resemble their literary namesake in that they help other Christians earnestly to seek God and his kingdom, and to grow in every way as their Father in heaven intended. The complex, twin-layered nature of the Mentor character in Homer provides an apt metaphor for the way in which divine assistance is mediated through those who allow themselves to be used by God as a blessing to others in mentoring.

Mentoring relationships in the Bible[25]

While the word 'mentoring' is not found in the Bible, the concept certainly is. In the following seven examples of mentoring-type connections in the Bible, you will notice that the personal interaction typically arises out of an ongoing relationship. The specific forms of interaction vary in each case, depending on the sort of relationship and the nature of the context. The over-representation of mentoring relationships containing a significant element of apprenticeship reflects the special concerns of biblical writers keen to document continuity of leadership in the redemptive narrative. However, some themes emerge that are helpful to our understanding of how mentoring might be exercised today in order to develop the next generation of Christian leaders.

Jethro and Moses

Running to escape punishment for his crime of murder, Moses fled Egypt and went to live in Midian. Aged forty, he met the local priest, Jethro, and married one of his daughters. Moses worked for Jethro as a shepherd, remaining in Midian for forty years until the Lord called him to lead the Israelites out of

Egypt (Exodus 2:11–3:1). A strong relationship would no doubt have formed between the two men, connected as they were by marriage, by employment and by the communal culture of which they were a part. Jethro's release and blessing, given freely and warmly when Moses sought his permission to return to Egypt, indicates that the relationship was close and strengthened by mutual respect (Exodus 4:18).

In the time that Moses was away in Egypt, Jethro took care of his wife and two sons. As he was returning, Jethro brought Moses' family to him at Horeb and the two met once more, with Moses greeting his father-in-law with affection. He was eager to share with him all the good things that had happened in Egypt. The conversations reported in Exodus 18 reveal a relationship of mutual influence. On the one hand, Jethro expressed delight on hearing that Yahweh had delivered Israel and affirmed, perhaps for the first time, that the God of Moses was supreme over all gods. This confession, and his sacrifice to Yahweh which followed, appears to be due to the strong religious influence from Moses over the forty years of their association. On the other hand, Jethro took the opportunity the following day to give Moses some pertinent advice about wise governance. His approach to mentoring is worthy of close scrutiny.

Jethro was present when Moses sat down to serve as a judge for his people. After a very long day of listening to disputes, Jethro simply asked Moses some open-ended questions about what he had observed (verse 14), drawing him into some critical reflection. Moses did not take affront at this, but fielded the questions honestly, if inadequately. In response, Jethro gave his candid assessment of the situation (verse 17), pointing out what Moses had failed to see. Jethro's mild rebuke was confrontational, but Moses took it on the chin, presumably because of the solid relationship they shared. It appears that this was a normal sort of conversation for these two to have.

Perhaps other leaders close to Moses saw what was happening, but if they did, they did not raise it with him as Jethro did. As a mentor, it was appropriate for Jethro to broach the subject. By drawing out the issue through questions and feedback, Jethro secured Moses' attention before going on to share some much-needed insight into how to deal with the needs and problems of large numbers of people. Jethro's preface to his advice in verse 19, expressing a desire that God would be with Moses, reveals that he was aware in some measure of identifying and promoting the work of God's Spirit in his son-in-law's life. His input contains warning, new perspectives and practical advice. Jethro put it to Moses that his leadership role needed developing from that of sole judge to a delegated, multi-level system of justice. He referred to a five-fold function for Moses himself:

- *Intercessor:* representing the people and bringing their disputes to the Lord.
- *Teacher:* instructing the people in God's decrees and laws.
- *Model:* showing the people how to live and the duties they were to perform.
- *Team builder:* choosing and appointing the right kind of people to share the leadership load.
- *Chief judge:* dealing with the cases too difficult for others to handle.

Although he had been addressing a serious problem, Jethro reinforced his message with a note of hope, painting a picture of a more preferable scenario – what we would call casting a vision. In conclusion, he set his advice in perspective, urging Moses to follow it only 'if God so commands' (verse 23). By doing so he puts the ball back in Moses' court for him to decide what he should do next. Such respect did Moses have for Jethro that he implemented everything he said.

It is not possible to prove beyond doubt that this was not simply an isolated incident of wise counsel rather than an indication of an ongoing mentoring relationship. However, the evidence within the narrative of the longevity and warmth of their connection, the subject matter encompassed by their conversations, the lack of surprise at Jethro's deep engagement on potentially controversial issues and Moses' amenable response all suggests that this is a representative example of regular exchanges of this sort.

Moses and Joshua

Moses' relationship with Joshua was complex, passing through several phases in their long association as Joshua grew from a boy into a fully mature adult. Starting out as an attendant, Joshua was successively an apprentice, a team-member, a senior leader and finally a successor to Moses. In Exodus 24:13 Joshua is described as Moses' 'aide' or 'servant'. The Hebrew word here refers primarily to a young boy and then by inference, to one who is an attendant. Rather than a domestic slave, this type of servant has a higher status, closer to what we might call a personal assistant. Since Joshua was old enough to command Israelite troops in Exodus 17 and had served Moses from his youth (Numbers 11:28), it appears that his association with Moses began no later than the time of the Exodus and possibly earlier than that. By the time of Moses' death, Joshua had served him for around forty years in a close relationship with daily interaction.

Mentoring may involve arranging special opportunities and experiences that promote the work of God's Spirit in the life of a mentoree. This was certainly the case between Moses and Joshua. When the Amalekites came and attacked the Israelites who were camped at Rephidim, Moses gave Joshua the responsibility of gathering a squad to fight them (Exodus 17:8–16). Throughout the skirmish, Moses was in support, interceding with the Lord. His prayers made the decisive difference to Joshua's success. Moses took a risk on Joshua, giving him the opportunity he needed to develop into an outstanding military leader. After the event, the Lord specifically instructed Moses to write up an account of the day's events and make sure that Joshua heard it (verse 14). This is a clear indication that Moses sought to further God's agenda in the young man's life.

Moses found opportunities not only to develop in Joshua

the military skills vital to God's call on his life, but also to deepen his inner, spiritual life. While everyone else was ordered to stay at a distance, even Aaron and the other senior Israelite leaders, Moses took Joshua with him into the presence of the Lord on the peak of Mount Sinai (Exodus 24:13) to receive the tablets of the Law. Subsequently, he took him into the tent of meeting with him when he met with Yahweh (Exodus 33:11). The text indicates that Joshua's presence at Moses' face-to-face meetings with Yahweh was part of their normal routine. Through these life-forming experiences Joshua gained confidence in spiritual matters vital to his future leadership.

Moses' mentoring of Joshua also extended to his personal example and influence of character. Moses modelled humility and gracious leadership (Numbers 12 and 14). By his behaviour in the most trying of circumstances, Moses demonstrated for Joshua that leadership requires sincere intercessory prayer and humility. In Numbers 11:24–30 Joshua responds negatively to two elders who were prophesying in a way that seemed to undermine Moses' authority. Moses asks Joshua an insightful question, drawing him to examine his motives for criticizing the two men. Moses opened up for Joshua another way of seeing the situation. From Moses' perspective, he wished everybody would be a prophet. He used this situation to teach Joshua a vital lesson about empowerment of others. Finally, Moses appointed his long-time servant as his successor. When Joshua was commissioned, Moses empowered him by giving him authority, imparting confidence to use the skills he had developed in him over the years.

Elijah and Elisha

Even before he met him, Elijah was very aware that God wanted him to identify and promote the work of the Spirit in Elisha's life. At a point of deep crisis, Elijah was at the end of his rope when God allowed him a fresh start. In 1 Kings 19:15–16 he was given instructions to anoint the next kings of Aram and Israel and also to anoint Elisha to succeed him as prophet. That succession was not to take place for approximately twenty-three years, during which time Elijah mentored Elisha in an apprenticeship model similar to that of Moses with Joshua. Elisha lived and travelled with Elijah constantly through these years. The bond between them grew to be that of spiritual father and son.

Elijah chose a dramatic way to mark Elisha's call to prophetic ministry. Finding him at his work as a junior ploughman, Elijah threw around Elisha's shoulders his distinctive prophet's cloak – a symbol of spiritual power. At first, Elisha did not fully comprehend the significance of this act, nor the urgency of it. He begged for time to bury his father and mother; in other words, to wait until they had passed away before he would be ready to leave his home and follow Elijah. Even though he knew what God's agenda was for Elisha, Elijah did not coerce him to comply with the call. Instead, he left the way open for him to go back to his parents, but challenged him through a pointed question to consider carefully what had just occurred. That moment of reflection switched on the light of insight for Elisha. In a total turnaround, he slaughtered his oxen, cooked them over a fire made with his ploughing equipment and gave the meat to his fellow workers as a kind of going away party. He irrevocably left everything behind to pursue God's call. This act of empowerment was performed publicly so that it left a deep impression not only on Elisha but also on those who witnessed it.

Mentoring is not always a form of apprenticeship as it was in this case. But even here it is important to note the way this arrangement came about. It was not a matter of Elijah casting about for someone to assist him or to carry on his ministry. Their relationship was God's idea, not Elijah's. What passed between Elijah and Elisha was not predicated on Elijah's agenda or what he had to offer, but on what God was doing in Elisha and how Elijah was in the best position to promote that work. Through witnessing Elijah's interaction with Ahab, Ahaziah and their commanders, Elisha learned how to deal with political and military leaders and how to respond under pressure. He watched how Elijah called upon God for miraculous intervention, something that would later become a hallmark of his own prophetic ministry. Beyond what might be termed prophetic skills, Elisha learned to appreciate the crucial value of the inner spiritual life for leaders through his relationship with Elijah. In their last moment together, Elijah asked Elisha what he could do for him before he was taken away. Of all the things he might have asked for, his one request was that he might have a double portion of Elijah's spirit. What he valued most was the inner qualities he had seen in Elijah, and his greatest desire was to emulate that deep spirituality.

Priscilla, Aquila and Apollos

Originally from Pontus, Priscilla and Aquila set up a tent-making business in Rome, but had to leave there in AD 49 when a disturbance over the Christian gospel caused Claudius to expel the Jews from the capital. They transferred to Corinth in Greece, where they met Paul in AD 50. Since they had just been through a conflict over the Christian faith, the fact that they took Paul into their home and business suggests that they were already Christians at that stage. They helped set up the church in Corinth and made very good friends there. When Paul left Corinth on his way back to Palestine, Priscilla and Aquila accompanied him as far as Ephesus, staying there to prepare the way for Paul's future mission in that city.

It was during this time that they met Apollos, an accomplished public speaker who was preaching a rudimentary form of the Christian gospel based around John's baptism. The account of their interaction is briefly recorded in Acts 18:24–26. It would have been clear to Priscilla and Aquila that the Spirit of God was active in Apollos' life, yet he was in need of some further development. Their invitation to him to come into their home suggests more than a mere casual acquaintance. Furthermore, the extent to which they were able to influence such a sharp mind indicates a mentoring relationship of some depth. Yet this phase, occurring around AD 53, probably only lasted a matter of several months, because Apollos had moved on to Corinth by the time Paul arrived back in Ephesus from Palestine.

Alexandria, from where Apollos came, was the intellectual capital of the ancient world. Raised in this environment, Apollos had a thorough knowledge of the Jewish scriptures and was trained to marshal his thoughts logically and present them convincingly. In addition, he had come to an accurate understanding of the facts about Jesus' ministry. Yet for all his impressive intellectual grasp of the faith, there was something missing. Luke only mentions specifically that Aquila and Priscilla 'explained to him the way of God more adequately' (verse 26). Given Apollos' background, this is unlikely to have been further lessons in propositional truth.

Luke uses the episode involving Apollos to foreshadow Paul's ministry a few verses later in Acts 19:1–7 where he encounters people in Ephesus with the same inadequate grasp of the faith as Apollos. It is reasonable to conclude that Priscilla and Aquila's work with Apollos would have been similar to that of Paul, involving not only instruction but also prayer, spiritual impartation and possibly baptism. Apollos did not need more information; like the believers of Acts 19:1–7, he needed inner transformation by the power of the Holy Spirit. As mentors rather than instructors, Priscilla and Aquila would have been able to reach him on this level.

The brothers at Ephesus encouraged Apollos to pursue his desire to do mission in Corinth and wrote letters of introduction to open up doors for him there. Although it is not clear from the text, it is likely that among those brothers Aquila (and perhaps Priscilla) would have been a key player, since he had excellent recent connections with the church in Corinth and had the best personal acquaintance with Apollos by which to offer a letter of commendation. Priscilla and Aquila provide a good example of short-term mentoring for a strategic transitional phase in a leader's life.

Barnabas and Paul

When no one else would believe that Paul was genuine in his conversion, Barnabas brought Paul to the apostles (Acts 9:27). Their friendship evolved over the years, beginning as a giving mentoring relationship from Barnabas to Paul, becoming a peer relationship as Paul matured, and going through a period of tension before being resolved at some point that we don't read about in the New Testament.

When Paul needed someone to vouch for him, Barnabas was prepared to do so, sponsoring him and introducing him to the apostles in Jerusalem. Paul went away for a long period of time into the desert. He may have been forgotten by others, but Barnabas remembered him, and brought him to Antioch. Barnabas, who was already a leader there, arranged for Paul to be appointed to the leadership team.

On the first missionary journey, he worked alongside Paul as the senior partner. He gave Paul speaking opportunities, so that Barnabas was regarded as Zeus (senior partner) and Paul as Hermes (speaker, herald) by the people of Lystra (Acts 14:12). Barnabas supported Paul as he developed his theology of mission to the Gentiles. He challenged him to take a risk with John Mark – a challenge which Paul refused, thereby causing a rift between the two. Paul eventually came to see that Barnabas was right – John Mark was useful in ministry after all (Colossians 4:10; 2 Timothy 4:11; Philemon 24).

Paul and Timothy

Born to a Greek father and a Jewish mother, Timothy was brought up in Lystra in southern Turkey. He was probably converted through Paul's ministry on his first missionary journey (Acts 14:6–23). On the second missionary journey, Paul and Silas picked up Timothy, most likely as a replacement for John Mark. Local leaders of his home church in Lystra affirmed him (Acts 16:2).

At first Timothy simply accompanied Paul, learning the ropes of ministry through observing him and giving practical assistance. He was then given emissary duty – specific, short-term tasks. Paul sent Timothy from Athens to Thessalonica, from Ephesus to Corinth, and from Caesarea to Philippi. Paul finally gave Timothy a major, long-term responsibility in Ephesus.

Since Paul was at least indirectly responsible for Timothy's conversion, and since he had such a close working relationship with him, he could justly call him his 'true son in the faith' (1 Timothy 1:2; cf. Philippians 2:22).

Paul mentored Timothy by taking his son in the faith on his missionary journeys with him, where Timothy was able to see first hand how the churches were strengthened in the faith and grew daily in number (Acts 16:1–5). He also saw what persecutions Paul had to endure in places such as Antioch, Iconium and Lystra, and how the Lord rescued him each time (2 Timothy 3:10–11). By doing so, the apostle taught and modelled to Timothy what the Christian life and ministry were all about. Paul demonstrated virtues such as faith, patience, love and endurance in the midst of his persecution.

When Paul thought that Timothy was ready to do so in his own right, he gave the young man opportunity to minister the gospel. Paul was always concerned for Timothy's well-being and ensured that he was looked after in ministry situations (1 Corinthians 16:10–11), not wanting ill feeling towards himself to overflow onto Timothy. The apostle also gave him fatherly advice, telling him to drink a little wine for his stomach complaint and frequent bouts of illness (1 Timothy 5:23). Wine was known for its medicinal purposes and Paul was thinking purely of Timothy's health and therefore suggested a remedy.

Throughout his life, Paul continued to exhort, instruct, teach and warn Timothy, even when he was in charge of the church at Ephesus. He encouraged his son in the faith to develop his personal character, spiritual life and ministry. In two letters to Timothy, he gave him instructions, teaching, strategies, encouragements, warnings, and various exhortations. Paul empowered Timothy by giving him direct input and many opportunities so that he could grow personally and develop in ministry.

Jesus and the Twelve

Tracing the mentoring relationship between Jesus and his twelve closest disciples requires us to piece together many incidental snippets of evidence from our sources. Since the Gospel writers' purpose lay elsewhere, we should not expect our information to be complete or even balanced. However, in spite of this difficulty, there is sufficient material to show that Jesus acted as a mentor and some of the ways he went about it.

Although the language of mentoring was not around in Jesus' time, in some respects rabbinical schools operated like mentoring networks. Religious formation of disciples was achieved not through formal classes such as were offered by Greek academies, but by conversations, questions and answers, observation and imitation. If you had asked any of the Twelve what sort of relationship they were in with Jesus, they would most likely have told you that he was their rabbi and they were his disciples. This was the language with which they were familiar. And yet, Jesus reinterpreted the traditional role of a rabbi in ways that sometimes surprised his contemporaries.

Significant social status was enjoyed by rabbis. Jesus' stinging criticism in Matthew 23:6–7 parodies their sense of self-importance:

> They love the place of honour at banquets and the most important seats in the synagogues; they love to be greeted in the marketplaces and to have men call them 'Rabbi, Rabbi.'

Jesus did not adopt a superior stance or hold himself aloof from his disciples but ate and drank and went to parties with them as a social equal. He took an individual interest in each one and considerately cared for their needs rather than demanding that they look after him. Instead of working them into the ground, he suggested they take time out with him on their own to get away and rest. He treated them as friends, not servants. When it came to teaching, Jesus was not just full of words. What he said was backed up by authority, action and a whole way of life that demonstrated his radical teaching about the kingdom of God.

Normally, disciples would choose their own rabbi. It was a consumer-driven market with the most highly regarded rabbis attracting the most talented disciples. Jesus reversed the custom by carefully choosing twelve people – all of them unlikely candidates – and entering into an intentional relationship with each one for the clear purpose of enhancing their effectiveness in serving God. We know this was an important distinction because Jesus reminded them of it at the Last Supper (John 15:16). He was saying, in effect, 'I believe in you.' In John 17:6–8 we get a rare glimpse into how Jesus thought of his relationship with the Twelve. Jesus was acutely aware that his Father had a purpose for each of these people and it was his task to further that agenda. He entered into a mentoring relationship with them only after extensive prayer (Luke 6:12–13).

Jesus adapted himself to the particular personalities and needs of his disciples. To Peter, the man of action, he gave the opportunity to walk on water. For Thomas, who struggled with doubts, Jesus went out of his way to provide the reassurance he craved. Jesus sensitively rehabilitated Matthew's dubious social acceptability by attending a party held in the former tax-collector's home. Nathanael's wall of cynicism was pierced by Jesus looking past this fault to affirm his lack of guile. By paying attention to the uniqueness of each individual, Jesus lifted his connection with them from functional contact to real relationship. Each of Jesus' disciples could be certain that they were loved and accepted for who they were.

Living and travelling together for around three years, Jesus was able to profoundly impact the lives of the Twelve because of his availability and vulnerability. His purpose in calling them was firstly that they should 'be with him' so that he could consequently send them out to preach and have authority over demons (Mark 3:14–15). He was available to them in terms of the resources he could bring to them – his wisdom, power and love. He was vulnerable in the sense that he allowed himself to be deeply known. The Twelve saw him operating in his strengths of teaching, healing and offering grace and also in his moments of extremity, when he was tired, hungry, grieving, exasperated and threatened. Krallmann summarizes well:

> [The Twelve] accompanied him to the synagogue, the Temple, into the fields and onto the Sea of Galilee, to villages and to Jerusalem; they were with him at a wedding and a funeral, when he visited friends and sick people, when he dealt with multitudes and individuals, women and children, religious leaders and outcasts, Jew and Gentiles, rich and poor; they heard him pray, preach and teach; they saw him heal and deliver; they experienced Jesus in public and in private, as joyful and saddened, thirsty and tired.[26]

Jesus mentored the Twelve by demonstrating what he wanted them to learn and become. They studied how he taught and performed miracles. They observed the way he engaged with people one-to-one and how he handled large crowds. They noted how he took time to look after himself emotionally and spiritually. They watched him deal with conflict, criticism and shallow adulation. Jesus modelled for them healthy rhythms of life: activity and rest, prayer and solitude, working and waiting. He expressly gave them an example of servant leadership which he expected them to follow.

Jesus gave the Twelve various assignments when he judged they were ready and empowered them for those tasks with clear strategies, delegated authority and the power of the Holy Spirit. Knowing that he would not always be with them, he worked to build inner strength into the Twelve so they would not remain dependent upon his physical presence with them. He used a wide range of methods to achieve this:

- *Debriefing.* Jesus facilitated reflection after key experiences (Matthew 17:19–20). He wanted to hear from the disciples and give them feedback. The way Jesus worked with the Twelve cycled between instruction, action and reflection.

- *Offering alternative perspectives.* Jesus unsettled the disciples' assumptions, such as the rich being preferred by God (Matthew 19:24–26) and disabilities being the result of sin (John 9:2–3). Once, he grounded their euphoria by pointing out that lasting joy comes from security in God rather than success in ministry (Luke 10:20).

- *Listening.* Observe Jesus' highly perceptive reading of the conversation around the table at the Last Supper in John 13–16. Jesus was also quick to pick up on important loose comments on the road (Mark 9:33).

- *Asking questions.* Jesus knew how to draw out his disciples and stimulate their curiosity (Matthew 16:13; 17:25; Mark 8:17, 27; 9:33).

- *Challenging.* When they were in a position to know better, Jesus was quite willing to confront, correct and even rebuke his disciples (Luke 9:55; Matthew 16:23; Mark 10:14).

- *Affirmation and encouragement.* When the disciples did well Jesus acknowledged it and when they failed he opened a way of restoration (Matthew 16:17–19; John 21:15–17).

- *Use of scripture.* Jesus employed biblical texts to help the disciples understand his mission and as an antidote to human tradition (Luke 4:18–19; Mark 12:10–11; Matthew 22:32; Luke 24:27).

- *Prayer.* Jesus both prayed for them (John 17; Luke 22:32) and taught them to pray for themselves (Matthew 6:5–13), thus helping them to access God's resources.

- *Giving access to special experiences.* For Peter, James and John in particular, Jesus did what Moses did for Joshua, opening the door to life-changing moments such as the transfiguration (Matthew 17) and his final hours in Gethsemane.

In all this, Jesus clearly expected his disciples to put into practice what they learned from him. His mentoring was far from being an exercise in gaining theoretical comprehension of his message. He said, 'Not everyone who says to me, "Lord, Lord," will enter the kingdom of heaven, but only he who does the will of my Father who is in heaven' (Matthew 7:21). Yet he also explained that he was not seeking mere external compliance of behaviour. His constant references to the importance of the heart and inner motivations show that Jesus was looking for deep, radical life-change in his disciples. Yet when their progress was slow, Jesus patiently bore with his disciples' ignorance, pride, laziness and failures and remained committed to them.

Of course, we must be careful not to claim too much for mentoring here. There were aspects of Jesus' relationship with the Twelve that do not belong in the realm of mentoring because of the unique nature of who Jesus is. He alone could rightly claim to be their Lord and Master. He was fully in possession of insights that will always remain at least partially obscured to mentors and mentorees alike. No mentor has the right to say, 'Apart from me, you can do nothing,' and, 'If you love me, you will keep my commands.' Jesus was able to claim personal allegiance and speak with absolute authority in a way that is not valid for mentors. Yet insofar as Jesus did engage the Twelve in mentoring relationships, he serves as the best role model for modern-day mentors of Christian leaders.

New Testament perspectives on mentoring

During his earthly ministry, Jesus not only gathered disciples into relationship with himself; he deliberately built them into an interdependent community. He even went so far as to *command* them to love one another! From Pentecost onwards the Spirit of Jesus has continued and extended this work, creating a church consisting of a web of relationships that are pathways of grace. Metaphors for the community of Christ's followers employed in the New Testament – body, house, temple, family and so on

– stress the interdependence of believers on each other for their progress in discipleship.

In the letters of the New Testament, the dynamic process of promoting the work of the Holy Spirit in another person's life – what I am now naming 'mentoring' – is presented as a natural outworking of following and serving Jesus Christ in the community he has created by his Spirit. Engagement in that process is especially urged upon Christian leaders but it is by no means confined to them. Five major themes concerning mentoring emerge from the New Testament: concern for both being and doing; the role of mentors as examples; the rejection of domination; the creation of future leaders; and Christ-centred formation. A representative sample of thirteen passages is here grouped around these five themes.

Concern for both being and doing

Therefore go and make disciples of all nations, baptizing them in the name of the Father and of the Son and of the Holy Spirit, and teaching them to obey everything I have commanded you. And surely I am with you always, to the very end of the age.

Matthew 28:19–20

[Christian leaders] prepare God's people for works of service, so that the body of Christ may be built up until we all reach unity in the faith and in the knowledge of the Son of God and become mature, attaining to the whole measure of the fullness of Christ.

Ephesians 4:12–13

Jesus makes it clear that the process in which he wants them to engage with new believers is not merely a matter of teaching knowledge that leads to an inner transformation of enlightenment. He is looking for disciples who are immersed and drenched in the Holy Spirit, and who live out their new, inner identity in the practical obedience of everyday life, doing the things he has commanded.

Paul reinforces that the ongoing process of following Jesus and becoming a mature member of his community has to do with both the 'doing' of competence and the 'being' of character. This suggests that mentoring – if it is to truly further God's purposes – will address what the mentoree does – 'works of service' – and the sort of person the mentoree is – 'mature', having the 'fullness of Christ'.

The role of mentors as examples

Whatever you have learned or received or heard from me, or seen in me – put it into practice. And the God of peace will be with you.

Philippians 4:9

Even though you have ten thousand guardians in Christ, you do not have many fathers, for in Christ Jesus I became your father through the gospel. Therefore I urge you to imitate me.

1 Corinthians 4:15–16

Follow my example, as I follow the example of Christ.

1 Corinthians 11:1

Join with others in following my example, brothers, and take note of those who live according to the pattern we gave you.

Philippians 3:17

For you yourselves know how you ought to follow our example. We were not idle when we were with you, nor did we eat anyone's food without paying for it.

> On the contrary, we worked night and day, labouring
> and toiling so that we would not be a burden to any
> of you. We did this, not because we do not have the
> right to such help, but in order to make ourselves a
> model for you to follow.
>
> 2 Thessalonians 3:7–9

The Christian mentor serves as an example of how to respond
to the grace of God, and what that grace can achieve in a human
life. It is important to remember that Paul did not expect those to
whom he wrote to be carbon copies of himself with exactly the
same personality, gifts, calling and ministry, any more than he
himself had exactly the same ministry as Jesus, whose example
he followed. Christian mentors do not expect to reproduce
themselves in their mentorees. Rather, they seek to impart ways
of identifying and responding to the work of the Holy Spirit that
they have discovered so that their mentorees can run the unique
race that is marked out for them.

The rejection of domination

> Nor did we eat anyone's food without paying for it.
> On the contrary, we worked night and day, labouring
> and toiling so that we would not be a burden to any
> of you. We did this, not because we do not have the
> right to such help, but in order to make ourselves a
> model for you to follow.
>
> 2 Thessalonians 3:8–9

> Be eager to serve: not lording it over those entrusted
> to you, but being examples.
>
> 1 Peter 5:2–3

Mentoring becomes ineffective when exercised from a position
of power. It is far more effective for Christian mentors to see
themselves clearly as servants of their mentorees, and not take

advantage of the relationship in any way. While purposeful, negotiated accountability is certainly an element in healthy mentoring relationships, the heavy-handed and intrusive approach adopted by some disciple-making processes that unilaterally demand accountability is to be rejected as contrary to the Spirit of Christ. Jesus' method is to extend an inspiring invitation rather than exercise power to coerce conformity.

The creation of future leaders

> You became imitators of us and of the Lord… and so you became a model to all the believers in Macedonia and Achaia.
>
> 1 Thessalonians 1:6–7

> And the things you have heard me say in the presence of many witnesses entrust to reliable men who will also be qualified to teach others.
>
> 2 Timothy 2:2

Paul is keen that those who receive help to progress in their walk with the Lord, in turn help others to do the same. Each of the passages above refers to four generations of disciples. Each new generation of leaders will need mentors to emerge into their full potential, and has the responsibility to pass on what they have received to the generation that follows them.

Christ-centred formation

> My dear children, for whom I am again in the pains of childbirth until Christ is formed in you…
>
> Galatians 4:19

> We proclaim him, admonishing and teaching everyone with all wisdom, so that we may present everyone perfect in Christ. To this end I labour, struggling with

all his energy, which so powerfully works in me.

Colossians 1:28–29

In every believer the Holy Spirit is working to form the image of Christ – not in terms of personality or ministry calling, but in terms of holy character. The mentoring process is rooted in serving this agenda as a matter of priority so that the mentoree grows in Christlikeness. It goes on to help the mentoree be ready to respond to the specific calling that God places on their life, just as Christ responded to his calling in full surrender, humility, wisdom, power and love.

Mentoring in the history of the church

This quick historical overview traces how processes akin to mentoring have been practised and written about in the period from after the New Testament to the present day.

The early church

During the third and fourth centuries, when the Roman Empire was in decline, many thousands of Christians withdrew to the deserts of the Near East for refuge against persecution. Among them arose 'fathers' and 'mothers', sought out by pilgrims for spiritual advice. Antony of Egypt (d. 356), Evagrius Ponticus (d. 399) and John Cassian (d. 435) were leading Desert Fathers. What has come down to us in documentary form may appear to be merely general pastoral instruction in discipleship. However, it should be remembered that these nuggets of wisdom were first delivered as personal insights addressed to particular people. The Desert Fathers and Mothers did their best to engage with pilgrims as unique individuals. A small sample of mentoring from Antony of Egypt is the following:

> A brother asked an old man, 'What thing is there so good that I may do it and live?' [Antony] answered, 'All works are not equal. The Scripture says that

Abraham was hospitable, and God was with him.
And Elias loved quiet, and God was with him. And
David was humble, and God was with him. What
therefore you find that your soul desires in following
God, that do, and keep your heart.'[27]

Basil (d. 379), bishop of Caesarea, urged Christians to find a
suitable person 'who may serve you as a very sure guide in the
work of leading a holy life.' Basil warned, 'To believe that one
does not need counsel is great pride.'[28] Ambrose of Milan (d.
397) and Augustine of Hippo (d. 430) also offered assistance
to other Christians on a one-to-one basis after the style of
mentoring through personal conversations and letters.

From the fifth century, Celtic Christianity flourished in
Ireland and Britain, growing up out of the roots of the Desert
Fathers. Prominent leaders included Patrick (d. 460), Brigit of
Kildare (d. 524), Columba of Iona (d. 597), Aidan of Lindisfarne
(d. 651) and Hild of Whitby (d. 680). One of the features of this
stream of spirituality was the emphasis on the ministry of the
anamcara or 'soul friend'. Edward Sellner comments:

The stories and sayings of the Celtic saints clearly
reveal that mentoring and spiritual guidance were
considered an important if not essential part of Celtic
Christian spirituality. All the saints seem to have been
changed profoundly by these relationships – whether
they offered a compassionate ear or a challenging
word.[29]

Such was the value placed on mentoring that Brigit is credited
with the saying, 'Anyone without a soul friend is like a body
without a head. Eat no more until you get a soul friend.'[30]

The Middle Ages

By the twelfth century, mentoring was mostly carried out by
and for members of monastic orders. However, there were

notable exceptions such as Bernard of Clairvaux (d. 1153) who wrote over 460 letters of spiritual counsel to seekers, helping them to clearly think through issues of faith and to make good life choices. Aelred of Rievaulx (d. 1167), whose family were custodians of Cuthbert's shrine at Durham Cathedral, was consulted widely on matters of spiritual guidance. Encouraged by Bernard of Clairvaux to produce books of his wisdom, he published his best known work, *Spiritual Friendship*, in which he writes:

> The gospel life, with all its twists and turns, is too much for us to handle alone. We need the counsel, guidance and support of others who will tread the path with us. That person is the spiritual friend.[31]

Likewise, Thomas à Kempis (d. 1471) in his widely read work, *The Imitation of Christ*, urged those seeking a life of deeper discipleship to 'ask counsel from a person of sound judgement; ask instruction from one better than you; avoid following your own proud ideas.'[32] Men and women who took heed of this advice had few alternatives but to seek out clergy and other members of monastic orders. Sadly, generous and tender mentors were hard to find. Medieval mentoring could be controlling and ascetic in the extreme, and tended to aim for conformity to monastic regulation rather than life and freedom in the Spirit.

The post-Reformation era

The Reformers reacted against the authoritarian dominance of the clergy, yet also understood the need for soul care. Martin Luther (d. 1546) and John Calvin (d. 1564) both offered spiritual guidance to searching souls from many walks of life. It is impossible to gauge how extensive the practice was. Because of the individual and confidential nature of mentoring, few records remain of particular mentoring relationships. What we do have is in the form of letters, but this probably represents only a small portion of the mentoring being conducted compared with that being carried out via formal and informal conversations. A string of important works touching on the ministry of mentoring published during the sixteenth and early seventeenth centuries would have been read and used by mentors and mentorees alike. That they achieved notoriety and high circulation gives some indication that the practice of mentoring was alive and well. Some of the better known works are these:

- Martin Bucer (d. 1551), *On the True Cure of Souls*
- Ignatius of Loyola (d. 1556), *Spiritual Exercises*
- Teresa of Avila (d. 1582), *The Way of Perfection*
- John of the Cross (d. 1591), *The Ascent of Mt Carmel*
- Francis de Sales (d. 1622), *An Introduction to the Devout Life*

Through the seventeenth century several famous writers, especially those from the Puritan tradition, continued to give their attention to promoting the work of the Spirit in the lives of others. This was a period of growing intellectual and spiritual destabilization as old religious authority structures were increasingly questioned. These writers produced books designed to provide spiritual anchors for those seeking to pursue their calling in difficult times:

- Richard Sibbes (d. 1635), *Discouragement's Recovery*
- Thomas Goodwin (d. 1680), *A Child of Light Walking in Darkness*
- Jeremy Taylor (d. 1667), *Holy Living and The Golden Grove*
- Richard Baxter (d. 1691), *The Reformed Pastor*
- François Fénelon (d. 1715), *Spiritual Letters*

The Society of Friends (Quakers) stressed the doctrine of 'inner light', by which God speaks directly to the soul, suggesting a somewhat independent approach to spiritual development. Yet their founder, George Fox (d. 1691), wrote more than 3,000 letters that helped seekers in their spiritual pilgrimage. John Wesley (d.

1791) set up what could be termed a mentoring network through his Methodist class meetings across Britain. These groups of a dozen persons plus a leader met for purposes of mutual spiritual nurture that included confession, encouragement and challenge.

The modern period

The rise of modernity from the early eighteenth century and the increasing influence of the philosophical movement we call the Enlightenment had a powerfully deleterious impact on the practice of mentoring in the church generally. This was especially so amongst Evangelicals and Pentecostals in the nineteenth and twentieth centuries. Matters of discipleship and maturity in the faith were addressed more and more through the exercise of reason alone. Pursuing one's calling in God through reflection, revelation and the power of the Holy Spirit gave way to more 'rational' and 'scientific' approaches. Training leaders for Christian service ministry became the exclusive preserve of theological academies and the modernist spirit of rugged individualism and entrepreneurial leadership undercut traditions of pursuing a journey of discipleship in company with others. For many Christian leaders, this led to disastrous consequences.

In spite of these trends, the twentieth century did witness some significant contributions to the ministry of mentoring from people such as the Anglican scholar and mystic Evelyn Underhill (d. 1941) and the Oxford don C. S. Lewis (d. 1963). In addition, custodians of the long tradition of spiritual direction in the Catholic Church such as Thomas Merton (d. 1968) and Henri Nouwen (d. 1996) have gained wide readership in Protestant circles. They have helped Evangelicals to access the wealth of resources for mentoring held within the writings around the topic, particularly from the early church and the Middle Ages.

More recent authors such as Richard Foster, John Mallison, Eugene Peterson and Dallas Willard have placed mentoring firmly on the agenda for anyone interested in developing leaders for mission. Dozens of books on Christian mentoring have been published in the past ten years. Influential Christian leadership magazines now carry regular articles on the topic and an increasing number of ministry training institutes are offering courses in mentoring and spiritual direction as part of their core curriculum. After a long period during the nineteenth and early twentieth centuries in which mentoring was not widely practised among Protestants, something is now changing that makes mentoring a powerful idea for our time.

An ancient art for a post-modern context

In the twenty-first century we are observing signs that the worldview and dominant philosophies associated with the modern period are slowly fading in influence while alternative ways of looking at the world are rising up. Science no longer holds the vaunted status it once enjoyed as we no longer believe it has the answers to our most pressing questions. No longer can rational argument command universal respect. Many people are deeply suspicious of authority structures and of anyone who appears certain of what they think they know. There is a growing sensitivity to context, appreciation of wonder and mystery, craving for authenticity, openness to all kinds of spirituality, valuing of subjective experience and cherishing of community.

The ancient art of mentoring scratches where post-moderns are itching. Moderns approach discipleship and training for leadership by stressing the importance of getting the right answer. Emphasis is squarely placed on what a person knows. The inference is that knowing something automatically translates into transformation of life and ministry. The current crisis among Christian leaders points to a flaw in that approach. Mentoring appeals to post-moderns because it goes beyond what a person knows to the condition of a person's soul. Mentoring gives people space and time, within the context of a sacred relationship, to journey toward transformation not by the power of propositional truth but by the power of the Spirit of truth. A Christian mentor is not so much a person with the right answers as a person with the right questions who walks the road of discovery with others.

Post-moderns respect love and wisdom, but will deny a necessary connection between knowledge and authority. Where moderns tend to trust the expert who is highly knowledgeable, post-moderns are more likely to resonate with a person because of who they are, responding to their integrity and energy. They are more likely to seek a relationship with that person rather than simply look for a set of principles that they can take away and apply by themselves. Mentoring provides precisely that sort of relationship in which the partners can move from objective comprehension to intersubjective understanding.

Individualistic notions of leadership that gained currency in modernity are less and less appealing to post-moderns as the negative consequences of such an approach become apparent. Contemporary Christian leaders crave connection as an antidote to the sterility and vulnerability that results from isolation in leadership. They are keen to find companions for the journey and see leadership more in terms of navigation than of governance.

Post-moderns like to explore the interconnectivity of everything, unlike moderns who tend to comprehend the world in discrete categories. Christian mentoring invites mentorees to respond to the God who is already at work within us in every aspect of our being and doing, inviting them into a deeper relationship and a richer life of love and service. The idea of paying attention to the work of God in our own lives, our experiences, our imaginations, our feelings, and responding in concrete, practical ways to the divine presence appeals greatly to post-moderns.

Mentoring is not merely a passing fad. It has been around for centuries and has deep roots in the Christian tradition and especially in the ministry of Christ himself. Although somewhat dormant through the modern era, mentoring is an idea whose time has come once again because it is so well adapted to the personal hunger and vocational needs of the next generation of Christian leaders.

Chapter 3

Navigating the Perfect Storm

Sarah is a disappointment to herself and, she imagines, to so many who watched her early development as a leader with such anticipation. Leadership came naturally to her at an early age. She was school captain, star of the debating society and leader of her church youth group. She was already engaged in ministry training when she married Ben. He was very encouraging, pursuing his electrical contracting business as a means of supporting Sarah through her undergraduate and postgraduate studies. Sarah's sense of call from God was clear and thrilling. She could think of nothing else she would rather do than to serve God in ministry.

Sarah has been at her present small church in Vancouver in Western Canada for ten years, but it feels like a lifetime. The ideal scenario was for her to serve this small community for a few years to get some experience and then go on to a more challenging role with greater scope for her talents. Leaders in her denomination had encouraged her to pursue this path, but early on things started to go awry. A conflict erupted with one powerful lay leader who turned out to be well connected in the denomination. At first it seemed like a minor setback. Sarah was assured that if she could hang in there and work through the conflict, all would be well. Despite her best efforts, the conflict still simmers after all these years. Sarah has had some great ideas to transform this struggling little church into a vibrant community of faith and mission. But every time things seem on the verge of breakthrough, something happens to make it all fall apart.

Expectations of what she could achieve were high and impossibly diverse. No matter what she has done, someone has been disappointed. Little by little Sarah's self-confidence has been eroded and she has begun to resent those who seem determined to make her life difficult. She thought of seeking another church, but those available to her were in other cities and Ben's business has them tied down. Nowadays, meetings with her area supervisor and ministry conferences with her peers are particularly painful times. Lately, Sarah has been making excuses for herself and even stretching the truth a little to have her performance appear better than it actually is. Once a gregarious and fun-loving person, Sarah has become isolated and morose. Her biological clock is ticking, but she fears that if she takes time out to have a baby she will never go back into ministry. That thought haunts her and she wonders if her sense of call was misguided after all.

Good leaders in crisis

The pressure is on for Christian leaders, especially those who commit themselves to achieve transformational change among God's people for the purpose of mission. The inspirational task of mission presents so many opportunities that they can become a pressing burden for those who dare to care. Good-hearted leaders are running themselves ragged trying to keep up with what they believe is expected of them. At the same time, conditions that can help to make Christian leadership sustainable appear to be lacking and, indeed, evaporating. Thus is created the current crisis for Christian leaders which could be substantially addressed through mentoring.

At a time when expanding opportunities for the gospel require leaders who can keep operating at a high level in a rapidly changing environment, many of our best people are struggling to survive or giving up altogether. They end up unproductive or out of ministry not because they don't have the right stuff, but because there is no one to walk the demanding journey with them, helping them stay fresh and on track. We desperately need solutions to the problem of good leaders underperforming or dropping out of Christian leadership. Considering the task of mission before us, the crucial role that leaders play in addressing that task and the training resources apparently being wasted, this must be a matter of considerable concern for everyone involved in strategizing for mission.

Research being conducted in Australia shows Christian leaders dropping out of ministry at an alarming rate. One outstanding expert in this field is Dr Rowland Croucher, of John Mark Ministries. He estimates that in Australia there is one ex-pastor for every currently serving pastor; about 13,000 at the present time.[33] My own informal survey of people involved in ministry supervision in the UK, Canada and the United States indicates that dropout rates for those countries are similar.[34] Roy Searle, a former President of the Baptist Union in the UK, told me in a personal conversation that dropout rates for evangelical and charismatic leaders in particular are quite phenomenal. Croucher has found that the highest dropout rates are suffered by those denominations with the highest involvement in church planting. From his research it is reasonable to conclude that the more intentional a group of leaders is about transformational leadership, such as those at the coal-face of mission, the higher their attrition rate is likely to be.

But the crisis is not confined to those who drop out. A large percentage of those who remain in ministry suffer from various degrees of stress and burnout. Analysis of the National Church Life Survey published in Australia in 2001 covering 4,500 senior ministers, pastors and priests has findings that are sobering indeed. It reveals that burnout is a major feature in the lives of nearly a quarter of all congregational leaders. In addition, a further half are bordering on burnout.[35] When half of our Christian leaders drop out and only one in four of those who remain are doing well, we have a serious crisis on our hands.

Can mentoring help?

For many years the Baptist Union of Great Britain has recognized the problem of Christian leaders dropping out of ministry. In an early attempt to stem the flow, the Baptist Department of Ministry in the 1990s instituted an assisted self-appraisal process for pastors. The idea was to raise relevant issues with pastors in an unintrusive way. 'Appraiser guides' were made available to help pastors to work through this voluntary process. The take-up rate for this system was very poor, and the attrition continued, with a worrying 20 per cent of ministers dropping out less than five years after graduation.

In 2001 a new system was established for newly accredited ministers in their probationary period of three to four years. This new approach departed from the voluntary self-appraisal approach, opting instead for the appointment of mentors alongside theological reflection groups and a continuing connection with their ministry training college. Several years on, each of their thirteen regional associations has a team of trained mentors in place and the scheme is having a remarkable effect. Robin Urwin from the Baptist Department of Ministry writes:

> In terms of statistics about the impact of the Newly Accredited Ministers' programme, especially mentoring, on the dropout rate from ministry, prior to the introduction of the scheme in 2001, the fall out was 20% in the first five years of ministry. This has now fallen to less than 5%. Across England and Wales, we currently have 320 trained mentors available on our books of whom about 200 are currently in a mentoring relationship with one or more Newly Accredited Ministers. At any one time we might have between 250 and 280 Newly Accredited Minsters at some stage in the scheme.[36]

You may already be convinced of the value of mentoring for Christian leaders, and that may be the reason you have picked up this book. But even if that is the case, what would you say if someone were to ask you why mentoring is such a great idea and whether it is appropriate for all Christian leaders in all contexts? I've been asked that question many times and this is the sort of response I make.

Firstly, I point out that leadership is a function that no one person can carry out alone. It is a team sport and no one has everything it takes to do the job. Furthermore, life was not meant to be a solo journey. Neither are we meant to navigate leadership on our own. We advance the kingdom of God together with other people. Healthy, effective leaders in this enterprise learn how to connect with key people who keep them sharp, on track, focused and in good shape as human beings and as servants of God. It is a strategy of Satan to isolate leaders so as to make them more vulnerable to negative forces and blunt their effectiveness in mission and ministry. So from the point of view of the needs of individual leaders, mentoring is a lifeline that can help them be their very best.

Secondly, I look at the big picture. Producing the next generation of Christian leaders is critical to the task of recalibrating the church as an agent of God's mission. Christian leadership training institutions around the world are grappling with the first part of this process, but what happens once leaders graduate from college? In ministry contexts of comprehensive, far-reaching, discontinuous change especially (but not exclusively) in the Western world, life is extraordinarily tough for Christian leaders who often feel ill prepared for what they encounter. As Eddie Gibbs remarks:

> How can any educational or training institute equip church leaders with the necessary tools to deal with the range of situations they are likely to encounter in the years of ministry that lie ahead of them? Any 'toolkit' approach will soon prove deficient because we do not know what lies ahead. Training... should provide a mentoring experience. Learning opportunities must be provided throughout a person's years of ministry.[37]

Unlike up-front, preparatory institutional training, mentoring travels the journey with the leader, flexibly addressing issues as they arise, ensuring leaders have the best chance to go the distance in a healthy, effective way. Mentoring is a nimble, low-overhead empowerment process capable of delivering just-in-time resources to Christian leaders in a format ideally adapted to their needs and availability. It is precisely the sort of thing denominational bodies and mission agencies are looking for to ensure their leaders stay on the cutting edge of mission.

Before we can fully appreciate the personal value of mentoring for contemporary Christian leaders, we require a more thorough understanding of the issues that lie behind the troubling statistics. We will look a little more closely at why leaders are underperforming and dropping out of ministry, and how mentoring can address those matters. Towards the end of the chapter we will return to further consider the big-picture, strategic value of mentoring for ministry and mission.

The perfect storm

In 1993, author Sebastian Junger was researching a book about the sinking two years before of a fishing boat in extreme weather off the east coast of the United States. In an interview, Bob Case from the National Weather Service explained to Junger that conditions became unusually intense because of the freak convergence of multiple weather events creating a 'perfect' scenario for catastrophic wind, waves and rain. From that conversation was born the term, 'the perfect storm'.

The perfect storm for Christian leadership occurs where systemic hazards meet the vulnerabilities in a leader's personality. By 'systemic hazards' I am referring to the adverse conditions that coalesce around Christian leadership. These conditions are sometimes simply a consequence of helping people deal with momentous issues of life, and sometimes they are dysfunctions of the communities that Christian leaders serve. We all know that leadership is hard. But it is made harder than it needs to be when systems function in carnal ways that are not reflective of the kingdom of God. Very few Christian organizations are thoroughly hazardous to their leaders; but none are completely free of hazardous conditions.

By 'vulnerabilities in a leader's personality', I am referring to those parts of the psyche that are still in the process of being brought into conformity with the image of Christ. These are the weaknesses, old wounds, dark secrets, immaturity and foolish ways that quench leadership capacity. All leaders – all people, in fact – have such vulnerabilities. They are never entirely eradicated, but through the power of the Holy Spirit significant growth and healing can be achieved and the ongoing negative effects can be neutralized.

Leaders and systems form symbiotic relationships. The individual and the community each affect the other both positively and negatively. Human nature being what it is, the negatives tend to have an increasing effect over time, unless outside intervention is interposed. The hazards in a system will exploit the vulnerabilities in a leader unless someone helps the leader to keep their feet in the midst of the storm. Mentoring helps Christian leaders navigate the perfect storm, leveraging their strengths to address their vulnerabilities so that the hazards present in Christian organizational systems are contained and systemic health is promoted.

Systemic hazards

Those who answer the call to Christian leadership find themselves drawn into contexts that are at times demanding, disempowering, emotionally dangerous, isolating and unforgiving. I don't mean to say that these qualities are unremittingly dominant in every Christian leadership context, yet they are present to some degree in virtually every church and Christian organization you may care to name. These hazardous conditions constitute a real danger to the sustainability of Christian leadership. Lauer puts it succinctly:

> Churches expect their ministers to do the impossible.
> His primary calling is spiritual, says the layman,
> but the minister is judged on organisational rather

than spiritual criteria. The minister is a social being
but tends not to have meaningful relationships with
church members... The ministry presents us with a
case of structure punishment.[38]

Let's take a moment to examine each of the five hazardous
conditions I have listed, as they frequently appear in a local
church setting. The leadership setting that you work in may not
be a local church, but you will probably be able to imagine how
these factors might play out in your context.

Demanding

Christians would generally agree that to be involved in the
mission of Christ is the highest, most valuable thing anyone can
do with their lives. It is a cause worthy of our utmost effort,
loyalty and devotion. The problem arises when that effort,
loyalty and devotion is demanded by Christian institutions such
as local churches, denominations, mission agencies, Christian
schools and so on, in the name of Christ. The demands of such
institutions can easily spiral out of control and place burdens on
Christian leaders that Christ himself does not require.

Influenced as they are by secular business models of
success, church organizational systems are greatly concerned
with the quantifiable results of attendances, offerings, baptisms.
Leaders are required to report on the programmes and ministries
being conducted by the church in terms of the number of people
involved and the amount of help they provide. These demands
may drive leaders to produce quantity over quality and pursue
success at any cost.

Christian leaders sign up to serve Christ, but are soon
confronted with a crowd of people with a consumer mentality
which demands that they be served. Their expectations are often
at variance with those of the leader. The leader expects people to
be willing to reset their expectations, while these people expect
the leader to fulfil their expectations. Should leaders allow
themselves to be drawn into this consumer–provider contract,

they soon discover that the crowd's expectations are diverse to the point of contradiction. It is impossible to please one person without displeasing another.

By nature, the roles and functions of Christian leadership are diffuse and multi-faceted. Particularly in local church settings, leaders are required at once to be educator, evangelist, organizer, pastor, preacher, priest, scholar, social reformer and all-round paragon of virtue. Outside Christian circles, such an impossible set of demands would be clearly recognized as unreasonable. Yet they are justified in Christian organizations in view of the high calling of serving Christ's mission, and are taken on by successive generations of leaders who idealistically dedicate themselves to the cause.

Furthermore, the demands of Christian leadership fall not only on the leader but also on their family. The time required to even begin to address the expectations placed upon them takes leaders away from home on a regular basis. Even when they are at home, their responsibilities consume their mind and emotional energy. Pastoral issues have a knock-on effect into family relationships, and it is expected that spouses and children will bear this burden for the sake of the leader's calling. They, too, are expected to react in an unfailingly Christlike manner to every situation.

Disempowering

If the high demands placed on Christian leaders were not enough, matters are made worse by the disempowerment they experience. By disempowerment, I mean the sense that leaders have of lacking the wherewithal to deliver on the expectations demanded of them. One leader described it to me as being told to build a wall, and then discovering he had to make his own bricks. To be fair, the individuals within local churches do not sadistically set out to create these conditions, but they exist for several reasons.

First, there is scarcely a Christian ministry anywhere that does not lack the financial and physical resources it needs to fulfil its vision. If ever the resources do catch up, the vision is soon expanded to embrace an even wider field of mission, leaving us short once again. We're all trying to change the world on a shoestring. Christian leaders find that those who readily applaud bold new initiatives may not be so quick to contribute materially to the achievement of the objective.

Second, the structures of local churches and other Christian organizations typically lack clarity. The organizational chart may look neat on paper, but in reality, the lines of informal influence and communication are usually very complex. Leaders are left a little unclear about exactly who is responsible for what. Who has authority? Who is setting the direction? It is not at all uncommon for Christian leaders to be encouraged to pursue certain projects only to have the rug pulled out from under them at the last moment.

Third, the diminishing respect for leaders evident in Western society in general has had a significant impact in the church. Experts are distrusted. After all, even the experts don't agree with each other. Everyone believes they can be their own expert and weigh the opinions of the so-called authorities. Christian leaders find themselves doubted and questioned every time they seek to lead their people in a direction that challenges their comfort or disturbs the status quo.

Fourth, local churches typically involve a high proportion of volunteers. Leading volunteers is a very different prospect from leading paid employees in business. Volunteers can pull out at any time without warning, without excuse and often without fear of repercussions. Since the power to get things done in and through a community of believers relies on teamwork, the capriciousness of volunteers results in leaders feeling disempowered.

Fifth, Christian leaders suffer from the ambiguity of the servant-leader model. As a leader, they rightly understand that they are empowered to exercise influence and bring about transformational change. Yet there is a sense that the humility required of a servant would have them be responsive rather than take initiative. One of my mentorees once commented to me,

'When I'm doing what they want, they affirm me as a leader. But when I don't, they quickly remind me that I'm a servant.'

Dangerous

Those who have never been in Christian leadership cannot imagine just how scary it can be. This is not just a game. The stakes are high. We are dealing with real people's lives, often at the very point that they are grappling with momentous issues that arouse intense emotions. Christian leadership is a loss-prone business and there are many casualties. Leaders are regularly caught in the crossfire between members of their community. They become targets in their own right for whoever may happen to be angry or frustrated about how they have been treated or the direction they think the organization is headed. Not to mention that Christian leaders are a favourite target for the powers of darkness.

Caring pastorally for people with various personal difficulties is inherently hazardous. Not all Christian leaders are trained counsellors, and yet they are often the first point of contact for people in crisis. Quite apart from the emotional strain involved in these processes, the dysfunctionality of those being cared for intrudes on the person of the leader. All manner of internal reactions are set running that may be difficult to resolve, and few leaders escape unscathed. Church systems tend to unwisely reward leaders who throw themselves heart and soul into every situation of need. Where leaders are encouraged to take on responsibility for others' actions and decisions, a breeding ground for co-dependent relationships is created.

It seems that every conflict in Christian organizations takes on larger proportions simply because of proximity to eternal issues. Simple differences of preference are blown out of all proportion as the parties make their particular viewpoint an article of faith. These conflicts might blow over or satisfactorily remain unresolved except for the fact that Christian leaders are generally expected to create unity and harmony in the system – a hopeless and sometimes misguided goal. The worst of it is when the leader is party to a conflict and there is no one to help work it through. When things are not going well in a church, a common reaction is to blame the leader. Criticism of a very personal kind may come from people the leader took to be friends.

Further dangers arise from the failure of organizations to put in place measures of transparency to ensure their leaders are seen to be above reproach. Excusing this dereliction of duty as trust of the leader, organizations give vulnerable leaders opportunities for indiscretion. Dangerous temptations of a sexual and financial nature are ever-present for many Christian leaders, and form part of the hazardous world in which they move every day.

Isolating

The old saying, 'It's lonely at the top' is nowhere more true than in Christian organizations. Paul and Libby Whetham write:

> [Our] research used a number of quantitative and qualitative measures to help understand church leaders' relationships with other people. Their scores on most measures were lower than average. In the area of general social relating their scores were lower than all other sub-groupings sampled, including psychiatric populations. Church leaders have few, if any, close friends inside or outside the church.[39]

Is this something that is simply part of a leader's profile, or do Christian organizations set their leaders up for isolation? Five factors point to the latter conclusion.

First, the notion of clergy/laity distinction is still deeply entrenched in many churches and Christian organizations, despite the Reformation. Leaders in general and clergy in particular are regarded as a breed apart. Of all the various ways in which this is played out, perhaps the most impactful is that Christian leaders are rarely if ever allowed to be out of role, even in social situations. No matter where they are or who they are with, they never cease to be a Christian leader, with all the attendant responsibilities such a role entails. Few other positions of leadership have quite this dimension.

Second, high mobility makes the enjoyment of long-term friendships difficult. Christian leaders move from one community to the next with above average frequency – second only to members of the armed forces. It is possible for most people to leave one place of employment and take up another job without necessarily leaving behind their entire social community. Christian leaders are required to become totally immersed in the community which employs them so that any change of job is thoroughly disruptive to friendships.

Third, the high demands we have already mentioned that are made of Christian leaders make them too busy to have time for friends. The hours of the day when most people are available for social contact are the times that Christian leaders are most busy working among their community.

Fourth, the friends that leaders make within their leadership contexts are also part of the group that employs them. Inevitably, role conflicts ensue that put strain on friendships. Christian leaders must always be on guard in such situations lest they say too much or act in ways that are later misinterpreted. Most people can choose whether or not to socialize with their work associates. The way the system works means that Christian leaders often do not have that choice.

Fifth, the structures established by networks of churches to connect leaders with their colleagues tend to exacerbate feelings of isolation. For example, area supervisors and bishops appointed by denominational networks do not operate pastorally but bureaucratically. Where a pastor to the pastors is appointed, they are stretched to the point that they are only dealing with the most desperate cases.

Unforgiving

It is disappointing to say that some of the most ungracious, harsh and vindictive organizations I have ever come across are churches. It would be a stretch to assert that the individuals who comprise these churches had those qualities. But somehow, when those individuals acted together, the organizational culture kicked in and took on a most un-Christlike tone. Anyone who dares to represent such a Christian organization in a position of leadership is liable to suffer wrath if they should bring discredit on that organization in any way. To defend the name of Christ, some churches will judge offending leaders in ways that are hardly consistent with the Jesus we find in the Gospels. There are few genuinely restorative processes in organizations where judgment triumphs over mercy.

The most severe treatment is reserved for Christian leaders who fall into moral failure, and news of this becomes public. Christian organizations respond rapidly to distance themselves not only from the offending behaviour but also from the offender. Codes of conduct and ethical charters are drawn up to identify actions that will not be tolerated and the consequences for those who transgress. The emphasis is on punishment rather than restoration. These codes of conduct are essential in the current context. Yet one cannot help but wonder if their adoption by Christian organizations is more about managing risk and avoiding litigation than it is about strengthening the integrity of Christian leaders.

It is not only moral failure that triggers an unforgiving systemic response to Christian leaders. Leaders who get into such deep trouble that they can no longer function through burn-out or depression may find themselves out of a job and on the scrapheap with little prospect of returning. This is another form of falling from grace. These former leaders sink without a trace and are never seen or heard of again. They are regarded as an embarrassment. Christian organizations do not easily forgive weakness in those who are supposed to be heroes. It has been said that the church is the only army on earth that shoots its own wounded, and many thousands of ex-pastors can attest to that truth.

The vulnerabilities of a leader

The systemic hazards that exist in Christian organizations, at whatever level they are found, would not be such a problem if leaders were not sitting ducks for these hazards. At the same time, common vulnerabilities that exist, not just in Christian leaders but in many people, would be of small concern if not for regular exposure to the conditions that exploit them. That is the nature of a perfect-storm scenario. Each element has a multiplier effect on the other. In this scenario, even the best of leaders are at risk of failing to reach their potential. Let's work through the aspects of leader vulnerability that are exposed by the systemic hazards I have described.

Demanding leadership contexts

Demanding leadership contexts will expose leaders who have not settled the question of their own identity in God apart from their identity in their role. Tendencies to be driven by performance will cause a leader in demanding systems to engage in compulsive behaviour, working harder and harder to meet the expectations of the system. If the leader should have any difficulty in managing time and planning effectively, the inevitable result is a lack of self-care. Leaders in these contexts often fail to give proper attention to their families. If these aspects of vulnerability are not addressed, burnout may result.

Disempowering leadership contexts

Disempowering leadership contexts will bring out the worst in leaders who are not especially resourceful or resilient. Out of insecurity they may engage in passive-aggressive behaviours – characterized by indirect or underhanded attempts to address unmet needs – in an attempt to control intolerable situations and overcome feelings of powerlessness. In addition, disempowering contexts will expose leaders with a tendency to fantasize. Compensating addictive behaviours commonly arise in these contexts as leaders try to find a way to find comfort or escape.

If these aspects of vulnerability are not addressed, depression may result.[40]

Dangerous leadership contexts

Dangerous leadership contexts are a special snare for leaders with a lack of self-awareness and a lack of emotional maturity. Without understanding how and why they are reacting to the emotional pressures around them, they will neglect to observe wise boundaries. Leaders with a strong desire to be helpful – the need to be needed – often fall into the trap of co-dependency by which they, perhaps inadvertently, perpetuate the self-destructive behaviour of others. If leaders are at all prone to temptations of lust and greed, churches may be places of great danger. Conflict will bring out the worst in a combative, defensive leader. If these aspects of vulnerability are not addressed, termination of tenure may result.

Isolating leadership contexts

Isolating leadership contexts are particularly poisonous for leaders who are prone to individualism. In such systems, leaders become unaccountable for their personal lives and miss out on the advantages of friendship. In their loneliness they may become either aloof, or paranoid, or both. At the very least they lose perspective on what is happening to them and around them and are more likely to make serious errors of judgment. If these aspects of vulnerability are not addressed, disconnection from the cause of Christ may result.

Unforgiving leadership contexts

Unforgiving leadership contexts cause leaders with character flaws to hide their inadequacies. Such leaders become shallow and hypocritical, maintaining a veneer of piety to cover their shame. Leaders in these contexts may not be aware of any major flaws, yet may grow narcissistic – inordinately obsessed with enhancing and preserving their image. Where judgment and unforgiveness dominate, leaders will resort to telling lies to avoid dealing with their struggles. If these aspects of vulnerability are not addressed, moral failure may result.

The following table summarizes the issues we have been considering:

Systemic Hazard	Leader's vulnerability	Likely outcome
Demanding	Performance driven Compulsive Fails to manage time Lack of self-care Takes family for granted	Burnout
Disempowering	Insecurity Compensating addictive behaviours Passive-aggressive (controlling)	Depression
Dangerous	Lack of self-awareness Crosses boundaries – lust, greed Combative, defensive Co-dependence	Termination
Isolating	Individualism Unaccountable Lonely Inadequate perspective Paranoia	Disconnection
Unforgiving	Hides character weakness Shallowness Hypocrisy Narcissism Tells lies	Moral failure

Of course, in real life, it's not actually quite that neat. Isolation contributes to burnout and disempowerment has an impact on moral failure, for example. This table is designed merely to begin to make sense of the exceedingly complex web of factors that play a part in the underperformance or dropout of Christian leaders. Now that we have this clearer understanding of the issues, we are in a position to consider how mentoring can address them.

The personal value of mentoring for leaders

In the light of the five areas of challenge for Christian leaders, mentoring firstly assists leaders struggling with massive demands by shifting the focus of attention to God's agenda. This gives a frame of reference for resolving clashing expectations. Secondly, mentoring connects leaders who are feeling powerless with spiritual resources. In this process, mentorees recover hope and confidence that they can rise up to answer God's call on their life. Thirdly, mentoring establishes a demilitarized zone – a safe relationship of acceptance and confidentiality. Mentorees learn to let go of their anxiety and carefully examine the relational dynamics going on within and around them. Fourthly, mentoring provides healthy relational support and accountability. Mentorees get the benefit of a broader perspective and learn the value of working through difficult issues in partnership rather than alone. Finally, mentoring is a relationship of grace and truth in balance where character is explored and strengthened. Character flaws are not excused, but neither are they a trigger for punishment and rejection.

Relevant to these issues, there are five capacities of mentoring which I have discovered that bring health and strength to Christian leaders and set them up to navigate the perfect storm with confidence. These capacities are: personal and spiritual preparation, relational connectedness, non-competitive partnerships, empowering structures and life-transformation.

Personal and spiritual preparation

There has been a worrying underemphasis on personal and spiritual preparation in training for Christian leadership and pastoral ministry over the past several decades. In too many training institutions it has been naïvely assumed that students with satisfactory academic results will also somehow have developed spiritual and emotional maturity sufficient to see them through a lifetime of difficult ministry. The growing number of leaders dropping out of ministry shows that this is not the case. However, the responsibility for developing this maturity cannot be left with training institutions alone. The most they may be expected to do is clearly flag the issue so that graduates are aware that they will need to access ongoing means of addressing it throughout their ministries.

This matter is all the more critical for those leaders engaged on the front line of mission where they are often without the support of a mature Christian community with attendant corporate spiritual disciplines. Christian ministry is difficult partly because we regularly find ourselves out of our depth dealing with complex, sometimes irrational human nature as well as awesome, eternal mysteries that go beyond our capacity to fully comprehend. Those who are committed to transformational leadership in mission find it additionally difficult because they enter a context of opposition from a committed spiritual enemy. These leaders accordingly have a complex relationship with their work and calling – alternately experiencing euphoria and despair.

Mentoring helps leaders to keep their heads in the midst of the difficulties they face by clarifying the issues in the light of God's goodness and greatness, and bringing to bear – amongst other things – spiritual resources to build strength into the inner life of the leader. By paying close attention to the work of the Holy Spirit, matters of identity and character for the leader are raised so that the leader is better prepared to tackle the spiritual and emotional hazards of ministry.

Relational connectedness

Christian leaders in both front-line mission work and pastoral ministry desperately need relational connectedness without professional strings attached, yet they are currently experiencing increasing levels of isolation and loneliness. Several factors are combining to produce this outcome. Those in both local church ministry and mission agencies are dealing with increased time demands. Tight budgets mean less staff members are available to service the growing expectations of parishioners and supporters. Short of time, leaders simply lack the opportunity to develop significant friendships outside the church or mission agency.

At the same time, growing consumer attitudes both inside and outside the church assign leaders to professionalized, non-reciprocal roles. Leaders are increasingly expected to deliver the service for which they are paid in a depersonalized transaction. Less and less does their work create the occasion for mutual ministry in which they are able to benefit from two-way giving and receiving. This vocational hazard puts Christian leaders at great risk of disillusionment and possible compromise of their calling.

It cannot be discounted that some isolation in Christian leadership is a result of poor choices driven by pride or laziness. Some leaders are sufficiently arrogant to suppose that they do not need personal spiritual and emotional support. Yet there are far more that fail to reach out because of insecurity. Those who supervise such leaders must bear some responsibility for providing opportunity and incentive for them to access appropriate support networks such as mentoring.

Non-competitive partnerships

Christian leaders need the kind of partnerships in their work that encourage the heart and provide a sense of solidarity in team. Yet there continues to be a tendency for relationships between Christian leaders to be competitive. Thus, when they make the effort to overcome their isolation by attending peer gatherings, they are exposed to conversations that are not conducive to honest disclosure and feedback. To be fair, this is most prevalent among male leaders and is less obvious in all-female settings. However, since the majority of Christian leadership gatherings are mixed gender and dominated by males, the result for females is, sadly, the same. Informal peer mentoring, that could otherwise be so helpful to leaders, is all too rare in an atmosphere such as this.

It is reasonable to ask why Christian leaders have become so competitive. If we are all on the same team, working in partnership for the same goal of extending the kingdom of God, why are we not more supportive and collaborative? The answer has partly to do with our tendency as leaders among God's people to admire and imitate the way the world conducts leadership. Taken in by appearances of cleverness and success, we imbibe values of competition and non-collaboration. Yet deeper down the reasons are rooted in personal insecurities and lack of security in God that cause us to default to a performance orientation in assessing our own value and worth.

By the nature of their ministry, mentors are on the side of the leader and work collaboratively with the express intention of encouraging the heart. They remind leaders of the values of the kingdom of God that stand radically opposed to the values of the world, and open up ways toward deep security in God. Mentors of Christian leaders will share a similar passion for serving Christ and his mission, providing mentorees with a partner in ministry who has no interest in playing competitive games.

Empowering structures

Christian leaders need to find a place to fit in structures beyond themselves that provide them with not only an essential line of professional accountability but also appropriate support and delegated authority to make decisions and put them into effect. However, leaders who look to their parent organizations to provide *personal and spiritual* accountability and support may find the structures of their denomination or mission agency to be bureaucratic and, frankly, disempowering.

In broad terms, according to the extent to which these

organizations exercise power, they compromise their capacity to impart power. Further, those assigned by the structures to provide support and accountability may be perceived to have a conflict of interest between what is best for the leader and what is best for the organization.

Some leaders opt out of organizational structures because of this and other related reasons, dismissing such structures as being irrelevant to their calling to leadership. They run the risk of drifting in and out of ad hoc networks that fail to deliver the meaningful support and accountability essential to spiritual empowerment. I have seen this happen on numerous occasions and see it as the major leadership integrity challenge facing the emerging church movement.

What is needed is ongoing, stable yet flexible accountability and support structures that are capable of imparting empowerment precisely because they do not exercise power over the leader. Competent mentors operating in a negotiated formal arrangement have the capacity to provide just those kinds of structures.

Life transformation

Christian leaders need opportunities to thoroughly process the information they receive about ministry, mission and leadership. Yet available in-service training opportunities generally fail to produce personal transformation. Seminars, conventions, workshops and the like are able to deliver information and even stimulate conceptual change. However, they are unable to facilitate deep change of heart and mind because they are short-term and piecemeal in nature. They cannot bring about integration of the content offered into the life of the leader concerned because these things take time and careful consideration of the unique intersecting factors that exist in the lives of each participant.

It may be too early to call it a trend, but I have noticed a shift in the way some Christian leaders are allocating their professional development budgets. My research into mentoring in the UK conducted in 1999 indicated that only a small fraction of pastors were willing to pay for the services of a spiritual mentor, yet they were attending several conferences each year. My observation now is that younger leaders in particular are being more selective about which seminars and conferences they will attend and are investing in one-on-one coaching and mentoring sessions. This is something which only a few years ago would have been out of the question. In Canada and Australia in particular the rush of younger leaders to employ ministry coaches is remarkable. This seems to indicate that these leaders believe the achievement of their goals will involve something beyond simply absorbing knowledge. They want someone to keep working with them until they 'get it'.

Mentoring recognizes the need for an empowering process that is long term rather than short term, holistic rather than piecemeal and that, through pursuing God's agenda for the individual, achieves the integration essential for genuine life transformation. Some forms of coaching may also achieve this. However, the ministry coaching I have observed is mostly about affirming and developing strengths, leaving out essential confrontation and challenge on the character issues that so often affect the long-term assimilation of new understanding.

In summary, mentoring has the capacity to significantly address all five of these needs of Christian leaders. Mentored leaders gain the benefits of help in maintaining personal spiritual health, a companion for the journey, a safe relationship in which to discuss vocational issues, accountability from a person without positional power, support which is not conditional upon ministry performance, integration of the theory and practice of ministry through reflection and effective help to achieve goals of inner transformation.

The strategic value of mentoring for the kingdom

We now return to the matter of the value of mentoring from a big-picture perspective in the midst of the current crisis of

Christian leadership. In addition to the benefit gained by the mentoree, the kingdom of God is strengthened through effective mentoring networks. This perspective will be of particular concern to mission agencies and what are now being called 'missional churches' – that is, churches that are seeking to creatively adapt to a changing context for mission in order to more effectively make disciples. In traditional models of church, damaged and failing Christian leaders may be able to remain in their posts undetected as long as they simply keep the wheels of the institution turning. But in missional churches, mere maintenance is not acceptable. Lasting personal health and effectiveness of their leaders is essential. This brings into sharp focus the need for sustaining processes for Christian leaders that continue on when initial leadership training is completed.

Leaders developed faster

Because mentoring maintains focus on agreed objectives by holding the mentoree accountable, the mentoree's development in leadership is accelerated beyond what is commonly observed in unsupported leaders. This is the 'fast-track' factor. As I expressed in my introduction, I have some concerns about this becoming the main reason for providing mentoring to a young Christian leader. Such leaders should never be regarded primarily as units of production in the machinery of the kingdom of God. Where this occurs, it simply contributes to the pressure that can make ministry unsustainable.

Mentoring does not accelerate development in leaders like certain drugs enhance the performance of athletes. Rather, mentoring supports the normal, healthy growth and strengthening of a leader, minimizing the stunting, debilitating factors that often abnormally delay development in leaders who do not have access to such support. Leaders typically report that much of the personal progress they make is offset by slides back into old habits, or the inability to cope with new pressures, or one of a range of other negative factors. It's the old 'three steps forward and two steps back' syndrome. Mentoring does not eliminate the inevitable ups and downs of life, but it does help to consolidate gains and reduce regression. Keeping the main thing the main thing provides for cumulative, compounding growth and strength in much the same way as a carefully designed physical training regime builds an athlete's capacity without resort to drugs.

Better quality leaders

A great deal of effort is put into producing and selecting high-quality leaders these days. Most organizations are very careful about who they place in positions of significant responsibility. Where leadership fails, the reason is more often than not a character flaw rather than a deficiency in mental capacity or lack of skills. The nature of Christian leadership means that nowhere is this more true than in the church. Other forms of preparation and equipping for leadership address a leader's head and hands. Academic institutions provide an intellectual grasp of knowledge and apprenticeship placements enhance proficiency in practical techniques. Mentoring is especially suited to address the heart, dealing with critical inner character issues.

It is altogether too easy for leaders without mentors to duck difficult yet real personal issues that may threaten the quality of their leadership in the long run. Getting to these issues is not a matter of the mentor proactively digging, trying to discover character flaws in the mentoree. On the contrary, the probing, investigative work of the mentor is focused on the good work of the Spirit rather than the deficiencies of the mentoree. But when the Holy Spirit begins to deal with character issues, the mentor can help the mentoree to work with the Spirit, thereby building a strong, inner foundation. When this is put together with the preparation and ongoing equipping of academies and apprenticeships, leaders have the all-round quality necessary for the development of significant, healthy ministries.

Leaders last longer

Rowland Croucher says that the statistics on ministry drop-out are getting worse and are related to at least forty different reasons for leaving, among which conflict was most prevalent.[41] No doubt, we might be able to prevent some leaders dropping out by providing, at the ministry preparation phase, better training in the theory and practice of conflict resolution – and we would need to do the same for each of the other thirty-nine reasons for leaving. Yet, in my experience, even leaders who do have adequate knowledge and skills in all the key areas still struggle with their actual experience because they lack the focused, personal support and accountability that a mentoring relationship can provide.

In the cut and thrust of a conflict situation, for instance, issues lurking below the surface are suddenly exposed. Uniquely challenging scenarios are thus created for which no entirely adequate theoretical or procedural preparation can be made. What is needed is a readily available relational solution. In such a vulnerable moment when quitting can seem like the best option, a mentoring relationship helps Christian leaders maintain perspective and access resources in God essential for sustainable ministry.

Other points of vulnerability widely acknowledged as common triggers for leadership dropout – sense of identity, personhood issues, lack of self-awareness, strain on marriage, tension within teams, lack of self-care, failure to cultivate adequate spiritual disciplines – are the very matters with which mentoring is most capable to deal. The relational dynamic of mentoring develops interdependence in leaders, making them less liable to burnout. It is my observation that the vast majority of Christian leaders who remain effective in ministry and finish well are easily able to identify the individuals who have acted as mentors throughout their ministry.

In the last three chapters I have discussed the nature, biblical basis, history and contemporary value of mentoring. Having set the scene in this way, I now want to move from theoretical foundation to practical implementation. There is too much at stake and time is too short for this matter of mentoring Christian leaders to remain merely an interesting topic for discussion. As you delve into the following chapters, I hope you will think of Christian leaders known to you, and consider how you might practically go about strengthening their ministry through mentoring.

Chapter 4

Getting Started

Getting off to a great start will give your mentoring relationship the best chance of developing into something that is both fulfilling for the mentor and effective for the mentoree. And the key to a great start is thorough preparation. If you take time up front to lay the groundwork for your mentoring you will reap the benefits later. I have had some mentorees who have found the preparation process a little tedious. Later on they are invariably grateful for the clarity it brings and the potential clash of expectations it avoids.

In addition to preparation, good formal mentoring relationships do need to be monitored and managed. Far more can be achieved in mentoring when the relationship moves from something occasional and haphazard into a more intentional mode. However, this intensification requires appropriate boundaries and processes in order to stay focused and on track. This chapter explores basic issues of preparation and management to be considered at the commencement of a mentoring relationship.

Who chooses who?

It is not uncommon for both mentors and mentorees to feel somewhat like teenagers at the High School dance. Lacking the confidence to ask the question of a potential partner, they sit on the sidelines, longing to get involved in the action but not sure how to go about it. Hesitation arises from several uncertainties: 'What are the rules here?', 'What if I get rejected?', 'Are they already linked up with someone?'

Mike Pegg, a professional mentor working in the secular field, thinks the way the relationship between mentor and mentoree comes about is of critical importance. His view is that mentorees should be able to choose their own mentor so that they can ensure they have a 'values fit'.[42] I would certainly agree that a close registration of values between mentor and mentoree is highly determinative of the eventual success of a mentoring relationship. However, I'm not so sure that landing the potential mentoree with the responsibility to always take the initiative is the only way to bring that about. In some cases, a crucial value may be expressed by the very act of the mentor approaching the mentoree, as it was for Jesus when he chose the Twelve (see Chapter 2).

My view is that either the potential mentor or potential mentoree could take the initiative to commence a mentoring relationship. For both parties, the values they perceive in the other will be of critical importance. In Christian leadership circles it is usually expected that the potential mentoree should do the asking. However, Bobb Biehl addresses potential mentors, questioning whether young adults are inclined to do this:

> Are they going to come up to you and tell you how much they admire you and ask you to be their mentor? When you were their age, did you tell the adults that you looked up to that you admired them? Did you ask them to be your mentor? Probably not! You probably hoped they would take the initiative by approaching you. The people you consider future leaders are probably looking at you and in their hearts saying, 'I sure wish I could get some time with that person!'[43]

Mentors and mentorees may work through this checklist to identify a potential person to approach:

- Write down what you are looking for in a mentoring relationship.
- Review the qualities listed in this book of good mentors (Chapter 5) or mentorees (Chapter 6).
- Make a list of up to three potential candidates who come to mind as you review those qualities, and with whom

you share the same fundamental values.

- Consider what Christian mentoring achieves: Within intentional, empowering, unique relationships, Christian mentoring identifies and promotes the work of God's Spirit in others' lives, assisting them to access God's resources for their growth and strength in spirituality, character and ministry.
- Identify which of your candidates best fits the criteria you have considered.
- Ask God to make his will clear to you.

Good Christian mentoring relationships get their start in prayer. So whoever makes the first move and the one approached to consider the proposal will both be wise to first hold the idea before God in prayer to find out if this is what he has in mind for the people involved. If it seems to both people that God is in it and it's worth pursuing, then an initial meeting can be arranged at which hopes and dreams will be put on the table. Only after that meeting will the parties be in a position to commit to an ongoing arrangement for mentoring.

The first session

The purpose of the first meeting is simply to get to know each other a little better, to get a sense of each other's heart and values, and to discover an approach to mentoring which appeals to both people. Ask each other, 'What would make this a successful mentoring partnership for you?' From the things the mentor says, the mentoree will make an assessment of the level of trust he or she is prepared to place in the mentor. From the things the mentoree says, the mentor will begin a process of discernment to perceive how the Holy Spirit is dealing with them and seek confirmation from the Lord about how to proceed.

Mentoring is a journey on which the mentor accompanies the mentoree from where they are to the place where God wants them to be. At the outset of a mentoring relationship many things about the journey are unclear. The destination is yet to be discovered and the next port of call is most likely undecided. The navigation for this journey is like any other; it takes account of conditions, clarifies the present position, identifies the destination and only then sets a course. These elements shape the way I approach an initial meeting with a mentoree.

Assess the conditions

To assess the conditions for a mentoree's journey, I begin by asking them to tell me a little about themselves. The question is deliberately left as open-ended as possible. If they should ask, 'Well, what do you want to know?', I respond, 'Just the things that you think are most important in your story.' The choices mentorees make about what to include and what to leave out are themselves important clues about the conditions of their lives.

The background that comes out of this part of the first meeting is like getting details of prevailing winds, currents, climate and seasons. Past environments and patterns of behaviour are vital pieces of information when the time comes to chart a course ahead. You do not need the skills of a psychotherapist for the purposes of this stage; neither should you be concerned to dig too deeply. A relatively small amount of information will begin to give you a sense of where the person is coming from. Deeper understanding will emerge as time goes on.

Unless you have an excellent memory for details, it is wise to make a note of the things that are mentioned at this stage. Some items that seem insignificant within this conversation will recur later, giving you a clue about their true importance. Your impression of the prevailing condition of the mentoree's life will also suggest ways in which you might tailor your approach to this mentoring relationship, taking account of their personality, experience and preferences.

Map the present location

Having heard a little of their past, I then ask, 'And how are you going now?' With this question I am trying to tease out the issues with which the mentoree is currently grappling, and especially the areas of life in which God's Spirit is most active. If there is some difficulty in identifying those areas, I may use a diagnostic tool such as the one found in Chapter 8. Alternatively, for an initial meeting in which I don't want to get too heavy, I might employ a simpler structure developed by my friend and colleague, Dr Keith Farmer. This provides prompts in the five areas of: spirituality, key relationships, emotional health, created rhythms of life and vulnerabilities. Keith explains his approach in the appendix at the end of this book.

Identify the next port of call

Next, I ask about the goals my mentoree wishes to pursue. Occasionally we may need to work together to generate several possible goal-options between which they can choose. However, most people have a ready opinion about where they want to go and which areas of their lives need attention. Their opinion may vary from God's agenda, but that need not be a concern at this point: any need to realign goals will become evident in time. It is necessary to begin where the person is at that moment. Reserve judgment on future directions your mentoree shares even when you're doubtful or sceptical about them. Keep in mind that the world is all too willing to tell your mentoree why she or he can't have that dream. You may be the mentor that helps it happen.

In this stage of the conversation I check to make sure that the mentoree fully owns the goals they have identified. It is possible that a goal may be articulated simply for the sake of having something to say, or because it was what they thought I wanted to hear. These goals will shape the direction of the mentoring process, so it is vital that the mentoree believes in them, is committed to them and takes responsibility for them. It is better to let this stage of the conversation flow over into a second session than to rush into the next stage with superficial goals.

However, even though the goals are identified by the mentoree himself or herself, it is normal in mentoring that these goals will evolve over time. This is not because they were arrived at whimsically, but because progress on the journey reveals deeper insights into God's agenda and the goals require adjustment accordingly. Therefore it is wise to have a structured way of recording the goals. I ask the mentoree to write them down and send them to me by email along with their summary of the session we have just had. This way we both have a written copy of the goals the mentoree is working on and the mentoree is fully in control of how they are articulated.

Set a course

The next stage of the conversation requires restraint on the part of the mentor. Without telling the mentoree what they should do, the mentor helps the mentoree to devise action steps that will carry them closer to their goal. The mentor is free to discuss and generate options. But it is essential that when the time comes for writing them down alongside their goals, the mentoree should freely nominate their action steps and commit to implementing them out of their own desire for progress. I encourage mentorees to devise action steps with SMART qualities: specific, measurable, achievable, relevant and time-framed.

As part of setting the course, I explain to the mentoree how the mentoring process proceeds from this point. At the next session, the action steps they have set are reviewed to find out whether they were carried out and how effective they were at achieving the progress for which they were devised. In that review process, the action steps will be refined or replaced. Indeed, even the goals may be reshaped according to the mentoree's evolving awareness of God's agenda.

Periodically, goals will be reached and new ones will be formulated. Occasionally, new goals will emerge that take precedence over the ones previously stated. Bit by bit, mentor and mentoree together will gain a clearer idea of what God wants to do in the mentoree's life. Goals and action steps are constantly being reviewed and reshaped in this iterative process.

The first session is now drawing to a close. By this point in your time together you can expect to have built up a degree of energy and expectation about being in a mentoring relationship together. If not, it is probably best to let it go, at least for the present. However, if the 'spark' is evident, spend the last part of the first meeting considering how you will proceed by drawing up a mentoring contract, following the guidance in the next section.

Establishing a mentoring contract

If you are both willing to establish a mentoring relationship, work out the ground rules and practical arrangements of how and when you'll meet or communicate before you begin. The questions that need to be settled up front are these:

- Over what period will the mentoring last?
- How and/or where will mentoring sessions be held?
- How often will sessions take place?
- How long will the sessions be?
- How accessible is the mentor to be outside those sessions?
- Who will initiate contact and confirm arrangements?
- What matters will the mentoring address?
- What outcomes are expected?
- Who has responsibility for those outcomes?
- What expectations does the mentoree have of the mentor?
- What expectations does the mentor have of the mentoree?
- What are the expectations of honesty and accountability?
- What standards of confidentiality are expected?
- Who will cover the cost of this mentoring?
- How will incidental expenses be handled?
- What process of review will be followed?

Although this list is designed to be fairly comprehensive, it is wise to ask if there are other special boundary issues that are a concern to either person. The responses to all these questions can then be summarized in a brief document, no more than two pages long. In most cases, this document will not be referred to again until the relationship is reviewed; the value will have been in the process of constructing it. However, situations may arise in which such a document will be an important point of reference to clarify clashing expectations and sort through misunderstandings.

Formal mentoring contracts can be constructed in a wide variety of ways to suit the specific circumstances of the individuals involved, and there is no one best way to structure them. But for the benefit of those who have little or no experience in mentoring and would like a place to begin, I will outline a typical mentoring arrangement that should serve for the majority of Christian leaders. Please remember that this is just one possible format. Although it is commonplace, it is not at all prescriptive.

Mentoring usually consists of a series of one-to-one, face-to-face meetings, roughly monthly, of around two to three hours' duration. In Chapter 9 I will deal with other ways of conducting mentoring other than face-to-face. These are best used when large geographical distance is a factor. When meeting face-to-face it is important to settle on a location in which concentrated conversation and prayer may take place. As a rule, it is not wise to choose a location in which you cannot be observed or interrupted, yet some degree of privacy is desirable. It is most common for the mentoree to do the major part of the required travel to such a location, yet from time to time there is benefit in the mentor being present in the mentoree's everyday environment. I recommend that the initial period for a mentoring contract be twelve months.

The usual pattern of monthly sessions, mentioned above, has a rationale behind it. For the typical mentoring relationship, this frequency allows enough time between sessions for new circumstances to arise that generate topics of conversation and enough time for the mentoree to take the agreed steps toward his or her goals. More mature and self-motivated mentorees may find meeting this frequently makes mentoring sessions tedious and redundant. In this case, sessions may be adjusted to quarterly or even annually. On the other hand, in certain periods of rapid change or serious upheaval, mentorees might find monthly sessions leave them feeling adrift in a fast-moving current. In these circumstances, more frequent sessions or other forms of contact between sessions may be introduced.

The duration of these sessions should be long enough for the mentoree to really get to the bottom of what has been happening in their lives, without the session becoming mentally or emotionally exhausting. My experience is that this is typically achieved in about two to three hours, although greater skill may enable a mentoree to engage with the relevant issues in a shorter time. If the time is too long it will become difficult to keep focused on the issues, and both parties may end up feeling that time is being wasted.

Mentoring sessions may vary from this pattern from time to time, and it may be helpful to specify this in the contract. For instance, they may occasionally involve other people besides the mentor and mentoree. An example might be a session that includes the mentoree's spouse, or the mentor's spouse, or both. Some mentoring partnerships find it helpful to make an occasional retreat together. This may be for just a day or perhaps longer, in order to spend an extended time together that includes informal socializing as well as focused concentration on the matters at hand.

It is normal for there to be some contact between mentor and mentoree outside the mentoring sessions in the form of emails or phone calls. This is to be encouraged as part of the real relationship between the parties. However, it is wise to put some boundaries around this, at least at the outset, to forestall the possibility of dependency developing. These informal contacts will generally be instigated by mentorees when there is something they wish to discuss briefly. During this sort of contact, the mentoree will normally take the initiative to confirm arrangements for the next session shortly before it is due to take place.

I raise the matter of what we will deal with in our sessions and the outcomes I think we will be able to achieve by sharing my understanding of Christian mentoring. This also provides the opportunity for me to express my desire to help mentorees take responsibility for their own lives. Although it has never yet become a point of debate, I would hesitate to enter into a mentoring contract that did not allow me to be true to my basic values concerning this area of ministry.

The matter of mutual expectations, including those to do with honesty, accountability and confidentiality, is worth taking some time over when constructing a mentoring contract. It may be helpful at this point to review past experiences of mentoring – if there have been any – which have not gone as well as was hoped. The most commonly articulated expectations are those which seek to avoid a repetition of past disappointments. The mentoree's goals will be a continuing focus of the mentoring process, but the mentor will also have goals and these are best declared from the beginning. There may be other interested parties who have a vital interest in the outcomes of the mentoring process, and whose expectations may be relevant; the mentoree's employer or spouse, for example. Be sure to document their expectations where they are relevant.

The costs associated with mentoring, including the mentor's time, travel and communication costs, are not normally borne by the mentor but by the mentoree or the mentoree's employer. If the latter is the case, consider clarifying with the employer that the mentor is not required to submit reports about the content of the mentoring process to anyone in the mentoree's organization. This is to make sure that the mentor does not become a person of power within the mentoree's life.

Even though there is no rule about this, it is extraordinary how many mentoring sessions include spending some time together at a café. But who pays the bill? My personal approach is to pick up incidental costs for things such as coffee and light meals that I share together with my mentorees. However, I have the freedom to do this because of my present financial circumstances and not all mentors are in that position. Neither party should feel any sense of obligation about this, but it is worth establishing a clear understanding so that each can be sensitive to the other.

A review of the mentoring contract should be scheduled towards the end of the period, and perhaps more frequently early in a mentoring relationship. Discuss how you will evaluate the mentoring process, what feedback you are prepared to give each other and how you will know when it is time to conclude your contract in a healthy way.

Administration for formal mentoring

Informal mentoring can be conducted in an ad hoc fashion with no more administration than diary entries such as you might make in the conduct of any friendship. Once mentoring is lifted to a formal, intensive level, the results are more noticeable and the administrative requirements are greater. In a highly intentional process it is more critical that you make the most of each session, that you stay on track, that progress is monitored, and that errors of judgment are guarded against.

Keeping notes

With the mentoree's permission it is advisable for the mentor to take notes during the mentoring sessions. Memory alone will not be sufficient to keep track of the complex developments taking place in the lives of mentorees. Privacy legislation in most jurisdictions will apply to how these notes are to be stored and who is able to have access to them. If taking notes during the session is distasteful to either the mentor or mentoree, the mentor may make a record of the session immediately after it has concluded.

Notes taken of what was said during the session, including agreements about goals and action steps, are normally available to the mentoree. Notes that the mentor makes about his or her own reactions, hunches, and tentative conclusions normally remain private to the mentor. However, the mentor should be fully acquainted with the obligations pertaining to such records in the jurisdiction in which he or she operates. A one-page template containing key prompts, such as the one given here, will help the mentor stay on track and capture the most important points raised in the mentoring session:

One-page template for mentoring notes

Mentoree name:

Location, date and time:

UNDERSTANDING

Current circumstances – how are things?

Mentoree's well-being – how are you?

God's fingerprints – what is God up to?

FOCUS

Review action steps from last time – were they completed/effective?

Revisit goals – do they need refinement/replacement?

Action steps – what will you do by next session?

REFLECTION (this section private to the mentor)

Mentoring process – what is working/not working?

Insights into the Spirit's activity – what hunches do I have?

Impact on me personally – what issues must I deal with?

Location, date and time of next session:

Written feedback to mentorees

Around once per year or at the agreed point of review of the mentoring contract, it is helpful for the mentoree to receive a written record of progress from the mentor. This can reinforce the value of the relationship and celebrate the progress made. It may contain a summary of what has taken place in the past year, along with observations and reflections from the mentor. It will indicate possible ways ahead and give encouragement. I have placed a sample of an annual summary as an appendix at the end of this book to provide an idea of how these might be constructed.

Evaluation and supervision of mentors

Mentoring is carried out for the purpose of facilitating the work of the Holy Spirit in another's life and derives its value directly from success in this regard. However, the extent to which that purpose is fulfilled in any given period is very difficult to assess. The outcomes of mentoring are often intangible, yet real; unquantifiable, yet precious. To evaluate the outcomes of mentoring, gathering anecdotal evidence from a conversation is a more productive method than using written, structured evaluation tools.

Beyond the outcomes of mentoring, it is also helpful to get an idea of the value of the mentoring process and the facilitator. One rough but generally reliable indicator about these things is whether mentorees express a desire to continue at the point of review. The shortcoming with this method of evaluation is that it really only gives the process and the mentor a pass/fail evaluation. It does not indicate precisely what has worked and not worked or how things could be improved. This is where structured evaluation tools can provide necessary feedback.

At the point of review, I ask my mentorees to complete in writing a short evaluation tool. They respond to the following questions about the process: What has been the most valuable aspect of the mentoring sessions for you in the past year? What has not gone well with the mentoring sessions from your point of view? What would you like to add to the mentoring relationship and sessions that has not happened yet? What are your reasons for wishing to continue or discontinue the mentoring sessions?

Then comes the very scary part for both me and my mentorees: they are asked to use a numerical rating and, where applicable, make a comment, assessing me, as the facilitator, in the areas of perception, acceptance, flexibility, patience, vision, encouragement, willingness to confront, and spiritual integrity. The feedback I gain from this process helps me to continually improve my mentoring skills and tailor my approach to the specific needs of each mentoree.

Mentors need to engage in regular self-evaluation, and

have a forum in which they can discuss in general terms the best ways to handle tricky situations. In addition, mentors need a way of monitoring the spiritual and emotional impact the ministry is having upon their soul. These functions could be carried out informally with a mature friend or in the context of the mentor's own mentoring relationship. In cases where the mentor is inexperienced, or the load is great, professional supervision of the mentor may be advisable.

Longevity for mentors

Mentoring is a role that requires a great deal of energy, and mentors need to take steps to look after themselves emotionally and spiritually. These pointers go part of the way to guiding mentors in how to go the distance.

Be sure to have adequate spiritual support

No matter how mature we may be as Christians, we do not outgrow the need for having someone alongside us as a soul friend. Whether it is a formal or informal arrangement, those who offer mentoring to others need a receiving or mutual mentoring relationship for their own well-being. I am so grateful for my mentor, Ray. We have known each other for over twenty-five years, and formalized our mentoring relationship just eight years ago. We meet together every six to eight weeks and he asks me the questions that keep me honest.

Furthermore, it is a great benefit for mentors to have someone gifted in intercession praying for them on a regular basis. An intercessor does not need to know details about what goes on in mentoring sessions. All they require is timely, general information that will guide their prayers for you and your ministry. This prayer-support base helps to guard the mentor against spiritual attack and is a means of grace and spiritual power for the mentoring relationship.

Weather the storms in prayer

Being a mentor can be emotionally and mentally demanding. There will be times of profound self-doubt when you ask yourself, 'Am I really making any positive difference in this person's life?' I have certainly known times when I have felt useless and a failure as a mentor. My conversations with other mentors suggest that this experience is not uncommon. At those times you can regain perspective and renew your hope by taking your doubts and questions to God. Recognize before the Lord the limited part you play in the relationship between him and your mentoree. Release responsibility for mentoring outcomes, and reaffirm your sacred responsibility only for your contribution. Ask God to help you see more clearly the godly potential of your mentoree and for the necessary patience to continue to play your part in bringing that potential to reality.

Learn to let go

Mentors need to be able to handle occasions in which mentorees unload significant amounts of negativity and, perhaps, pain and anger. This consumes emotional resources in the mentor, but it goes with the territory if you're going to ask how someone is and really want a truthful answer! The only way to stay sane is to put some reasonable boundaries in place. For example, when writing up your notes after listening to someone expressing their distress, it is perfectly in order to spend a little time in prayer for that person. After that, I would advise you to learn to leave the issues with God and resist the tendency to continue turning them over in your mind.

Learn to say 'no'

Some mentorees will take as much of you as they can get, and then come back for more. The only way to keep on loving these needy people is to say 'no' once they try to overstep the boundaries you've established. Be completely settled in your own mind that your 'no' is, in fact, an expression of love for the long term.

Concluding a mentoring relationship

It is perhaps a little surprising to be reading a section on concluding a mentoring relationship in a chapter called 'Getting Started'. However, it is wise to begin a mentoring relationship with a clear idea of how to bring it to a healthy conclusion when the time is right. Although mentoring is a covenantal relationship, it is not a marriage. If this is not grasped, mentoring partnerships are bound to conclude with a sense of failure – as if somehow the partners were sadly unable to make it work. But if it is acknowledged that it is perfectly normal for mentoring relationships to run their course, then they may be honourably concluded with a sense of fulfilment.

For many years through the 1980s and 1990s, Barry was my mentor. When I moved overseas we put our mentoring relationship on hold with the plan to revive it again later. When I moved back to Australia we caught up again, but both of us knew something had changed. Our old pattern of relating was not satisfying for either of us. We decided to end our mentoring as it was and transition into a mutual peer relationship, which we still enjoy today.

While long-term mentoring relationships are generally very beneficial, none are guaranteed to last forever. Relationships can last longer or end earlier than expected. The annual feedback report to the mentoree and evaluation of the mentor presents the opportunity for a review of the mentoring relationship. Any one of several factors may indicate it is time to transition or conclude the relationship.

Once a mentoring relationship has been unproductive for several months, it should be concluded without further delay. Possible triggers include the following:

- Mentoree claims to have reached all their significant goals.
- Mentoree is seeking help elsewhere.
- Agenda fizzles out – no new issues are being raised.
- Other priorities are taking precedence – repeated

      rescheduling is a sure sign.

- No follow-through in action on part of mentoree.
- Action steps are not leading to achievement of goals.
- Mentor is not 'getting it' and feels stumped.
- Feeling drained after every session – a sign of an unhealthy relationship.
- Loss of respect for the other person.
- Consistent breach of confidence.
- High dependency.
- Unreasonable demands.

Sometimes one or both hang on indefinitely through sentimentality or an unwillingness to create an awkward moment. There should never be any disagreement about this point of concluding. Even if only one person wants to end the mentoring relationship, it is undoubtedly time to end it.

Finishing well is a serious challenge, but one worth meeting with creative energy. Mentoring partners may not have experience in ending relationships positively, so several factors need to be taken into account. Be prepared to deal with feelings of rejection, anxiety, resentment, surprise, relief, grief, fear, joy, excitement, disappointment, discomfort and awkwardness. Be aware that the other party might simply run away to avoid this moment.

If the mentoring relationship is to end, make sure it is a blameless, no-fault separation. If possible, make it a celebration and let it end on a note of gratitude and appreciation. I try to leave the door open, setting a date in the medium future to catch up again to find out how each of us is progressing. You may wish to enjoy a meal together as a concluding ritual at which you reminisce, or exchange symbolic gifts. If so, ensure the value of gifts is modest and that they are relevant to the journey you have shared together.

Guiding principles for mentoring

In this section I want to bring together a brief 'rough guide' to mentoring that will help mentors quickly get their bearings and begin to chart a course ahead as they commence a new mentoring relationship.

Build genuine relationship

Mentoring as an empowering process is inseparably connected to deep interpersonal dynamics between the mentor and the mentoree. This is, in fact, true of all mentoring, both secular and spiritual. For those who aim to take Jesus as their model for mentoring, this fundamental principle is especially compelling. Christian mentoring is more than an arrangement set in place for pragmatic purposes and cannot be conducted from an emotional distance. Beneficial mentoring processes for Christian leaders, in particular, require an environment of mutual positive regard, respect and heartfelt care.

The kind of mentoring we see Jesus engaging in takes place in an interpersonal relationship in which both the mentor and mentoree learn how to grow, live and love in the spiritual life. (I will have more to say about taking Jesus as a model for our mentoring at the conclusion of this chapter.) This does not mean that the mentoring relationship lacks appropriate boundaries, but that those boundaries include a valuing of one another beyond the mentoring function.

Establish mentoree responsibility

Mentoring is effective only when the mentoree takes responsibility for his or her own spiritual growth and health. Positive accountability, the 'conscious melding of self-responsibility and rigour',[44] rests on this foundation. If the mentoree should hesitate to take responsibility for the decisions and actions taken as a result of the mentoring process, it may default to the mentor. This is unacceptable because it gives the mentor too much power. There is absolutely no domination or control in mentoring. Some mentorees would actually like their mentor to take over responsibility for their decisions. No matter how tempting it may become, we urge mentors to firmly resist telling a mentoree what to do for the sake of the mentoree's long-term health and strength. It is better to sit with a floundering mentoree for a while and to be mistaken for being uncaring than to short-circuit an important learning moment with well-meaning rescuing intervention.

Prioritize the inner life

While the whole person is of interest, development of the inner life is fundamental to Christian mentoring. This principle is based on the conviction that our doing flows out of our being. While it is true that our doing may also impact on our being, the principal means of bringing about deep inner change is the power of the Holy Spirit in the life of the mentoree. Enhancing personal and spiritual growth through seeking God's agenda and eliminating isolation through the mentoring relationship will, in time, bring benefits to all the outward aspects of the mentoree's life, including greater vocational effectiveness in serving God.

Put aside other agendas

If mentors are going to move mentorees onto God's agenda, it is vital that they recognize whatever agendas they might personally have for the mentoree concerned and consciously put those agendas aside. This is a matter for ongoing vigilance for, even if a mentor does not have an agenda at the outset, ideas can start to form as the relationship progresses. For this reason, mentors require a sense of being 'established' in God, and should not be prone to push their own agendas, no matter how well intentioned. Otherwise, they are too dangerous to be allowed into the soul space of others to influence their spirits.

Mentoring that starts with some ministry role in mind for which an attempt is made to find and mould a suitable candidate lacks authenticity. It may produce enhanced performance in the short term, but it is unlikely to result in a mature, Spirit-empowered life. The mentor's concern is for the spiritual growth of the mentoree, beginning where the person is at, and working toward what God has designed them to be.

Discern God's work

Discernment is a highly valuable spiritual gift in the work of mentoring, and one which mentors do well to seek. Mentoring involves a process through which one person helps another to understand what God is doing and saying. This does not need to be an obscure, mystical process. Thoughtful conversations linked with prayer comprise an effective setting in which a mentor, with the Spirit's help, may discern God's activity in a person.

Facilitate reflection and goal-setting

Encouraging reflection and goal-setting in mentoring is aimed at achieving experience-based learning through following the threefold model of:

action ➡ reflection ➡ planning

Adults learn best by actively participating in everyday life and then reflecting on the experiences they go through. Reflection turns experience into learning. It is the central factor of experience-based learning. It is the process by which we revisit our experiences and seek to analyse what was happening, to identify behaviour, ideas, feelings and the consequences of our own actions and the actions of others.

You may find it helpful to structure reflection on the mentoree's experience in a particular situation around a set of standard questions such as these:

- What happened?
- How did I respond to the circumstances in the moment?
- What do I think/feel about the experience now?
- What have I learned through it?
- What should I do as a result of that?

Reflection on God's activity in particular and welcoming that work are essential to personal transformation. Christian mentors find appropriate ways to help mentorees think clearly and deeply about who they are, what is happening in their lives and how they are responding to those things. Once they get insight into where they are on their journey and where God is taking them, they are in a position to set goals and action steps that will take them further along that journey.

Having better understood the cause-and-effect connections operating in their lives, mentorees are in a good position to identify and commit to goals and to action steps appropriate to those goals. Goal-setting is an essential part of an effective mentoring process, but there are several caveats.

Firstly, it is vital that the goals are set by mentorees rather than mentors. Secondly, as far as possible within the limits of a facilitative framework, ensure that the goals are not simply about performance but also take account of the inner life and being of the mentoree. Thirdly, encourage mentorees to keep their goals flexible so that they are open for realignment and development. Finally, work together with mentorees to progressively shape their goals around what they believe are God's goals for them.

Provide positive accountability

Mentorees set goals and action steps for themselves and commit to achieving them. In doing so, they also give their mentor permission to hold them accountable for following through on these commitments. This is an invitation to the mentor to ask the tough questions. It is vital that this accountability be exercised faithfully and positively. If mentors should fail to remind mentorees of their goals and action steps, then the value of the process diminishes sharply. These reminders are to be constructed in such a way that they are moments to prove progress rather than to expose failure. Whatever a mentoree's actions in regard to their goals and action steps, the mentor's response is to be one of encouragement rather than judgment.

Prepare thoroughly

Before each session, allow adequate time to prepare. You will expect that your mentoree will have put some thought into your time together, so it is only right for you to do the same. Begin by reviewing the notes that you have made from previous sessions to refresh your memory of the material you have covered. Pray over these notes and open your awareness to any insights from the Holy Spirit. Jot notes about this and prepare a few questions designed to spark the interest of your mentoree. Make sure that you have completed any undertakings you gave at the last session.

Pursue mentoring energetically

It is necessary for mentors and mentorees to be deliberately proactive about their mentoring relationship. The default mode of operation in mission in our contemporary culture is highly individualistic, even among those leaders who are highly motivated about their own personal growth and development. This militates against deep, accountable and generous relationships. If mentoring is not made a priority it will certainly be edged out by the huge number of competing demands on a leader's time and energy.

Encourage mentorees to mentor others

Once mentoring has been received, it is easier to provide it for others. Where a mentoree takes on the role of serving another future leader, the benefit they have received through being mentored is more firmly established in their own life. There is strong biblical and historical evidence that God has ordained that there should be mentors among his people. It is part of the structure of love in the kingdom of God. There is a great need for mentoring to be multiplied as a normal function of Christian community and missional leadership in our time.

Learn from Jesus

As I explained at length in Chapter 2, Christian mentoring is a biblical process, modelled most perfectly by Jesus. He mentored his disciples by who he was, what he said and what he did.

Mallison says:

> Jesus provides our one and only truly perfect model, message and method to direct our mentoring under the guidance and empowerment of the Holy Spirit. We must learn how he went about being with his disciples, from their immature first steps to their becoming leaders who would be strong pillars of his kingdom, after their Pentecost experience. He provides not only our best example but he is our own best mentor.[45]

Bruce Demarest helpfully summarizes sixteen aspects of Jesus' ministry with others that can guide us in our mentoring:

- Jesus made himself available to people.
- Jesus ministered in the power of the Spirit.
- Jesus dealt with persons as unique individuals.
- Jesus engaged people in creative dialogue.
- Jesus asked probing questions.
- Jesus listened attentively and empathetically.
- Jesus skilfully applied the word of God to people's lives.
- Jesus affirmed and encouraged people on their faith journeys.
- Jesus identified obstacles to spiritual growth.
- Jesus challenged, confronted, corrected and rebuked.
- Jesus patiently bore with people's ignorance, pride, laziness and failures.
- Jesus was fervent in prayer for those to whom he ministered.
- Jesus ministered soul care in community.
- Jesus experienced resistance.
- Jesus ministered with a sense of lightheartedness.
- Jesus cared for his own soul.[46]

While I am substantially in agreement with Mallison and Demarest, I would want to say that in some respects Jesus serves as an excellent model for today's mentors, and in some respects he does not. For example, as their Lord and Master, Jesus was in a position of authority over the disciples in a way that is not to be reflected in contemporary mentoring relationships. Mentorees owe obedience to Christ, not to their mentor. In the next section I want to revisit and expand on the word of caution I mentioned in Chapter 2 about this most important subject.

Jesus as a model for mentoring

Over the years Jesus has come more and more to be my model for ministry, including my mentoring. At first, this did not happen as a result of any careful theological reflection. Ministry just seemed to work better that way. Yet it is worth careful consideration to figure out why Jesus is a good model for ministry, and what the limits of that position might be.

Several years ago my boys started wearing bracelets with the letters WWJD – an acronym for 'What Would Jesus Do?' This is a pretty handy theological tool for a great many situations in life, and a reasonable question for mentors to ask themselves when deliberating how to move forward with a particular mentoree. Moulding our responses around our understanding of how Jesus would respond to a similar situation often proves to be a good guide. But a cautionary note must be sounded.

This caution has to do with the limits of our understanding of Jesus and what he would do in any given situation. What I imagine Jesus might do could be well wide of the mark. Neuhaus puts this problem quite starkly:

> We tend to conform Jesus to what is already known and accessible. The result is that we tend to live not by reliance upon the promise of the gospel but by a myth of Jesus that is finally of our own construction.[47]

Neuhaus has accurately identified a real problem, but his solution is even worse! He suggests that we help people understand that Jesus is distanced from us by a huge gulf of two thousand years, and urge them to abandon ideas of the immediacy and relevance of Jesus. I most strongly disagree with his unsupported assertion that:

> The New Testament does not present Jesus as a moral
> model on which our lives are to be fashioned.[48]

The Gospels, while not *simply* biographies of Jesus, are certainly centred upon him in a way that calls the reader to follow as disciples – apprentices – to the Master. The Apostle Paul, who Neuhaus says makes scarcely a reference to the personality and character of Jesus, urges us to have the same attitude that was in Christ and to follow his example as he follows the example of Christ.[49]

It is a grave mistake to drive a wedge between the Jesus of history and the Christ of faith. It must be acknowledged that the same Jesus who walked the earth is alive here and now, not distanced from us by two thousand years. He can be known, and he communicates directly to believers by his Spirit, as a shepherd speaks to his sheep who know his voice.[50]

Dallas Willard, in a chapter called 'A Curriculum for Christlikeness', takes this view:

> Jesus' disciples are those who have chosen to be with
> him to learn to be like him. As they move along...
> they increase in the amount and quality of grace they
> have in their real life. That is the same as increasing
> in their experiential knowledge of the real person,
> Jesus Christ.[51]

Yet in taking Jesus as a model for ministry Willard makes two further cautionary points. Even if we were to gradually overcome the errors of perception of what Jesus would do, we must still guard against falling into the trap of external conformity to what Jesus said and did, or the trap of merely professing a perfectly true doctrine about ministry.[52]

Clearly we do not take Jesus as a model for ministry in the specifics of his place and time, nor of his Messianic role. We do not need to dress as he did, walk where he walked, or literally die on a cross as he did. However, his example of incarnation and giving of himself is certainly a model that can properly be applied to the ministry of mentoring.

While affirming that we should model ourselves on Jesus in terms of his *moral character traits*, there is an important distinction to be made. The *non-moral personality traits* of Jesus – even if we could accurately identify them from the Gospel accounts that give us little to go on – are not a matter for imitation for those who would minister in Jesus' name. Each of us has a unique personality of our own and we are at our best when we allow God to align and invigorate our uniqueness for his purposes.

Certain grey areas remain for me in taking Jesus as a model for ministry. The big themes and general thrust of his ministry are one thing, but I am not sure how closely to follow some of his particular methodologies. On the one hand, his practice of early morning prayer and regular times of solitude seem to me to be things I could well adopt and recommend as a model for surviving and maintaining focus in ministry. Also, his procedures in ministering with people seem at times to be so universally appropriate – for example, his practice of affirming people before challenging them – as to be worthy of my imitation.

On the other hand, there were times when his way of doing ministry seemed dependent on his context – his use of parables, and his methods of healing, for example. I am not convinced that I should practise telling oblique stories to my mentorees simply because that's the way Jesus did it. If Jesus' specific methods of mentoring are appropriate in our time (and many of them are), it will be because Jesus' context and ours happen to be similar in terms of accepted and preferred learning styles.

Nevertheless, that Jesus intended to serve as a model for ministry at the level of principles is clear from the way he trained his disciples and then gave them the task of passing on that training to ensuing generations of believers.[53] The writer to the Hebrews urges imitation of leaders, but also sets apart Jesus as the author and perfecter of the faith.[54] Paul expressly commands believers to imitate God and Christ, particularly in the areas of love, goodness, righteousness and truth.

Taking Jesus as a model for mentoring ministry is confirmed by the conviction that mentors must lead out of their relationship with God in the same way that Jesus did. Jesus took his cue from his heavenly Father, as he reminded both his critics and his followers on a number of occasions:

> 'My food,' said Jesus, 'is to do the will of him who sent me and to finish his work... I tell you the truth, the Son can do nothing by himself; he can do only what he sees his Father doing, because whatever the Father does the Son also does... By myself I can do nothing; I judge only as I hear, and my judgment is just, for I seek not to please myself but him who sent me... For I have come down from heaven not to do my will but to do the will of him who sent me... My teaching is not my own. It comes from him who sent me.[55]

Jesus set himself to do whatever his Father wanted. He lived responsively, seeing what the Father was doing and getting involved in it, hearing what his Father was saying and teaching it. The keys here seem to be openness and responsiveness. This, above all else, is an excellent model to guide mentors in their ministry.

Chapter 5

Giving Your Best to Mentoring

Young Emma from the house next door had just started to play the violin. She was a lovely lass but, my goodness, she produced some appalling sounds. Passers-by could be forgiven for thinking that a poor, defenceless animal was being horribly mistreated inside that home. The reason for the horrid tone was nothing to do with the instrument. Emma's parents had purchased a good-quality instrument for her. No, without being unkind, it has to be said that those discordant wails were due to the level of competence of the player. Fortunately, this phase did not last forever. As the months passed, the sounds coming from next door became far more pleasant as Emma gradually mastered her instrument. These days Emma's skilful use of a quality instrument produces music of rare beauty.

So far in this book I have been explaining my approach to mentoring of Christian leaders, where it has come from historically and biblically, and why it is needed today. Yet mentoring even at its best is just a tool – a quality instrument, if you will – in the hands of the people engaged in the mentoring relationship. When used skilfully, very beneficial results can be gained. However, when mentoring is employed by people with undeveloped aptitudes for this kind of relationship, it is possible for the results to be disappointing or even negative. Both mentors and mentorees have responsibilities in this regard, so in this chapter and the next I will address each partner in turn.

Even mentors with many years of experience find that the inherent complexity of human relationships creates an environment in which there will always be much left to learn about this process. Part of this complexity comes from the fact that human relationships function on many levels. On the first level, it is clear that mentors' words and actions have an impact on mentorees. What may not be quite so obvious is that on deeper levels, other factors within a mentor – such as inner attitudes, emotional health and the condition of the soul – are all in play, affecting the way the relationship functions and develops.

Mentoring is a relational process involving multiple behavioural functions. Norman Cohen says mentoring requires a relationship emphasis to establish trust, an information emphasis to offer tailored advice, a facilitative focus to introduce alternatives, a confrontation focus to challenge, a modelling process to motivate and inspire, and a visioning process to encourage initiative.[56] I would agree, and go beyond that to say that mentoring is not only about what you do; it's about who you are. In this chapter I invite you who are mentors to stir up your awareness and understanding of the interconnectedness between who you are, what you do, and the outcomes of your mentoring. Issues most pertinent to Christian leaders are at the forefront of my mind as I present this material, but these points have much wider relevance. Growing in the following traits and aptitudes will help you to become a better mentor, no matter who you are serving in that capacity.

Be godly

When I first moved to the United Kingdom from Australia, finding a local mentor was high on my list of priorities. I approached Herb Works, a retired American pastor doing some short-term mission work in the city where we both lived. Herb was a 'foreigner' like me, but his ability to empathize on that issue was not the main reason I chose him. There was a spiritual integrity about him that I found engaging and inspiring. Even though he was not quite sure what I was looking for in a mentoring relationship, he agreed to meet with me on a regular basis. Our times together were valuable to me not because of anything Herb said but because, in the totality of his life, he reminded me of Jesus. In a quietly empowering fashion, this quality of his soul called me back into connection with Christ.

In the year we had together before he returned to the United States, the greatest gift he gave me was his godly presence in my life.

True disciples

The first requirement of a mentor who will seek to promote the work of God's Spirit in another's life is that they should be pursuing the same goal for themselves. Good mentors are wholeheartedly committed to Christ with steadfast passion and a desire to keep growing in the things of the Lord. Godliness arises as a character quality where there is profound reverence for God and perseverance through testing circumstances. Its source is the presence of the Spirit of God, dwelling in and rearranging a person's life. It is developed only by progressive surrender to the work of the Spirit, and it does not come cheaply. Mentorees generally discern this quality intuitively and it is one of the first things Christian leaders look for in a mentor. Godliness in a mentor is the signal that this person has, in their own way, walked the path that the mentoree seeks to navigate.

Settled in God

Godly mentors have deep satisfaction in keeping company with God. Prayer is a welcome activity for them because it is part of their ongoing conversation with the one who is the centre of their life. They hunger for intimacy with God, but are not frantically desperate about it. Their life in God is secure, unthreatened and a source of deep joy. Out of their own experience of knowing God and his work in their life comes the conviction that God – and only God – can satisfy the deepest human longings and bring the restoration and empowerment necessary for effective service. Their confidence in God's goodness and greatness encourages mentorees to access God's resources for their own growth and strength.

Anchored in the Bible

Godliness is anchored in the Bible and derives specific shape from the character and ministry of Christ as revealed in the Gospels. Godly mentors are at home in God's word. They internalize and obey its truth so their lifestyle is rooted in the Christian scriptures. By constantly putting God's word into practice they are able to discern what is right in practical contemporary situations that are not specifically addressed in the Bible. As a result, the wisdom and moral perspectives they share with mentorees are highly valued for their authority, authenticity and relevance. Christian leaders need mentors with the spiritual integrity that comes from being with Jesus in private and walking with him in public.

Sensitive to the Holy Spirit

Godly mentors are attuned to the prompting of the Holy Spirit. Out of a deep desire to live a life pleasing to God, they are able to discern the 'still, small voice' and are in the habit of following that leading. Within mentoring, this sensitivity is of great value in helping identify what God is doing in the lives of mentorees.

Be safe

Brent is a gifted leader working as the pastor of a recently established congregation in a large Australian city. Within his denomination he is regarded as one of the huge success stories, although he is more aware than anyone of the precarious nature of church planting. He contacted me as a result of the recommendation of a colleague who was concerned that Brent was struggling.

We met and as we made our introductions he asked, 'So, Rick, what is your profile within our denomination? How are you connected?' He made the assumption that I was part of his wider network of churches, even though I am not.

So I said, 'Brent, I have absolutely no profile at all, and no connections except with the person who recommended me to you.'

He shot back: 'Good! Because if you were in any way

connected with the hierarchy it would not be safe for me to open up to you.'

In my experience, a large proportion of Christian leaders are concerned about how safe a mentoring relationship will be. They are particularly wary of the possibility of such a close relationship winding up in betrayal, manipulation or coercion and seek reassurances on these points as a matter of priority. Mentors who are safe have three qualities in particular: they keep confidences, have selfless motivation and do not wield power over their mentorees.

Confidentiality

Breach of confidentiality is disastrous in mentoring relationships. It occurs more frequently than it should largely because people have differing expectations of what confidentiality means. Some people feel uncomfortable about sorting out these expectations. Talking about it seems to imply a lack of trust and they fear that raising the subject might be considered offensive. Often it is assumed that the other person will guard what you confide in the same way that you would. Without a discussion about it, this is unlikely to be the case. To begin a conversation about this, you might consider which of these statements best represents your view of what confidentiality means:

- What we discuss stays between us for as long as we are engaged in our mentoring relationship.
- If asked by someone you report to, I can freely disclose our conversation.
- I can only disclose our conversations to others if they really need to know.
- What we say between us stays there unless you give me permission to talk about it with others.
- The things we ask to be kept confidential will be kept between us, otherwise not.
- It is okay to discuss how we relate to one another but not the content of the discussions.

- It is okay to talk with others about our conversations as long as it is positive.[57]

Good mentors ensure that they honour at least the form and degree of confidentiality that their mentorees consider to be safe. Such a commitment forms an essential part of the foundation upon which trust may be built. Trust opens the way to discovery of the truth which, combined with the application of the grace of God, sets people free. I will return to this theme in Chapter 6, and consider categories of confidential information and some of the implications for mentoring.

Motivation

So much about mentoring can be learned along the way. There is no need to have everything right before you start. However, motivation is one of those matters which does need to be examined before you begin. Although it is difficult work, it is necessary for mentors to get their hearts in tune with the Spirit of God if they expect to be used by him to bring benefit to others through mentoring. What motivates mentors to do what they do? For most of us, the reality is a mix of noble and base motivations. We may wish it were not so, but there is no use pretending. Having acknowledged that, it befits mentors to propagate the noble motivations and weed out the base ones.

Motivational forces may be either internal or external. Mentors require internal motivation if the mentoring relationship is to be healthy and sustainable. However, some mentoring relationships are established because of an organizational requirement or some other form of obligation. External demands and expectations like this may be present, but they do not predominate in healthy mentoring relationships. To paraphrase 1 Peter 5:2, our message is this: be eager to serve as mentors – not because you must, but because you are willing.

However, even internal motivations deserve scrutiny. Self-serving motivations make a mentor unsafe and not worthy of being trusted with access into the soul space of a mentoree.

Two motivating factors in particular are to be avoided. The first is the motivation that the mentoree will be useful in some cause to which the mentor is committed. This leads directly to manipulation of the mentoree. The second unsatisfactory motivation has to do with someone needing the title of 'mentor' in order to feel worthwhile. Mentors who become aware that their work has become more about what they can get out of the mentoree rather than what they can give are best advised to withdraw from mentoring, at least temporarily, in order to find their worth and security in God.

On the other side of the coin, there are many noble, selfless motivations which mentors can cultivate in their hearts to make sure they remain an asset in the lives of their mentorees. Among them, five are worthy of special mention. Firstly, mentors may have a sense of responsibility under God, responding to a moral urge to do what is right in making a contribution to Christ's cause. Secondly, they may mentor others out of gratitude, desiring to give back something in return for blessings they have received. Thirdly, they may be motivated by a sense of convergence, where mentoring is a fulfilment of God's purpose and call at the present time. Fourthly, mentors may be motivated by hope, having their imagination fired by the prospect of seeing God at work. Finally, mentors may be motivated by love – simply seeking the best for the other person. This final motivation seems to me to be the strongest and purest of them all, and one to be especially cultivated through prayer as the mentor seeks to take on God's attitude toward the mentoree.

The message of 1 Corinthians 13 is particularly pertinent to mentoring. Even though mentors may have an impressive array of skills to bring, if they lack the motivation of genuine care for the well-being of the mentoree, the results are likely to be disappointing. Once a mentoree is certain that the mentor has their best interests at heart and is not simply operating in a task-oriented contractual arrangement, the relational environment is safe. Trust and confidence in the mentor may then develop, opening the possibility of addressing the real issues and overcoming obstacles to growth. Without the trust that springs from love, it is very difficult for the mentor to make any worthwhile contribution to the life of the mentoree.

Power

Over time, mentors accrue a certain amount of power within their relationships with mentorees. To put it crudely, mentors are able, if they so choose, to get mentorees to do things that they would otherwise not choose to do. Accrual of power occurs for reasons which vary from one relationship to the next, but are broadly to do with either personal power or positional power. Mentors are faced with the question of what to do with the power they accrue; whether to use it or refrain from using it.

While the power of the Holy Spirit is welcome within mentoring relationships, the exercise of human power is problematic. By this, I do not mean the 'power within' of a spiritually mature person or the 'power for' exercised in affirmation and encouragement. I am referring specifically to the 'power over' that is present in coercive and potentially coercive interactions. It is this sort of power that may be detrimental to mentoring relationships, rendering them unsafe for the mentoree.

The operation of 'power over' in mentoring relationships is directly impacted by the motivation of love mentioned above. Logically speaking, the opposite of love is hate (or perhaps apathy). But psychologically, the opposite of loving someone is dominating them. Over sixty years ago, Carl Jung astutely observed the inverse relationship between these two dynamics in human relationships:

> Where love rules, there is no will to power, and where power predominates, there love is lacking. The one is the shadow of the other.[58]

In other words, if a mentor is truly expressing love toward a mentoree, they will not attempt to wield power over them. To the degree that power is exercised over a mentoree, the expression of love is diminished in the same degree. If mentoring relationships are to promote the work of God's Spirit and be conducted in a manner consistent with God's agenda, they must be rooted in love, not power. Operating in love, the mentor may appear to be in a 'powerless' or 'weak' position to bring about change and growth in the mentoree. Yet this is a crucial prerequisite for pursuing the Holy Spirit's agenda, for God's power is made perfect in weakness.

This kind of thinking about power is revolutionary. Worldly wisdom would suggest that in order to effect change in any situation, a certain measure of power over that situation must be exercised. Hersey and Blanchard represent the commonly accepted secular understanding of interpersonal power when they write:

> First of all, realize that power is finite. There is only so much power around. If someone else has it, you don't. If your power is negotiated away, it is no longer there. The amount of power available does not expand in different situations.[59]

Christian mentors are able to see things quite differently. For a start, they may understand that power is infinite and that there is far more power present in a mentoring relationship than that which resides in the human participants. Christian mentors know that God's power at work within us is able to do immeasurably more than all we ask or imagine. Also, they can appreciate that the operation of power in human relationships need not be a zero-sum game. Interpersonal transactions involving power need not always result in win–lose scenarios; win–win is possible. That is to say, it is possible to give power away and still be left with as much or more power as before.[60]

Some mentors find it difficult to accept that they should not use power over a mentoree; although they may prefer to use the term 'authority' or call it 'giving direction'. If a mentoree is constrained against their will it amounts to the same thing, and it is contrary to the wisdom of the New Testament. Late in Paul's life, he wrote to Timothy advising him about the use of gentle, non-coercive approaches in influencing others:

> The Lord's servant must not quarrel; instead, he must be kind to everyone, able to teach, not resentful. Those who oppose him he must gently instruct, in the hope that God will grant them repentance leading them to a knowledge of the truth.[61]

Paul knew that effecting a change in behaviour through coercive power is worthless, for it does not change the heart. Meaningful repentance must be freely chosen. Even when sorely tempted to exercise coercive power when dealing with the Corinthian crisis, Paul showed restraint. To those who were apprehensive that he would use his authority to punish his opponents, he says in 2 Corinthians 10:6, 'we will be ready to punish every act of disobedience, once your obedience is complete.' In other words, his intention was to resist using his power to punish until such time as his loving formation of Christ in them had rendered such punishment redundant.

Mentors who choose not to exercise power over their mentorees are being biblically responsible. Yet, in some cases, their admirable restraint may not be enough to create an environment that feels entirely safe for the mentoree. This situation arises when the mentor occupies an organizational position or has personal connections to which power is attached. Even though a mentor in this position may intend never to use that power, the possibility is enough to stifle the candid openness that is essential to an effective mentoring relationship. Brent, in the story I shared above about being safe, was fearful of this dilemma until he was reassured that I had no access to positional power.

After many years of observation it is my conclusion that it is not only the actual exercise of 'power over' a mentoree that is detrimental to the effectiveness of a mentoring relationship. Even the possibility of such power being exercised may have the same effect because of the apprehension of mentorees.

Therefore, it is helpful for a mentor to minimize the sources of their power over mentorees. I noted above that the accrual of power to mentors stems from either personal power or positional power. A mentor's personal power is largely derived from the esteem in which they are held by their mentoree, and little can be done to eliminate this. However, positional power is more readily addressed. I recommend that mentors of Christian leaders in formally appointed roles be independent, holding no position of power in relation to their mentorees so that the threat of power is neutralized. That independence entails that the mentor not be a supervisor or formal authority figure of any sort, nor even a part of the same organization. I will return to this theme in Chapter 7 where I discuss alternatives to the use of power in creating a liberating relationship between mentor and mentoree.

Be authentic

If good mentors are committed to being safe in order to allow mentorees to be real with them, then they will also be committed to being real themselves. Authenticity involves allowing yourself to be known, being honest about your weaknesses and having the courage to speak the truth even when it is confronting.

Transparency

Good mentors practise transparency, letting mentorees get to know personal details about them which are relevant to the issues that surface in mentoring conversations. Mentoring takes place in a genuine relationship, not a functional transaction. Professional distance and pretence have no place in a genuine relationship. Mentorees are interested to see if their mentor's life aligns with the things they say; this is especially true of those influenced by post-modernity. If they are unable to see much of their mentor's life, it not only denies them the reinforcement of the spoken message; it may also arouse suspicion about the mentor's authenticity.

I encourage mentors to occasionally invite their mentorees into their personal context. This might mean holding a mentoring session in the mentor's home, or asking the mentoree to share in a family meal. One summer I invited one of my mentorees to travel with me and my young son on a preaching tour to Ireland. His only responsibility was to share the driving. The experience was one which deepened and opened up our communication in a way I cannot imagine could have happened otherwise. Mentorees draw motivation and inspiration from being able to observe a respected Christian living out their calling amid the demands of everyday life.

Vulnerability

A special case of transparency applies when dealing with weaknesses, struggles and failures. Vulnerability is a risky business. It is a point at which the mentor, too, must rely on the confidentiality of the relationship. Yet vulnerability is worth the risk because of the reassurance and encouragement it brings to mentorees. Bobb Biehl comments:

> [My mentorees] often get the false impression that I am always 'Feeling like I'm on top of the world' because I am typically 'up' when I'm with them. When they learned of the fact that I have several days a year when I am deeply discouraged and feel depressed it seemed to them like perhaps the position of a [leader] wasn't only for 'super positive' people but regular human beings could get the job done.[62]

I suggest to people looking for a mentor that they find someone who is familiar with human pain and struggle through personal experience. Mentorees need someone who sees their own partly healed wounds not as a matter of shame but as signs of God's grace at work in their life. One word of warning: any self-disclosure on the part of the mentor must be for the benefit of the mentoree. There is no room in a giving mentoring relationship for the mentor to 'dump' their burdens on the mentoree.

Confronting

While mentors do not need to express all their impressions to their mentorees, authenticity demands that they do not create false impressions or continue to conceal what they really think. It is easy to be truthful about positive or neutral aspects of a mentoree. Negative factors are more difficult to deal with and many mentors shy away from it. Good mentors grasp the fact that helping mentorees to reach their goals is not just a matter of nurturing the positives through vision and encouragement. Effective mentoring is not blandly therapeutic hand-holding. It seeks to remind people of their best insights and their best intentions and hold them to the mark. At the right time and in the right way, negative factors that compromise those insights and intentions will also be addressed through constructive confrontation. This, too, is part of authenticity and commitment to the truth.

People say that what they want from a mentor is a boot up the rear. They should not be taken at their word! However, the same result can be achieved through asking some hard questions and giving candid responses when invited to give a perspective. For confrontation to occur in a healthy fashion it is necessary, for the sake of the mentoree's progress, for mentors to be ready to risk personal rejection and the possible derailing of the relationship. Having built up a credit of trust, the time will come for mentors to trade on that credit. When that time comes it is vital that the confrontation be handled in a constructive way. No blame or punishment is to be communicated. The emphasis is on clarifying the present position and finding a way forward. It is the negative obstacle which is to be torn down, not the mentoree. Good mentors have the capacity to differentiate between the two.

Be calm

Anxiety is infectious. If not checked it has the capacity to distort perceptions, strain relationships and lead to misguided actions. Good mentors are not anxious in the sense that they are differentiated, are prepared to wait patiently for the right moment, are tolerant of personal differences and remain calm under stress. They have the ability to tolerate high degrees of frustration, pain and uncertainty without 'losing it' in an anxious state. As a result they can maintain direction in confusing circumstances. Consider the potential negative impact of the repressive effects of anxiety on a mentoring relationship:

- Decreases our capacity to learn.
- Replaces curiosity with a demand for certainty.
- Stiffens our position against another's.
- Interrupts concentration.
- Floods the nervous system with adrenaline so that we cannot hear what is said without distortion.
- Simplifies ways of thinking (yes/no; either/or).
- Prompts a desire for a quick fix.
- Arouses feelings of helplessness or self-doubt.
- Leads to an array of defensive behaviours.
- Diminishes flexibility in response to challenges.
- Creates imaginative gridlock – not being able to think of alternatives, options or new perspectives.[63]

In contrast to this, consider Jesus asleep in the back of the boat as the disciples become more and more anxious about the storm raging around them. His ability to remain undisturbed by the circumstances and the reaction of others to those circumstances is a powerful metaphor of the less-anxious presence that good mentors maintain.

Differentiation

Good mentors are not easily thrown off-balance by the emotional state of their mentorees. Their responses can be thoughtful and creative rather than reflex reactions because they have a clear sense of self. Murray Bowen, a pioneer in the study of family systems, described the ability to know who we are apart from others as 'differentiation of self':

> Differentiation of self deals with the effort to define oneself, to control oneself, to become a more responsible person, and to permit others to be themselves as well. Differentiation is the ability to remain connected in relationship to significant people in our lives and yet not have our reactions and behaviour determined by them.[64]

Undifferentiated mentors tend to be instinctive, reactive, defensive, and make ill-considered decisions. Differentiated mentors tend to be intentional, responsive, open, and make well-considered decisions. Clearly, coming to differentiation is a lifelong journey. Progress in this direction yields greater capacity for good mentoring.

Patience

Mentors cannot afford to be in a hurry. When a particular approach proves not to be helping the mentoree to progress toward his or her goals, a good mentor is prepared to work at the pace of the mentoree, and gently seek to discover the factors that are causing difficulty. This is one of the points that make it so hard for a person's supervisor for a particular task to also serve as their mentor. Conflict arises over whether it is more important to get the job done or to maintain the integrity of the mentoring relationship.

Personal, spiritual and vocational growth are lifelong processes. Lasting outcomes are rarely achieved quickly. Good mentors will be content to wait for the fruit of their efforts to appear. To allow time for this, I recommend that a mentor and mentoree commit to a new mentoring relationship for at least a year up front, and entertain the possibility that they may work together for five to ten years. There is no advantage in overwhelming people by presenting them with a seemingly impossible programme of change through which they must work as quickly as possible. Mentorees need to know that it's okay to work through things at the pace God sets for them. The direction they are moving is more important than the point at which they have arrived.

Tolerance

Because Christian mentors are not trying to reproduce themselves in others, they learn to handle the inevitable differences that arise between themselves and their mentorees with tolerance and acceptance. Intolerance drives people to either eliminate interpersonal differences through changing the other person, or to end the relationship. Even on those matters in which the mentoree accepts responsibility for the need to change, acceptance of the reality of the mentoree's less-than-ideal starting point is essential.

Mentorees need a spiritual companion who will allow them to bring deep, dark realities out into the light without condemnation. Tolerance does not imply that these dark realities are okay; it conveys that it's okay to talk about them and the relationship will survive. Actively working to develop a high tolerance for differences will help mentors become virtually unshockable. The value of this is that mentorees can afford to canvass personal matters that they themselves find disturbing, disorienting or anxiety-producing in a context where the other person will maintain stability.

Keeping calm

One of the keys to remaining calm under stress is to keep track of the personal impact that the mentoring relationship is having on you through your session notes, and debriefing with your own mentor. It is important for the mentoree that you don't allow your own history to interfere with your ministry with them. If your mentoree's journey stirs up issues for you, take that as an opportunity from God, but deal with it away from the mentoring relationship.

Another helpful habit is to learn not to take personally the tensions that arise in a mentoring relationship. For example, frustration and disappointment are normal reactions when mentorees do not seem to be taking you seriously. You may recommend an action step which the mentoree takes on, only to see it apparently ignored. Remember that this is not about you. Since they freely accepted the assignment, it's not you they have let down but themselves and perhaps God if he was guiding them to do so.

When you become aware of anxiety starting to emerge within, work through these four phases. First, examine and identify your feelings. Are you mad, sad, glad, or scared? Second, own those feelings and resist blaming others for how you feel. Third, process those feelings, deciding what to do with them. Having cast your anxiety on God in prayer as we are urged to do in 1 Peter 5:7, you may decide to let the feelings go, or seek some change in the circumstances. Fourth, monitor the feelings you have identified in ongoing management, not just in crisis moments.

Be relational

Charles Schultz, the creator of the 'Peanuts' cartoons once wrote, 'I love mankind; it's people I can't stand.' You may firmly believe in the value of mentoring, but it's very hard to be a good mentor unless you really like people. Mentoring takes place within intentional, empowering, unique relationships. It cannot be delivered from an emotional distance or provided as a functional service outside of a real relationship. So it follows that the relational capacities of mentors are crucial to their effectiveness. Good mentors listen perceptively, communicate clearly, apologize and forgive readily, and adapt themselves to the needs of mentorees.

Perception

Along with love, it is vital that mentors have a growing capacity for acute interpersonal perception. This involves listening, close observation, intuition and spiritual insight. Without this, it will be a case of the blind leading the blind. Mentors need to be able to help others grasp what is going on in their lives, and this usually – though not always – involves the mentor being able to grasp it first. In addition, mentors need well-developed self-perception to minimize blind-spots that may inadvertently bring a negative impact to the mentoring process.

Communication

When the mentor comes into possession of a crucial piece of information or identifies a certain perspective helpful to the mentoree's progress, there are choices to be made about how to effectively communicate that information or perspective. Good mentors learn how to read each mentoree and appropriately employ verbal and written skills backed up by other, more subtle, means of communication.

In mentoring, the way information and perspectives are communicated is not at all like the didactic approach typically used in rudimentary educational curricula. Rather, the communication is designed to be facilitative of the mentoree's process of discovery. It may be factual knowledge, an observation, pertinent feedback or a suggestion to pursue a certain line of enquiry. This capacity empowers mentorees to make connections between what is communicated and the things they already know so that they can draw their own conclusions.

Apologizing and forgiving

All relationships are susceptible to disruption from offences committed either wittingly or unwittingly by one or both parties. Mentoring relationships are no different. Good mentors have the relational capacity to work through difficulties by taking responsibility for their offences, and forgiving those offences committed against them. Good mentors do not let these matters fester. Rather, they address the issues and seek reconciliation.

Flexibility

Every mentoree is a unique individual. It is the mentor's responsibility to adapt their mentoring style to suit the mentoree's personality, temperament, preferred mode of learning, level of experience and maturity, theological framework, family situation, ministry commitments, and so on. In an extended mentoring relationship of several years, some of these factors will slowly evolve, while others may be altered abruptly. A good mentor will be flexible enough to adapt along with those changes.

Be positive

Taking the work of God's Spirit as the principal focus has the effect of making mentoring essentially positive and hope-filled. Problems and difficulties are tackled in an atmosphere of confidence as steps toward the good outcomes which form part of God's intentions for the mentoree. Generally speaking, mentorees are painfully aware of their shortcomings and failures. They genuinely wish to address these matters, yet are fearful of being judged and condemned. Good mentors are not judgmental because they see beyond the negatives and convey the hope that springs from confidence in the grace of God. They truly believe in their mentoree, are good encouragers and grasp opportunities to celebrate progress.

Vision

Although 'vision' is an overused word in Christian leadership literature, it is appropriate in this connection because good mentors are eager to 'see' not only the present reality but also the possible future for their mentorees. Sharing realistic, positive scenarios with mentorees generates and sustains hope. Without hope, a mentoree will lack motivation to pursue God's agenda for them, and be inclined to give up when things get difficult.

The mentor needs the relational capacity to lift mentorees' eyes towards the future result of the work of the Holy Spirit in their lives. With the impartation of vision, the mentoree is empowered to take the initiative.

Encouragement

The capacity to strengthen the heart through effective stimulation and affirmation is the second element essential for sustaining hope. The presence of people who will support and stick with us makes all the difference to our ability to face the difficulties of life with hope. Lawrence Crabb says, 'Mentors speak three messages: It can be done. You are not alone. I believe in you.'[65] The presence of a credible, respected person alongside the mentoree, cheering them on, builds their heart to stay the course and reach their goals. Good mentorees will be doing their best to participate constructively in the mentoring process. Review the qualities in the following chapter. Wherever you see devotion to Christ, openness, determination, honesty, careful thought, initiative, responsibility, respect or courtesy being exercised by your mentoree, take the opportunity to affirm them.

Celebration of progress

As a mentor you will have the privilege of being present at some wonderful breakthrough moments in the lives of leaders. Take every opportunity to celebrate with them. Consider ways you can fashion symbols and mementos when a major goal has been achieved. This is not only affirming in the moment; it creates a sustaining memory for later times when progress seems slow or when a setback is encountered.

Be self-aware

From time to time I hear embarrassing stories of would-be mentors who blunder around like a spiritual Mr Magoo. You might recall that cartoon character of the 1950s and 1960s with the voice of Jim Backus and the signature line: 'Ah Magoo, you've done it again!' Mr Magoo gets into all kinds of sticky situations as a result of his near-sightedness, compounded by his refusal to acknowledge the problem. He always escapes unscathed, oblivious to the mayhem he leaves in his wake. In contrast to that, good mentors have a realistic assessment of their abilities and limitations, do not boast about their spiritual accomplishments, and acknowledge the impact of their emotions, experience and preferences in what they bring to a mentoring relationship.

Realistic self-assessment

In Romans 12, Paul cautions us not to think more highly of ourselves than we should, yet at the same time urges us to purposefully apply whatever gifts and abilities we possess in God's service. 'Sober judgment' is required – a realistic assessment of our capacities that neither exaggerates nor minimizes them. Good mentors do not pretend they have more experience or ability than is actually the case. Nor are they falsely modest. Instead, they employ whatever knowledge or skills they have that may be of benefit to their mentorees.

Disinclined to boast

Good mentors are secure enough in themselves not to feel the need to parade their achievements so as to impress others. At a deeper level, they do not see their spiritual advancement as their own achievement so much as the work of the Spirit. This attitude extends to the ministry of mentoring, where good mentors acknowledge their role to be secondary. The primary relationship in mentoring is not between the mentor and the mentoree but between the mentoree and the Holy Spirit. Therefore, the mentor's role is somewhat like that of John the Baptist playing the 'bridegroom' role for Jesus. There is no room for boasting about what you achieve in mentoring. Good mentors learn to play second fiddle.

Personal impact

Mentoring relationships are shaped by both mentor and mentoree through words, actions and the very nature of the people involved. Good mentors recognize that their own personality, preferences, background, experiences and emotional responses have a profound effect on the person they are seeking to assist. The point of such awareness is not to try to change these things, since that would be self-defeating. Rather, this awareness allows the mentor to acknowledge personal factors, discuss them with the mentoree and take steps to compensate for those that are problematic. By minimizing our personal blind-spots we increase our potential effectiveness as mentors.

Be self-controlled

When someone comes to the point of seeking out a mentoring relationship, it often arises from the realization that their life is not going where they want it to go. Perhaps they sense that, in spite of their best intentions, they mostly drift along. They may realize that they allow themselves to be shaped and pushed around by forces they would be better to deny. Sometimes the driving factor is simply a sense of not staying on top of things and feeling somewhat out of control. In the light of these very common feelings, leaders need mentors who have dealt with these factors and mastered them. Good mentors are able to live out the demands of everyday life wisely, are free from destructive addictions and compulsions, and maintain good habits of personal and spiritual health. In short, they can stand their ground and be self-controlled amid complexity and pressure.

Dealing with demands wisely

Mentors are free to assist others with their lives because they are not overwhelmed by their own lives. This is not to say that they do not find life challenging, but they handle pressure well by effectively managing their personal resources – especially their time and energy. Good mentors are able to make decisions, get organized, set priorities, maintain boundaries and keep track of what is important and what is truly urgent. Mentors who are frazzled, distracted, edgy or simply not coping with their lives are not credible as helpers in the endeavour of identifying and promoting the work of God's Spirit in another's life. When circumstances overtake careful self-management – as will happen from time to time – good mentors are able to 'roll with the punches' with patience, perseverance, flexibility, optimism and inner peace from the Holy Spirit.

Freedom from addictions and compulsions

When Paul wrote to Timothy and Titus about the qualities they should look for in potential church leaders, he put some emphasis on this matter of self-control. Although they work at an individual rather than a corporate level, mentors, like church overseers, are also engaged in 'God's work'. Paul's reasoning in Titus 1:7–8 is therefore relevant for our purposes here:

> Since an overseer is entrusted with God's work, he must be blameless – not overbearing, not quick-tempered, not given to drunkenness, not violent, not pursuing dishonest gain. Rather he must be hospitable, one who loves what is good, who is self-controlled, upright, holy and disciplined.

In similar vein, Paul writes in 1 Corinthians 6:12 and 10:23 that while everything is permissible for Christians, not everything is beneficial or constructive. Therefore Christians should not allow themselves to be mastered by anything, but should exercise self-control.

It should be self-evident that good mentors will not engage in substance abuse. Yet just as destructive as physical addictions such as narcotics, alcohol and food are non-substance addictions such as desires for power, control, money, affirmation, or sexual gratification. Gerald May discusses this, pointing out that the patterns of feedback, habituation, and adaptation – even the physical cellular dynamics – are essentially the same whether the addictive behaviour involves substances or not.[66] May paints a picture of the insidious nature of addiction:

> Addiction attaches desire, bonds and enslaves the energy of desire to certain specific behaviours, things or people. These objects of attachment then become preoccupations and obsessions; they come to rule our lives. Addiction breeds wilfulness within us, yet paradoxically, erodes our free will and eats away at our dignity. It is the absolute enemy of human freedom, the antipathy of love.[67]

Good mentors live in the freedom they recommend to their mentorees. Without this quality, the mentoring ministry lacks integrity and is robbed of its power both psychologically and spiritually.

Healthy habits

Beyond resisting the negative impact of addictive behaviours, the self-control good mentors practise is employed to establish and maintain life-giving habits. Some of these have already been discussed above, such as those that relate to godliness – surrender to the Lord and routines of prayer and deep engagement with the Bible. Four further habits requiring self-control are worthy of particular mention.

First is the habit of reflection. This may be practised through keeping a journal, taking regular times out for retreat and by conducting a periodic personal review. One helpful daily awareness exercise involves focusing on one or at most two particular moments of the day, examining the feelings that arose in those moments, reviewing the response those feelings evoked, seeking the self-understanding revealed and how the Spirit of God was present in those moments. The habit of reflection creates an opportunity to identify the work of God's Spirit.

The second habit is accountability. Good mentors will

recognize their own need to be mentored and submit to the accountability of that relationship. They also get into the habit of being honest with trusted friends, sharing their goals and intentions and confessing their shortcomings. The habit of accountability also entails paying attention to feedback and being willing to act on sound advice.

Third, self-control is vital to develop the habit of lifelong learning. This might be expressed through formal study, but not necessarily so. Informal learning can also take place through self-motivated research, reading several books around a particular topic, or simply asking several people for their thoughts on a certain issue.

Finally, good mentors exercise self-control to develop the healthy habit of rest. They do not give in to the compulsive tendency to work incessantly. Building in adequate time for recovery and recreation is among the most important habits mentors can develop. It provides a way to be alert and ready to meet the relational and spiritual demands of the mentoring process, and presents mentorees with a good example of how to conduct a sustainable ministry.

Be other-centred

Other-centredness is the distinctive essence of divine love. It is this kind of love to which good mentors aspire within their mentoring relationships. They delight to give to others selflessly for their benefit. They do not rely on reciprocity to maintain motivation and do not seek recognition. Good mentors are not looking for their own benefit but have generous spirits. They are content that it is not up to mentorees to supply something lacking in the mentor. Good mentors put their own needs aside for the sake of serving God's agenda in the life of the mentoree. They do not set out to build a personal empire or even a network of influence through mentoring, but seek to extend God's kingdom.

Let's recap these nine ways to give your best to mentoring:

1. *Be godly:* Good mentors are true disciples, settled in God, anchored in the Bible, and sensitive to the Holy Spirit.
2. *Be safe:* Good mentors keep confidences, have selfless motivation, and do not wield power.
3. *Be authentic:* Good mentors allow themselves to be known, are honest about their weaknesses and have courage to speak the truth.
4. *Be calm:* Good mentors are not anxious, are highly differentiated, patient and tolerant, and deal effectively with stress.
5. *Be relational:* Good mentors listen perceptively, communicate clearly, apologize and forgive readily and are flexible.
6. *Be positive:* Good mentors truly believe in their mentoree, are good encouragers and love to celebrate the grace of God.
7. *Be self-aware:* Good mentors have a realistic assessment of their abilities and limitations, do not boast about their spiritual accomplishments, and acknowledge the impact of their experience and preferences.
8. *Be self-controlled:* Good mentors live out the demands of life wisely, are free from destructive addictions and compulsions, and maintain good habits of personal and spiritual health.
9. *Be other-centred:* Good mentors delight to give to others for their benefit, do not rely on reciprocity to maintain motivation and do not seek recognition.

Chapter 6

Getting the Most from Mentoring

If you will permit me, I would like to change hats for this chapter. So far, I have mostly been writing as a mentor for those who would like to develop their understanding and practice of mentoring. Now I would like to write as one who receives mentoring and pass on to you some of the things I have learned – and am still learning – from that position.

Those of us seeking mentoring naturally look for a competent mentor. But we need to keep in mind that the actions and attitudes we bring to the table as mentorees will have a huge bearing on the outcomes of our mentoring relationship. Even those mentors who genuinely give their very best to mentoring in the ways described in the last chapter will be limited in their capacity to assist us if we do not fulfil our part of the equation.

Be devoted to Christ

The first thing I have learned about mentoring that aims to promote the work of the Holy Spirit in my life is that it is not going to get anywhere unless I have a genuine determination to follow Christ, to serve him and become more and more like him. If we are relying on our mentor to supply the energy to drive the process along we will wind up disappointed. The force that carries us along will be the wind of the Spirit of Christ. The sail that catches that wind is our devotion. It is important that this devotion to Christ takes priority over other motivations that will no doubt be present as we approach a mentoring process.

We may come to be mentored with a desire to be more effective in our ministry, or to sort through a complex challenge, or to work on a particular area of our character, or to invest the better part of our conscience in someone who will keep us honest, or simply to open ourselves to the influence of someone we respect. These agendas are fine so long as they are held within the framework of devotion to Christ and submission to the work of his Spirit which marks the mentoring as distinctively Christian.

Our pride immediately becomes an issue when we think in these terms. It requires humility to submit to the work of the Holy Spirit. Without humility before God, the divine grace essential to personal and spiritual transformation will be stymied, for 'God opposes the proud but gives grace to the humble' (Proverbs 3:34; Matthew 23:12; James 4:6; 1 Peter 5:5). Our determination to follow Christ may wax and wane over time, depending on circumstances. If we maintain humility, that determination may be renewed by God's grace.

Being devoted to Christ means being committed to change. From time to time, crucial matters arise in mentoring that the mentoree finds confronting and challenging to the point of resistance. Whether or not such challenges arise from the Spirit's agenda is up to the mentoree to determine. But if the resistance is, in fact, against the Spirit, the mentoring process will only regain momentum once that resistance is broken down by a deep and sustaining devotion to following Christ.

Be open

Some mentoring relationships founder because the mentoree only desires affirming strokes to bolster their shaky confidence. They will choose support over challenge every time and have no desire to learn anything new or tackle fresh opportunities. If a mentoree is closed to the new, the mentoring relationship will also become closed, stagnant and eventually unsatisfying to both mentor and mentoree. The alternative is to develop an attitude of openness and interest in what might be next on the Holy Spirit's agenda for your life.

Soon after I moved into our present home, I met an elderly neighbour who needed help re-hanging his front door. Now, I consider myself a reasonable handyman and I was only too willing to give him the benefit of my competence. Feeling like a modern-day Good Samaritan, I went over to do the poor old guy a favour. But it didn't quite turn out that way. He let me get to work, watching what I was doing with great interest. To my consternation, what had seemed like a simple job was, in fact, quite complicated. I was soon out of my depth and feeling a little embarrassed.

It was then that I discovered my neighbour had called me in not because he lacked the skill to get the job done. He just needed someone strong enough to lift the door. He was a master carpenter whose arms had lost a little of their strength but whose mind had lost none of its sharpness. He guided me through the process and I learned some neat tricks of the trade.

Afterwards I asked him why he had let me go so long before stepping in. 'I have enjoyed carpentry for most of my life,' he said, 'first as a career and now as a hobby. Working with wood is so wonderfully complex that it offers a lifetime of learning. I constantly learn things that make me wonder how I got along before I knew them. I wanted to see if there was anything I could learn from you.' Like a whack across the side of the head, I got the message! It is so important to remain open to receive new insights; to be a lifelong learner.

To get the most from mentoring you will do well to recognize the fact that all of us are never anything beyond beginners. It does not help to try to impress your mentor with your maturity and knowledge. It is far better to take the plunge and expose one's immaturity and ignorance. To hide these things from a mentor is as foolish as hiding your sickness from a doctor. The wise person is always more aware of their ignorance than their knowledge.

Fred Smith, who in his lifetime was an author and regular contributor to the journal *Christianity Today*, relates the following story:

> Dr Walter Hearn, a biochemist at Yale University, surprised me once by saying, 'Fred, every night when you go to bed you ought to be more ignorant than

you were when you woke up.' I took this as facetious until he explained that if I considered my knowledge as a balloon and every day that balloon increased in size, it touched more and more ignorance on the periphery. Therefore my knowledge brought me into contact with my greater ignorance. The arrogant are proud of their knowledge; the humble are acquainted with their ignorance.[68]

As a mentoree, maintain a teachable spirit; be receptive and listen closely to discern the whispers of the Spirit amid your mentoring conversations. Cultivate an eager expectation that God will use the foolishness of mentoring as a context in which he will reveal his agenda and wisdom for your life. That is the most important openness of all.

Be determined

To get the most from mentoring you will do well to continually stir up your discontent with the status quo. I do not mean that we should become so discontented as to be driven to despair! There are many things over which we can be thankful and feel satisfaction. Yet fostering holy discontent is vital to overcome the resignation, lethargy and complacency that can so easily take hold of us when our energy begins to flag from our efforts to live faithfully and well. The apostle Paul put it well in Philippians 3:12–14 where he writes:

Not that I have already obtained all this, or have already been made perfect, but I press on to take hold of that for which Christ Jesus took hold of me. Brothers, I do not consider myself yet to have taken hold of it. But one thing I do: Forgetting what is behind and straining toward what is ahead, I press on toward the goal to win the prize for which God has called me heavenward in Christ Jesus.

Good mentorees are determined to press on to overcome whatever obstacles there may be between them and the fulfilment of God's agenda for their lives. The person with this determination will meet with opposition of many kinds. Some suffering is unavoidable in the process of personal and spiritual growth, so our determination is tested on a regular basis! Paul tells us to 'rejoice in our sufferings, because we know that suffering produces perseverance; perseverance, character; and character, hope' (Romans 5:3–4).

When we engage in physical exercise, we have to push through barriers to reach new benchmarks of fitness, strength and endurance. Runners feel as if they cannot take another step, yet press on to complete that last lap. Weightlifters don't know how they are going to endure the next repetition, but summon up their strength to get to a new level. Character growth works in the same way. We must face things we're not sure we can handle. Good mentorees exercise the necessary self-discipline to carry out what is right even when it is painful.

On several occasions in the course of my own mentoring I have felt like giving up. I have wished that I had set easier goals, and doubted whether I could possibly have heard God right. Once I even contemplated changing my mentor so I could find someone who didn't know so much about the call on my life! The thing that has kept me hanging in there is my determination to run the race marked out for me. The words of Hebrews 12:2–3 remain an inspiration:

> Let us fix our eyes on Jesus, the author and perfecter of our faith, who for the joy set before him endured the cross, scorning its shame, and sat down at the right hand of the throne of God. Consider him who endured such opposition from sinful men, so that you will not grow weary and lose heart.

Be honest

From time to time your mentor may ask probing questions which aim to help you discover more about your interactions with the work of the Holy Spirit in your life. Let me be clear: you are not under an obligation to answer those questions. The process is a journey of discovery, not an interrogation. However, if you do give an answer, you do best to make it an honest one. If you prefer not to answer, say so clearly and give your reason.

It is vital to the integrity of the mentoring process that mentorees are not evasive or disingenuous. Honesty is not just a virtue. It is also the only way you will develop depth in your mentoring relationship. The litmus test of honesty may demand that you take the trouble to reflect deeply before making a response to some questions. This is an unavoidable part of the responsibility of the mentoree. Like any relationship, mentoring can only grow in the good soil of truth. In the end, it is the truth that will set you free.

Furthermore, honesty in a mentoring relationship goes beyond the way in which you respond to questions. It also involves being forthcoming – proactively raising pertinent issues within your life of which you have become aware. Your mentor may not think to specifically ask you about the 'hot' issue you are dealing with unless you are honest enough to provide the cue. Keeping such things secret may spare you from becoming uncomfortable or emotional or from some other situation you would prefer to avoid. But it is clearly most counter-productive to the purpose of the mentoring relationship and you certainly won't be getting the best from the experience.

Honesty in mentoring requires that each party is transparent about their opinions and passions. If a mentor should express a point of view with which the mentoree disagrees, it is not helpful for the mentoree to instantly acquiesce or remain silent. To 'push back' with an alternative perspective can be awkward for reasons of culture, temperament or age difference. Yet unless these difficulties are surmounted, mentoring conversations will devolve into polite superficiality.

Associated with this sort of honesty is resistance to the tendency to create false impressions through silence or oblique inference. It is natural, when we are in the presence of someone we respect, to desire them to think well of us. When we become aware that the person we respect has a favourable impression of us which is not quite true, many of us are inclined to let it go and simply enjoy it. We may go even further, dropping hints and telling half-truths that seem to indicate positive things about ourselves that are false, without ever actually telling a lie.

Although these tendencies are very common, they are not right or helpful – certainly not within a mentoring relationship. If your mentor makes a positive assumption about you which is not based in fact, my advice is to catch it early, and do not allow it to take root. The longer false impressions are allowed to remain, the harder they are to bring out into the light of truth.

Think

By now you will be getting the idea that being a mentoree is hard work, and it certainly is! Much of this work is carried out in the necessary business of thinking. This is not good news for those of us who would by far prefer to roll up our sleeves in action rather than take time out for reflection, but there is no way around it. Of course, this is not an either/or situation; without action there would not be much to reflect upon. Yet without reflection, our actions tend to get stuck in ruts – ruts that do not always take us where we want to go.

Figuring out what God is up to in your life is not an easy matter. This is not to say that God is being furtive and deliberately making things hard for us. It is rather to assert the truth that our spiritual sensitivity and acumen has been greatly attenuated by sin, and our process of healing and recovery is long. This is work we need to do for ourselves. We cannot take the insights others have gained about how God is working in their lives and apply those to ourselves. Each of us is an individual, and God works with us uniquely. As Carl Jung observed, this individuality creates a challenge:

> To find out what is truly individual in ourselves, profound reflection is needed; and suddenly we realize how uncommonly difficult the discovery of individuality is.[69]

Nevertheless, with the Holy Spirit to help us, we can meet the challenge if we are prepared to think. The apostle Paul holds out the promise that we can be transformed by the renewing of our mind (Romans 12:2) and assures us that, through the Holy Spirit living within us, we have the mind of Christ (1 Corinthians 2:16) so that we can learn to think like him. This thinking is not just navel-gazing. The goal is not mere understanding but a transformed life that has positive outcomes for our character, our relationships and our actions.

Don't look for the easy way out and expect your mentor to do your thinking for you. This will only weaken rather than strengthen you. The first part of your thinking as part of mentoring will be given to preparation for meeting with your mentor. Consider the events of the period since you last met and your actions in response to those situations. Jot down anything that makes you curious or suggests to you that God was involved in a particular way.

Next, prepare one or two questions that you would like to tease out with your mentor. There's power in a good question! Just as your mentor will have prepared questions for you, so you have the responsibility to think carefully through the questions you want to explore. Excellent questions come from consideration, reflection, analysis, and discernment. The best way to get to the heart of the matter and cut through unnecessary waffle is to write the question down. Throwaway or off-the-cuff questions will not get the best out of a mentor, while excellent questions will stimulate excellent responses.

The second part of your thinking as part of mentoring comes during and after your meeting. Take notes as you talk with your mentor and go over them later. Consider carefully what is said and capture any insights that start to emerge. Bring the thoughts that especially arrest your attention before God in prayer and ask him to prepare your mind to receive his truth. Then you will be in a position to make some decisions about the actions you plan to take as a result.

Take action

While some mentorees have difficulty taking time out from their activity to think and reflect, others wrestle with the opposite challenge. Garry was in this predicament. He came from a conservative, evangelical home with strong parents who took seriously their task to raise their son in the training and instruction of the Lord. Garry had graduated from a Christian school and, to his parents' delight, was training to be a pastor. But he was just drifting with the current.

As I began mentoring him, I noticed that he would think endlessly about issues, around and around in circles. His passivity arose out of his difficulty in arriving at clear decisions. He would sometimes try to get me to make his decisions for him and tell him what he should do. His goals were many and vague, with little commitment to pursue them. We would agree on steps he was to make before our next session but he would regularly fail to complete them. He was like the student who goes to piano lessons but never practises in between.

Curiously, Garry was not very concerned about this at first. He took the view that life had always just 'worked out by itself'. He even spiritualized it by saying that he was 'surrendering to God's will' by not actively taking control of his direction in life. The truth emerged that he hesitated to take decisive action for fear of failure. Even when he was in trouble, he would wait to be rescued rather than take the steps necessary to solve the problem. Garry made little progress until he resolved to overcome his passivity and rouse his initiative from its long hibernation.

To get the most from mentoring, good mentorees will refuse to be passive, will make clear decisions, commit to specific plans and carry them through. Passivity is not a spiritual virtue. Henry Cloud and John Townsend make the point forcefully:

Action is always an integral part of growth. Spiritual growth does not 'happen' to us; it requires a great deal of blood, sweat and tears. This doesn't mean either that we must do it all on our own or that God does it all. Our sanctification is a collaborative effort between God and us.[70]

The apostle Paul expresses the nature of this collaboration in Philippians 2:12–13 where he writes, 'continue to work out your salvation with fear and trembling, for it is God who works in you to will and to act according to his good purpose', and again in Colossians 1:29, 'To this end I labour, struggling with all his energy, which so powerfully works in me.' As I have observed above, there is a time to be still, to wait on God's activity and to reflect. Yet it is also true that our active participation is essential to the advancement of God's agenda in our lives.

Finding our way forward in mentoring involves a large amount of trial-and-error experimentation. On the principle that it is impossible to steer a stationary ship, the important thing is to get moving. Then you can make the necessary adjustments in direction to get on course. Inevitably, the actions you take will not always be the wisest and best. Even misguided action, when undertaken conscientiously in an attempt to pursue God's agenda, will contribute to the overall mentoring process. The good news is that you don't have to get it exactly right every time in order to make progress. In fact, much learning may be gained from mistakes. Over time, the actions you take as a result of your mentoring sessions will open up a pathway of God's grace into your life and accumulate into transformation.

Take responsibility

In learning to exercise initiative and take action, Garry came to the crucial realization that he was responsible for his own life and growth – not me, not his parents, not his teachers and not his pastor. When his life was over and he stood before God, he and no one else would be giving an account of what he had done with the resources and opportunities he had been given. A sense of God-given dignity and accountability struck him like a thunderbolt and he began to take charge of his affairs.

To get the most from mentoring, good mentorees will shoulder their own load, fulfil their commitments and own their failures and successes. Shouldering one's own load means being willing to take on the things that God requires. This includes both the general responsibilities of a godly lifestyle and the specific implications of one's own calling. It does not mean the drivenness that results from viewing every need as a call and every opportunity as an assignment.

Shouldering one's own load is intrinsic to the business of following Jesus. In Luke 9:23 Jesus said, 'If anyone would come after me, he must deny himself and take up his cross daily and follow me.' Accepting the call of God on our lives is not just a matter of affirming the glorious destiny to which he beckons. It is also a matter of undertaking the tasks and burdens of everyday life as we walk the journey towards our final goal. As the apostle Paul wrote, 'Each of you must take responsibility for doing the creative best you can with your own life' (Galatians 6:5 *The Message*).

In mentoring, it is up to us as mentorees to accept the task of addressing our shortcomings, deepening our spirituality, strengthening our character flaws, disciplining our time, guarding our vulnerabilities, developing our gifts and focusing our passions. Like the servants in Jesus' parable who were entrusted with a certain number of talents, we will be held accountable for what we do with what God has given us. Therefore, we must take ownership of the mentoring process and accept the ministry of our mentor as an assistant who will aid us to do what we must do for ourselves.

Taking responsibility also means that you may be relied upon to do what you say you will do. In the context of mentoring this involves keeping appointments, being punctual and well prepared, abiding by other aspects of the mentoring contract and following through on the action steps you undertake. Those mentorees who do not take these responsibilities seriously will certainly fail to get the most from mentoring.

It's no good protesting that an assignment you took on was not relevant or interesting. It is crucial for mentorees to take personal responsibility by only agreeing to assignments they believe are worthwhile and to which they are glad to commit themselves. If the suggested assignment is not a good one, don't agree to it. If it is, then follow through to the best of your ability. Some mentoring contracts require mentorees to email their mentor one to two days before their scheduled appointment indicating that they have completed or at least made progress towards the action steps agreed upon at the last meeting. If action has not been taken, the mentoree takes responsibility to postpone or cancel the appointment.

Finally, taking responsibility means owning your failures and successes. As a mentoree myself, I know how easy it is to fall into making excuses for why I have not completed action steps that I have undertaken. I can be quite creative, but my excuses are all variations on the old 'The dog ate my homework' theme. If we are going to get the most from mentoring we must stop habitually blaming others and painting ourselves as the victims of circumstance. Since Adam in the Garden of Eden, humans have been denying fault and seeking to avoid responsibility. If we are going to grow in grace, this has to stop.

At the same time, we will gain more from mentoring if we can learn to accept credit and praise when it is due. It is surprisingly common for Christian leaders to receive affirmation from their mentors with a degree of awkwardness or even to deflect it towards God or others who had a hand in the success. Such false modesty is unnecessary. Growth also comes when we are able to recognize and acknowledge the occasions when we do well. The positive reinforcement that we experience from taking responsibility for our successes stands us in good stead for the next time we face similar circumstances.

Respect boundaries

In these final two sections on how to get the most from mentoring, I want to address some of the 'dos' and 'don'ts' of how you relate to your mentor on a personal level. Indirectly, the quality of the relationship you have with your mentor has an important bearing on the benefits you will receive from the mentoring process. It is in your own interest to avoid straining the relationship and to look for ways to positively strengthen it. Let's begin with some 'don'ts'.

Mentors are often busy people. The time boundaries they put in place for the mentoring relationship are intended not so much to limit you as to enable them to continue to function at a high and intense level. Therefore, be careful not to demand more of your mentor's time than they have indicated they are prepared to give. If in doubt, check on your mentor's availability before sending long, involved emails or launching into a deep and meaningful conversation on the phone.

Also, respect the privacy of your mentor. Good mentors will seek to be authentic with you, but the provision of mentoring does not require the same degree of disclosure as is appropriate from the mentoree. Your mentor will make sure the relationship is safe for you by keeping your confidences. It is essential that this courtesy be returned and that anything he or she shares with you about themselves for your benefit stays with you. Your mentor will have other personal boundaries such as those to do with personal space, touch, and other signals of intimacy and language. There may be certain behaviours with which he or she is not comfortable, such as smoking. It is simple courtesy to respect these boundaries.

A person with a well-known mentor can be tempted to refer to her or him in ways that take advantage, particularly in quoting something out of context. Mentorees should not trade on the currency of their mentor's reputation, seeking to gain advantage by the association. A mentor is for progress in grace, not ego satisfaction.

Show appreciation

On the other side of the coin, there are some 'dos' that will help to enhance your relationship with your mentor. Firstly, it is a good thing to encourage your mentor with positive feedback about the value you are receiving from your sessions together. You do this to bless them, but you will also reap the benefit of a motivated mentor!

You can also show your appreciation of your mentor with small acts of consideration such as doing the greater amount of the travelling required for you to meet, and adjusting your diary to suit your mentor. Some mentors like to absorb incidental costs such as for coffee, meals, fuel, telephone and so on. However, it is better for mentorees not to presume upon this generosity but to considerately offer to meet the mentor's costs if at all possible. This is one of the matters that is best settled at the first meeting and may be included in the mentoring contract so that there is no misunderstanding.

While the mentoring relationship and the sessions you spend with your mentor are clearly set up for your benefit as the mentoree, there is still room for you to be a blessing to your mentor by praying for him or her. Do you remember how Jesus asked Peter, James and John to pray for him in the Garden of Gethsemane? Though he had expertly mentored these men for years, the hour came when he was in deep need and they were given the opportunity to minister to him. Supporting your mentor in their ministry may be something that you include in your private prayer time, or you might offer to pray for them once you have received prayer at the conclusion of your mentoring session. A note from time to time with a prayer for your mentor inscribed on it is a wonderful gift that will express your appreciation eloquently.

Let's recap these nine ways to get the most from mentoring:

1. *Be devoted to Christ:* Good mentorees desire to be like Christ, serve him wholeheartedly, and submit to the work of the Holy Spirit.

2. *Be open:* Good mentorees recognize that they are beginners, are ready for new ideas and change, and listen for God's voice.

3. *Be determined:* Good mentorees are not satisfied with the status quo, push through barriers and exercise self-discipline.

4. *Be honest:* Good mentorees are not evasive, are proactive in raising pertinent issues, own their opinions, and do not create false impressions.

5. *Think:* Good mentorees reflect on their lives, prepare good questions, and consider what is said.

6. *Take action:* Good mentorees refuse to be passive, make clear decisions, commit to specific plans and carry them through.

7. *Take responsibility:* Good mentorees shoulder their own load, fulfil their commitments and own their failures and successes.

8. *Respect boundaries:* Good mentorees are sensitive in their demands, maintain confidentiality, and do not take advantage of their mentor.

9. *Show appreciation:* Good mentorees acknowledge the value of mentoring, are considerate and pray for their mentor.

Chapter 7

The Mentoring Relationship

Throughout this book the importance of the relational nature of mentoring has been emphasized. In a sense, the operation of this relationship is the 'soul' of mentoring. Over forty years ago, Felix Biestek described the essence of the interaction between caring professionals and their clients.[71] This chapter takes its cue from his seminal work and builds upon it with theological reflection and the use of insights drawn from many years of mentoring experience.

In teasing apart this sort of relationship we should not lose sight of the fact that it is a deep, complex reality that goes beyond that which can be analysed and neatly categorized in words. When a mentoring relationship works well there is invariably a certain 'X-factor' which seems to come from outside the two people involved. Receive this gratefully as a gift from God.

Yet there are several facets of the mentoring relationship which, once identified, suggest a range of attitudes and actions which the mentor may adopt to deepen and strengthen that relationship, thereby facilitating the mentoring process. In this chapter we will consider ten of these facets that I consider to be essential and worthy of close attention.

Sacramental: Grace is conveyed

To understand what I mean by saying that a Christian mentoring relationship is 'sacramental', let me explain the derivation of the term. The Latin word *sacramentum* originally referred to an oath or pledge, especially a soldier's oath of allegiance. This is the language of covenant, conveying the ideas of promise, fidelity and commitment. As time went by, the meaning of *sacramentum* evolved and came to be the word Latin scholars used to render the Greek word *mysterion* when translating the

New Testament. In this use it came to be associated especially with the 'mysteries' of baptism and the Lord's Supper; moments of grace and spiritual power that flow from God in the context of covenant. Hence, we have Augustine's classic definition of a sacrament as 'the visible form of an invisible grace'. Both these aspects – covenant and a means of grace – relate to the mentoring relationship.

Mentoring as both covenant and a means of grace

Christian mentoring relationships are sacramental in the covenantal sense in that the mentor signs up to be for the mentoree, to cheer on, to delight in wins, to extend himself or herself for the sake of the mentoree. But at an even deeper level, the mentoring relationship is sacramental in that it is a visible sign of the invisible Master Mentor, Christ, who by his Spirit is on the side of the mentoree, cheering, delighting, and extending himself for the sake of the mentoree. In a mysterious way the grace of God, the power of the Spirit, and the love of Christ are mediated through the mentor to the mentoree. Bearing in mind Marshall McLuhan's famous adage, 'the medium is the message', it is up to mentors to make sure that they, as media, do not obscure or twist that which is mediated.

The grace of being

This sacramental dimension is not only expressed in the doing of mentoring – the words, the actions or even the subliminally communicated attitudes and feelings. It is also expressed in the very being of the mentor in relationship – simply being there, being in this relationship with another person is a means of grace. For this reason the spiritual integrity of the mentor is critical and fundamental to the whole enterprise of Christian mentoring.

Purposeful: Growth is pursued

Early on in my mentoring I began specifically asking for feedback from my mentorees about how they felt our relationship was working. One of the first pieces of feedback I received was from Rob. He was very affirming in many ways, but the words that stayed with me were these: 'You know, what I really need more of is a good boot up the rear. I'm so sick of drifting along. Please hold my feet to the fire. I want to know we're really going somewhere with this.' I quickly realized that effective mentoring was going to take more than time and kindness. Growth and strength in spirituality, character and ministry will not occur automatically but require the mentoring partners to be focused and intentional. The Christian leaders I work with appreciate understanding of their situation and sympathy for their difficulties, but they know they need more than that. Because they want to make progress, they desire a purposeful relationship that keeps the overall objective clearly in view and spurs them on to develop in every area of life according to God's agenda.

As I observed earlier, mentoring involves a real relationship, not just transactional contact whereby a mechanical process is carried out. However, it is primarily a functional relationship and only secondarily an affective one. This is one of the key features of a mentoring relationship that sets it apart from Christian friendship. That is not to say that Christian friendship cannot be purposeful; just that it is not the primary feature in such a relationship. Mentoring is primarily a functional relationship; it exists to carry out a function. Friendship is primarily an affective relationship; it exists because of the affection two people share for one another.

If a mentoring relationship should cease to function according to its purpose, it should be brought to closure. Friendships, on the other hand, do not have to achieve anything to justify their existence. Their validity is not based on productivity. Mentoring is validated by what it achieves in terms of identifying and promoting the work of God's Spirit in another's life. A good mentoring relationship does not meander along waiting for something to happen. Mentoring is active, investigating and pressing into new areas, breaking open new possibilities, planting seeds of thought and bringing nourishment to the soul. A mentoring relationship has the purpose of saving the mentoree from frittering away their days, drifting along in a sub-optimal existence that does not fully grasp the destiny God has designed for them. If mentor and mentoree have positive mutual regard and enjoy each other's company, that is all well and good, but it is not enough.

Sometimes I am asked, 'Can I mentor a friend?' I don't want to rule it out, but it should be understood that it will create some role conflict. Such arrangements rarely work effectively. Where they are pursued, the pure friendship is typically compromised by the functional element of mentoring. Under this relational pressure, the relationship usually lapses back to where it was without an effective mentoring element. This happens because the partners are unwilling to allow the function of mentoring to lead them into places where the affection of friendship would hesitate to tread. My experience suggests that a choice must be made to either maintain the friendship or pursue a mentoring relationship.

Adult: Maturity is respected

One way to see mentoring is that it creates a learning environment in which a person is helped to identify the work of the Holy Spirit in their lives and to cooperate with that work for their growth and strength in spirituality, character and ministry. Mentors take responsibility for making the learning environment appropriate to the needs of the mentoree. Part of being an effective mentor involves understanding the relational setting in which adults best learn, grow and develop.

Compared to children and teens, adults have different, special needs and requirements as learners. Clearly, an adult is not going to respond very well to the kind of learning environment that exists in, say, a primary school classroom. Despite this apparent truth, adult learning is a relatively new area of study. The field of adult learning was pioneered by Malcolm Knowles back in the 1950s and 1960s.[72] He identified six important characteristics of adult learners and showed that taking these characteristics into account when designing learning environments resulted in significant benefits for everyone involved. Consider these characteristics from the point of view of mentoring.

Adults are autonomous and self-directed

Adults have a valid need to be free to direct themselves. Good mentors actively involve adult mentorees in the learning process and serve as facilitators for them. Specifically, they make sure to identify mentorees' perspectives about what topics to cover and let them work on projects that reflect their interests. We find it best to allow mentorees to assume responsibility for what is discussed in our sessions together.

As mentors, we take care to act as facilitators, guiding mentorees to their own knowledge. If we inject facts, these are more in the nature of clues rather than conclusions. Adults respond better to mentoring processes that help them to think for themselves and find their own way forward, rather than one which gives directions into a pathway determined by someone else.

Adults have accumulated a foundation of life experiences and knowledge

These experiences and knowledge may include work-related activities, family responsibilities, and previous education. Adult mentorees find satisfaction when they can connect their learning to their unique base of knowledge and experience. To help them do this, a good mentor will draw out mentorees' experience and knowledge which is relevant to the topic under consideration at any given time.

If a mentor introduces a theory, conceptual framework, or any other clue to help the mentoree see things more clearly, it is vital to build a bridge of connection to what is already understood by the mentoree, thus recognizing the value of their experience.

Adults are goal-oriented

Upon commencing mentoring, adults usually have at least a sketchy knowledge of the goals they want to attain. That is to say, there are certain results that they find motivating in prospect. Energy is released into the mentoring relationship when mentors show mentorees how the mentoring process will help them attain their goals. They are attracted by an approach that is organized and has clearly defined elements that are predicated on where they want to go. Identify and classify goals and objectives early in the mentoring relationship. Revisit them regularly, because the mentoree's goals will almost certainly change along the way.

Adults are relevancy-oriented

Adults are only truly motivated to learn something when they can see the point of it. Learning has to be applicable to their relationships, their sense of well-being, their work or other responsibilities to be of value to them. Therefore, mentors work to identify what is of importance for their mentorees in the early phases of a mentoring relationship. This also means that mentors work at making connections, relating theories and concepts to a setting familiar to mentorees. The need for perceived relevance is fulfilled when mentorees are fully involved in designing the action steps they undertake.

Adults are practical

Adults focus on the aspects of a session and assignments most useful to them in their life. They may not be interested in knowledge for its own sake. Mentors help mentorees see explicitly how the session and the assignments that flow out of it will be useful to them in real life.

Adults need to be shown respect

This is, of course, the case with all learners. But whereas children and teens usually lack the power and opportunity to object to disrespect, adults will not hesitate to respond. Where due respect is not given, adults might occasionally take the opportunity to confront the situation, depending on the degree of assertiveness they feel comfortable expressing. More often, adults simply withdraw their cooperation from a process in which they are not respected.

Respect involves inviting a mentoree to freely voice their opinion and taking these opinions seriously. Adult mentorees more gladly engage in the mentoring process where mentors acknowledge the wealth of experiences that adult mentorees bring to the mentoring relationship.

Personal: Uniqueness is affirmed

The mentor builds a sacramental, purposeful, adult relationship with a mentoree who is not just *any* person, but *this* person, with all his or her personal differences which taken together comprise their own singular character. Some of those differences may be interesting, pleasant and comfortable. After all, the saying 'opposites attract' does have some validity. However, personal differences may also include particular preferences at variance with the mentor's, quirky idiosyncrasies and annoying habits. The mentoring relationship is not designed to produce standard outcomes and so is not concerned to eliminate these differences. Mentoring focuses on the individual not simply as another case or an additional resource to be developed for the kingdom but as a unique and loved child of God. As far as possible, the mentoring process is adjusted to suit the mentoree, rather than the mentor.

Facilitating personalization

Christian leaders of the current generation are especially keen to enter into empowering processes that respect their individuality. They do not accept the notion that they have to conform to externally imposed customs and sensibilities. There are several capacities that mentors can develop within themselves and certain approaches they can employ that help to avoid mentoring declining into a 'cookie-cutter' process. This begins with encouraging mentorees to tell their own stories in their own way. When it is done genuinely, this communicates an attitude of attention to the unique individual. The great benefit for mentors is that with understanding of the root causes for certain differences, many irritations simply fall away.

Mentors need to nurture in themselves freedom from bias and prejudice, for which most of us require the help of a perceptive supervisor. Becoming irritated with a mentoree is a signal to pay attention to this area. In addition, personalization is facilitated by mentors developing their ability to listen and observe, resisting the tendency to jump to conclusions or make unfounded assumptions. Once understanding is gained, mentors respect the individuality of mentorees by adjusting their pace to match the one they are seeking to help.

Personalization does not entail resetting the frame of reference for the relationship to the point where the mentor loses perspective. Rather it involves conveying an attitude of flexibility whereby the mentoree's uniqueness is taken seriously and informs the shape of the mentoring process. Communicating this attitude involves many little things such as thoughtfulness in arrangements, remembering details, privacy in conversations, care in keeping appointments, adequate preparation for sessions and creative adaptation in the approach taken.

Expressive: Feelings are explored

The action of God's Spirit in the life of a mentoree, potential or actual, arouses feelings in the mentoree that are integral to the process of growth. There is no way into the relevant issues in a mentoree's life that avoids his or her feelings. So the mentor creates an environment in which the mentoree will be comfortable giving expression to his or her feelings.

Why feelings are important

While the skill of asking good questions is invaluable in mentoring, it is ineffective unless the expressive aspect of the mentoring relationship has been developed. The degree to which feelings are expressed is a barometer of the depth of a relationship. Such expression of feelings within mentoring may serve a number of purposes. Examples of these purposes include: relieving pressure or tension, thus freeing the mentoree to see his or her situation more clearly and act upon it constructively; helping the mentor to appreciate what a situation means to the mentoree; enabling meaningful emotional support from the mentor; exposing a problem that consists of the feelings expressed; and deepening the mentoring relationship in preparation for a new area of work.

Managing the mentor's feelings

The mentor can help these purposes be achieved by being relaxed, ensuring a relaxing setting for the session, and not having a cluttered mind. There is no advantage in 'cramming' for a mentoring session! It is vital to listen attentively and purposefully, not interrupting the flow of expression. The mentor should be sensitive to the mentoree's rate of movement toward an emotionally difficult subject, avoiding premature interpretation or reassurances, and not rescuing the mentoree from tears or silence.

Dangers of inhibiting the mentoree's feelings

The expression of feelings is a dynamic element of mentorees' participation in their own growth. If they are not free to express their feelings but have their mentor's feelings and suggestions imposed upon them, mentorees are not active in their own growth and development. If this occurs, one of two results will ensue: either the mentoree will drop out of the relationship, or he/she will place total responsibility on the mentor and become overly dependent. Both of these results are fatal to the mentoring relationship. The mentoree must necessarily involve himself or herself in any real change. Dealing with feelings is an unavoidable part of the process.

Responsive: Hearts are engaged

The expression of feelings within a mentoring relationship calls for a response on the part of the mentor. It is only natural that the mentor should become involved with the mentoree at an emotional level. Sympathetic understanding and warm, human care are essential. Clinical detachment is not appropriate.

Yet entering into this emotional involvement requires care because without appropriate boundaries it may become a liability rather than an asset within the mentoring process. It is most unhelpful for the mentor to take on the emotional load of the mentoree in an indiscriminate fashion. If this were to happen it would prevent the mentor from bringing valuable objectivity to the relationship. In balancing sympathy and objectivity, mentors will develop two dimensions of their emotional involvement: understanding and responding.

Understanding emotions

Mentors work to understand the meaning and significance of their mentoree's feelings in relation to their journey of personal and spiritual growth and vocational effectiveness. The mentor needs to know what emotional effect their own words and actions are having on the mentoree, what is going on when the mentoree is stimulated to express their feelings, and know how this expression is contributing to the achievement of the mentoree's goals and God's agenda in their life.

This understanding will, inevitably, be partial at best. Growth in understanding feelings is aided by knowledge of human behaviour, reflection upon one's own life experiences, practice in mentoring, supervision by an experienced mentor and making private guesses about possible meanings of feelings, checking these in the light of the understanding that comes as the relationship develops.

Wise emotional responses

The mentor's response to the mentoree at the feeling level is the most important psychological element in the mentoring relationship. Other elements of a spiritual nature are more important overall, but this is the most powerful part of the human interaction. It is also, possibly, the most difficult to get right. The response is not necessarily verbal. Essentially it is an internal response of attitude and feeling. The internal response is then communicated through a word, facial expression, tone of speech or action.

There is no advantage in a mentor attempting to fake emotional engagement when it does not spontaneously arise in their heart. The mentoree will see through it, the mentor's authenticity will be compromised and trust will be eroded. However, it may be appropriate for a mentor to moderate their emotional response rather than allowing it to be expressed freely.

Knowing how and when to express an emotional response is a matter of sensitivity to the prompting of the Holy Spirit and an educated intuition. The intuition is educated through reflection upon instances of such expression and their effect. Mentors are wise to guard against expressions of emotional response that cannot be maintained or would leave the mentor in an emotionally depleted state.

Accepting: Reality is acknowledged

In any relationship where the parties have a strong desire for the relationship to work, there is a temptation to idealize the other person; to relate to them not as they are but as one would like them to be. This is most clearly the case in romantic love, but it is somewhat true of many other sorts of relationships, including mentoring. Mentors are able to be of much more help to mentorees when they begin where the mentoree is. This allows for each stage of the mentoring process to be tailored to fit the current state of the mentoree. Certainly, the mentor will be more concerned with the direction of the mentoree's journey than with the point at which he or she has currently arrived. Yet, discerning the present reality is a vital step in navigating the way forward.

Acceptance and approval

There is a world of difference between acceptance and approval. The mentor accepts negative elements in the character and behaviour of the mentoree as a doctor accepts a patient's symptoms. These negative elements are not affirmed as a true part of the person and there remains a commitment to overcoming them in the power of the Spirit. Acceptance has to do with acknowledging reality.

A vital aspect to the reality of each mentoree is that they have intrinsic value and dignity derived from being created in the image of God as his child and with his purpose in mind. Any failing is extrinsic and redeemable in Christ. Most mentorees do not start from a position of self-acceptance. Further, they do not have confidence that the mentor will accept them as they are either. In this situation it is possible to spend a great deal of time dealing with unreality.

Breaking through to reality

The mentor's unrelenting, unconditional acceptance of the mentoree drives at dealing with things the way they really are. The mentor does not need to know everything and does not need always to dig down to origins, but is interested in the real person. This is threatening at first, but only because of the fear of rejection. Once this is overcome and the mentor is no longer perceived as a threat, mentorees begin to be themselves – thus developing their greatest strength.

There are several possible obstacles to acceptance of the mentoree by the mentor. These include non-acceptance of something in the mentor's own self, transferring the mentor's own feelings on to the mentoree, biases and prejudices, theological differences, unwarranted reassurances, confusion between acceptance and approval, loss of respect for the mentoree, and over-identification with the mentoree.

An accountable relationship: Progress is mapped

The difference between accountability and judgment

The New Testament clearly cautions us against judging others. In James 4:12 we read, 'There is only one Lawgiver and Judge, the one who is able to save and destroy. But you – who are you to judge your neighbour?' Jesus, too, in Matthew 7 has this to say: 'Do not judge, or you too will be judged. For in the same way you judge others, you will be judged, and with the measure you use, it will be measured to you.' He goes on to warn those who seek to extract splinters from the eyes of others to first attend to the planks in their own eyes. Where does this leave mentors, who quite obviously have not totally sorted out their own 'plank' issues? How can they help others with their 'splinter' issues?

The way forward is for mentors to carefully distinguish between accountability and judgment. Judgment in the sense of condemnation has to do with the consequences of actions; assigning guilt, blame and punishment. (Of course, judgment may also mean discernment, and this is perfectly in order for a mentor, as described above.) Accountability has to do with considering an account, story or narrative about actions. It is a reckoning; comparing an actuality to an ideal. Mentors may validly provide mentorees with a point of accountability while being careful not to allow accountability to become judgment.

How mentors deal with judgmental thoughts

Having established a non-judgmental attitude at the beginning of a mentoring relationship, mentors cannot thereafter take it for granted that they will be able to maintain that approach effortlessly. It is to grow and deepen along with the relationship at every point in its development. Failure of the mentoree to actually deliver on an ideal undertaking is not an occasion for the mentor to pass judgment. Accountability stops at the reckoning. What is to be done about any failure – the allocation of consequences – is up to the mentoree.

When judgment starts to stir within the mentor, as it almost certainly will at some point, it is important for mentors to deal with these thoughts and feelings before the Lord in prayer. It becomes an occasion to reaffirm that the mentoree belongs to the Lord and is responsible to him alone. If mentors do not resolve these feelings, they will inevitably be communicated to the mentoree and damage the mentoring relationship. No words can effectively convey a non-judgmental attitude if the mentor does not really have it internally.

Leaving room for the Holy Spirit

While Christian mentoring does not get into judgment, it is nevertheless not a value-free relationship. The ethical standard about which Christian mentoring revolves is the life and character of Christ, and is rooted in the Bible. There is no wishy-washy compromise, no indulgent winking at sin for the sake of being gracious. Yet it is not the role of the mentor to convict the mentoree of failure to measure up. This is the role of the Spirit.

Mentors follow along in the wake of the Spirit, holding mentorees accountable for those things the mentorees perceive as the conviction of the Spirit. Mentors can only hold mentorees accountable validly when invited to do so on the basis of the work of the Spirit. Mentors should be alert to pick up when mentorees may be suffering from neurotic guilt over innocent actions or attitudes.

Terms of accountability

If the terms of accountability are constructed wisely, the process can be extremely encouraging as progress through difficult stages of growth is mapped. However, if the terms are unrealistic, the opposite effect may occur. I recall supervising a mentor who was disappointed about a mentoree's failure to achieve their goal to lose weight. There was no doubt that this was a good and necessary goal for this particular individual, but each month the story of failure to make progress was becoming more and more depressing. The dynamic was only turned around once the terms of accountability were adjusted to focus on specific matters over which the mentoree had direct control and for which practical support was established.

Some mentors inadvertently set up their mentorees for failure when they do not challenge unrealistic goals and action steps or neglect to develop the action steps to involve the employment of necessary help. Being held accountable for the outcomes of attempts to do the impossible merely sets the scene for the mentoree to be repeatedly humiliated. Even if certain action steps are well suited to the achievement of appropriate goals, the inclusion of appropriate empowering assistance will be part of the terms of a helpful accountability process.

A liberating relationship: Freedom is guarded

On one occasion when I was teaching on this subject, one of the participants on the course asked, 'How is discipline exercised in mentoring?' This touched off a very animated discussion in the group. Some maintained that 'discipline' in the New Testament was exercised by leaders to control and bring order to Christian communities and their individual members. Others countered that the word actually means 'to train' rather than 'to govern'. Although this was ostensibly a theological discussion, it seemed to me that cultural background and personality type were the major factors driving the opinions expressed.

In real-life situations, it is very tempting for a mentor to take control of a mentoree, especially when they are floundering and in a vulnerable place. It is common for someone at their wits' end to throw out the question, 'What am I going to do?' At that point the mentoree might welcome someone they trust simply taking over. From the mentor's point of view, it might seem the kindest thing to put an end to the agony and take charge of the situation. It is because it is so easy for a mentor to exercise power over a mentoree that it must be strenuously resisted at every point and at all costs. There are two reasons for this.

Firstly, there is a theological reason. The mentor seeks to promote the Lord's agenda, but never seeks to take the Lord's place. The lordship of Christ is to be emphasized, along with the servant nature of the mentor's role in the mentoree's life. Control or lordship over the mentoree's life is ultimately with Christ. But as far as the mentoring relationship goes, the control is with the mentoree. This means that the mentoree gets to have the last word about what the Spirit of God is doing in his or her life. The mentor may disagree, but should never press his or her conviction in a controlling manner.

Secondly, there is a pragmatic reason: mentoring does not work when the mentor is in control. The universal observation is that mentoring is truly effective only when mentorees make their own judgements, choices and decisions. Ownership of the process by the mentoree is essential to true progress in spiritual growth and vocational effectiveness. When alternatives are presented coercively, mentorees are likely either to comply in a weak, ephemeral way, or to respond defensively and become entrenched in existing positions. Walter Brueggemann notes:

> What we need is a safe place in which to host ambiguity and to notice the tension and unresolve without pressure but with freedom to see and test alternative textings of reality. An inviting effective alternative does not need to be toned down in its claim or made palatable. It does, however, need to be presented in a way that stops well short of coercion that is threatening and that evokes resistance to hearing or appropriating the new text.[73]

Alternatives to the use of power

Mentors need to be aware that control staying with the mentoree will make every mentoring process slower. But to push for a quick-fix solution is no alternative at all. With this in mind, there are several strategies available to mentors as alternatives to the use of power and taking control.

First, help the mentoree see his or her situation clearly and with perspective. In the midst of very complex decision-making scenarios, many mentorees would gladly hand control to someone else to escape feelings of confusion. Use of a conceptual tool such as six-hat thinking, which is described in the next chapter, may be useful in these instances as a way of empowering mentorees.

Second, stir up faith and hope in the mentoree with respect to the fulfilment of God's purposes in his or her life. Review past episodes known to you which have been resolved with God's help.

Third, direct the mentoree toward God and his grace. Pray with them, encouraging them to articulate their own prayer and affirming that God has heard their appeal. Suggest dwelling on appropriate passages from the Bible, perhaps using the *lectio divina* method described in Chapter 8.

Fourth, work with the mentoree to generate options for their own action to cooperate with the action of the Holy Spirit. Rather than rushing to choose one of the options, allow time for the mentoree to decide their next step for themselves.

Fifth, make links to relevant resources. Acquaint the mentoree with people and materials you believe would be helpful for them to follow up in their own time. Introduce stimuli that will activate the mentoree's own dormant inner resources. By these strategies a mentor may resist taking control and create a liberating relationship environment.

At the same time the mentor needs to avoid taking principal responsibility for the spiritual growth or vocational effectiveness of the mentoree, or letting the mentoree play a subordinate role. It is not helpful for mentors to insist on knowing every detail about a mentoree's life, whether or not the mentoree sees those details as relevant to his or her agenda. Mentors should not manipulate, either directly or indirectly, or even attempt to persuade in a controlling way.

A protected relationship: Confidentiality is maintained

Why confidentiality is essential

It is essential that mentoring relationships get at the truth of what is going on in the lives of mentorees. To that end, mentors are responsible for creating a protected environment, a place of trust and emotional safety, through maintaining confidentiality. In order to secure this sense of safety it is not sufficient that the mentor be a safe person during the time of the mentoring sessions or other contact with the mentoree. It is also necessary that the mentor can be relied upon outside the mentoring sessions to protect the secrets and privacy of the mentoree.

Classes of confidential information

There are three classes of confidential information:

- *The entrusted secret:* This is information communicated with the understanding, either explicit or implicit, that it will not be divulged to anyone else. This is the clearest case for confidentiality. It may, nevertheless, be hard to maintain, for entrusted secrets often are of significant consequence for others for whom the one entrusted may also have a duty of care.
- *The natural secret:* Natural secrets may become known directly or indirectly. It is information that, if revealed, would defame, injure or unjustly sadden the person concerned. Even if there is no contract for not divulging this information, it should be kept in confidence.
- *Unguarded comments:* These arise routinely in mentoring. Mentorees say things in unguarded moments that, even if quoted verbatim, would misrepresent their true, considered attitudes and feelings. It is also possible that these comments might be self-revealing to an extent that would be entirely inappropriate for knowledge outside a safe relationship.

Record keeping

Mentorees should be aware of any written records that are being kept of their mentoring sessions. These should be kept with sufficient security to assure the mentoree that any confidential information cannot be accessed by anyone other than the mentor.

Supervision

Mentors receiving supervision, or who operate within an agency providing mentoring services, may sometimes be required to relate details of their mentoring sessions. Therefore, consideration needs to be given to the concept of a 'group confidence', in which others with a valid interest in a particular mentoring relationship are given access to relevant confidential information. Mentorees should be made aware of the policies relating to any such arrangements at the outset of any mentoring relationship.

Understanding the soul of mentoring as a relationship that is sacramental, personal, expressive, responsive, accepting, accountable, liberating, safe and adult helps to explain what is for many an intuitive practice and is sometimes presented as a pseudomystical experience. Paying attention to these aspects of the relationship has borne fruit in my interaction with those I have mentored. Nevertheless, there is still mystery attached to a good and fruitful mentoring relationship for, beyond all these elements, it is ultimately a gift from God.

Chapter 8

Mentoring Methods

Back in Chapter 1 I urged caution when using materials produced as guides for mentoring sessions, including anything you might find in this book. This is now the chapter which requires that caution to be exercised. It is not that any of these methods are suspect or risky. Rather, it is that you can't just randomly pick up a method from here – *lectio divina*, or an interesting question, or journalling, or mind mapping, or writing a personal mission statement – and expect that using it will greatly promote the work of the Holy Spirit in a mentoree's life.

These methods are tools, and as such must be chosen according to the particular piece of work to be done. It would be pointless to pick up your orbital sander at random and wander about the house seeing what you might be able to do with it, when the most pressing need is to unblock the kitchen sink. First, identify the work to be done, and then choose the right tool. Lest you should conclude this means that diagnostic methods which identify the work to be done are universally appropriate for any and every mentoring situation, let me assure you that mentorees will find it most irritating if all you ever do is dig around to find out what's going on and never do anything about it. Identifying and promoting the work of the Holy Spirit go hand in hand, both processes requiring careful selection of the right methods.

The purpose of methods

Disclosure, feedback and reflection

In order for Christian leaders to take responsibility for their own lives, their growth and strength in spirituality, character and ministry, they will need to work at discovering what God is doing in their lives. Mentors help them do that work using a range of methods that we will discuss in this chapter. But before we get to the methods, let us pause to consider what is going on as a mentor and a mentoree work together to identify and promote the work of the Holy Spirit in the life of the mentoree.

Essentially, the work of mentoring revolves around the mentoree disclosing what they know or guess about themselves and God's work in their lives, receiving feedback from the mentor about that, engaging in reflection and then designing action steps that cooperate with the work of the Holy Spirit and further his agenda. One way of picturing what is going on in this process is to use a schema known as the Johari Window.[74]

The Johari Window

The insight behind the Johari Window is that self-knowledge is limited – there are some things about oneself which are known to self and some which are not. At the same time there are some things about oneself which are known to others and some which are not. Because of this there is not only the open arena of one's life which is known both to self and to others, but also the blind arena in which things are known by others which are not known to self, and the hidden arena in which things are known to self but not to others. In addition there is the unknown arena, in which are things known neither to self nor to others. This is depicted in the figure below:

	Known to self	Not known to self
Known to others	OPEN	BLIND
Not known to others	HIDDEN	UNKNOWN

Comparing what is known to self with what is known to others may yield several results. There can be affirmation as open-arena items perceived both by self and others are shared. This affirmation is empowering to the extent that one feels understood by others. Through the process of feedback, self-knowledge can be extended so that some of what was previously in the blind arena is brought into the open arena. Through the process of disclosure the public arena can be further extended as things from the hidden arena are shared with others. Through the process of reflection by both the mentor and mentoree, part of the unknown arena may also be discovered. The effect of these three processes is depicted here:

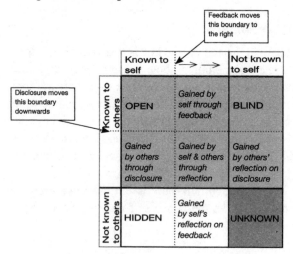

Methods serve God's agenda

Given the model of mentoring that I have been describing, it is not possible to provide precise details of exactly how you should spend your time in mentoring sessions. The content of mentoring sessions will be formed fresh within each mentoring relationship as the partners seek to discover how the Spirit is working in the mentoree's life. The methods to be used will be decided upon as the issues emerge on the basis of how they serve God's agenda.

Having said that, there are some ways of operating in practice that are foundational and others which are optional. Methods such as prayer will be used constantly. Journalling is used often, but not always. Other methods may be held in reserve and employed occasionally as the need arises. All of these methods are tools to help achieve disclosure, feedback and reflection to promote the work of the Holy Spirit in another's life. As you gain experience in mentoring you will no doubt add to this list.

Diagnostic methods

While most people commencing a mentoring relationship have a fair idea of what they want to work on, it is helpful to have a diagnostic method to investigate other potential issues. I have developed the method below for use both with mentorees who find it difficult to know where to start, and as a 'health check' for those who may have important, unidentified issues hidden in blind spots. It is designed to help the mentoree consider the whole of their life in a systematic way.

On numerous occasions I have heard mentorees say something like, 'Well, I haven't thought much about this, but now that you've asked the question...' The nine areas are prompts for asking open-ended questions which can lead to disclosure from the mentoree, feedback from the mentor and reflection together on the issues identified as in need of further consideration.

Spirituality

This area of investigation covers the mentoree's prayer habits, their reading of the Bible and other devotional literature, the impressions and insights they have gained from their prayer and reading and the decisions they have taken as a result. The mentor is attempting to tease out the level of hunger for God, his kingdom and his righteousness (Matthew 6:33) as a matter of first priority.

Character

Because God opposes the proud but gives grace to the humble (1 Peter 5:5), a good place to start investigating character is to ask questions probing the mentoree's humility and pride. Other pairs of traits to explore are: love and apathy, patience and courage, generosity and selfishness, integrity and compromise, kindness and cruelty, self-control and impulsiveness.

Ministry/professional work

Mentoring of Christian leaders often begins with a presenting agenda of ministry enhancement. It is an area in which goals and levels of satisfaction may change over a short period of time. It is worth regularly sifting through such matters as the mentoree's performance within his or her role, what is most exciting about their work, what the current challenges are, what development opportunities are being made available and whether or not the mentoree has a sense of meaning and significance in connection with their work. Check, too, whether the relationships with the person to whom the mentoree is accountable and those they supervise are healthy and positive.

Key relationships

The true state of a mentoree's inner life is usually demonstrated most clearly in the context of the relationships with those to whom they are closest. Where the mentoree is married, review the condition of their relationship with their spouse and children, if there are any. Canvass whether there are currently any relationships with persons not their spouse that present a possible danger. Ask about relationships that are particularly challenging and require extra grace to maintain. Finally, inquire about possible new relationships that may open up God-given opportunities.

Emotional health

Even the most effective Christian leaders are subject to becoming emotionally unhealthy. It is wise to remain informed about a mentoree's emotional well-being, being proactive rather than reactive by investigating this area regularly. Assess the impact of losses they have suffered, and whether or not this is making them susceptible to depression. Take note of incidents of anger and expressions of frustration over struggles of any sort. Ask about what they have been enjoying and special achievements they have attained so that you can celebrate along with them.

Physical health

From time to time, scrutinize mentorees' energy levels to ascertain whether they are getting sufficient rest. Where sickness or injury prevents a regular mentoring session, be sure to find out details and follow up on the outcome, as these events can have a significant impact on other aspects of a person's progress in discipleship. Air the subject of sleep patterns, habits of eating and exercise regime.

Intellectual development

Good mentors will ensure that their mentorees have plenty of energizing intellectual stimulation so that they do not become bored in their calling. Explore with mentorees what conversations they are having that cause them to think, what they are reading that expands their minds, and what writing they are undertaking to marshal their thoughts for the benefit of others. Keep abreast of the formal and informal learning they are engaged in and what teaching opportunities they have. Through questioning in these areas, seek to stimulate and encourage a desire to love God with the whole mind.

Material welfare

Attitudes towards material things are critical in Christian life. Jesus made it clear that his followers could not serve both God and money. Yet those we mentor still have material needs and may be caught by conflicting values in this regard. Ask probing questions about whether the mentoree's salary level is sufficient, what debts may be of concern, saving targets, and what housing arrangements are in place or planned. Be alert to your mentoree's attitudes towards possessions.

Life balance

It is of little value for a mentoree to be outstanding in one area of their life yet fail miserably in others. Christian mentors seek to address the whole person, and so are interested in how the mentoree integrates each part of their life into the whole under the lordship of Christ. Review how your mentoree is learning the 'unforced rhythms of grace', how they are putting sound, biblical priorities in place, what steps they are taking to introduce multiple 'facets' to their recreational time, and how flexible they are generally to make adjustments to their lives when unforseen circumstances arise.

Spiritual methods

Christian mentoring goes beyond secular models of mentoring in this fundamental respect: the Christian mentor is one who encourages others in spiritual things, through the spiritual world, by spiritual means. The beauty of Christian mentoring is that God does all the real work of transformation, while mentors merely assist him and have the enormous privilege of seeing people flourish under his hand.

Prayer

The first and indispensable method of Christian mentoring is prayer. It is in this place of priority precisely because success in the work of mentoring is utterly dependent on the grace of God, and it is essential that we mentors never forget it. By ourselves, we cannot produce a single good result in the lives of the Christian leaders in which we are investing so earnestly. Jesus put it succinctly in John 15:5: 'Apart from me, you can do nothing.' Our conversations with the Lord about matters to do with the life of our mentoree and our involvement in it are indispensable for several reasons.

Firstly, prayer recognizes that God is in charge. Each mentoree belongs to God and the real work of inner transformation that is going on in their lives is work that is being done by the Spirit of God. Prayer focuses the attention of the mentoree on their true source of hope. Prayer reminds mentors that their work is secondary, ancillary – that they are privileged to witness the development of a mysterious and wonderful relationship between heavenly Father and earthly child in which they play a minor role.

Secondly, prayer provides mentors and mentorees with the insights, perspectives and ideas necessary to make progress towards identifying and promoting the work of the Holy Spirit. This requires that times of prayer within mentoring sessions will not be all talking and no listening. Paying attention to the quiet whispers and gentle promptings of the Spirit in silence in the company of a mentoree is among the most productive methods a mentor can employ.

Thirdly, it is through prayer that actual change is effected at the core of the mentoree. Changes in behaviour may be brought about in other ways, but only God can transform the heart, the inner being of a human soul, and he does so in response to prayer offered in humility.

John Mallison sums up his emphasis on prayer in this way:

> Prayer has a significant place in my mentoring sessions. I pray beforehand for wisdom and grace, recalling the specific needs of my mentorees. During the session we may occasionally pray to celebrate something or to address a deep need. We never conclude without prayer to lift up to God the matters discussed. I frequently contact my mentorees between sessions, often only to pray with them.[75]

How encouraging it is to have someone pray for us. Not just to say, 'I'll pray for you', but to actually pray *with* us, so we can hear and join with their prayer for God's intervention in our lives. The Apostle Paul knew the power of this experience. So even when he was apart from the congregations he cared about so much and was not able to pray with them personally, he sent them letters in which he spelled out in detail exactly what it was he was praying for them. In Philippians 1:9–11 he writes:

> And this is my prayer: that your love may abound more and more in knowledge and depth of insight, so that you may be able to discern what is best and may be pure and blameless until the day of Christ, filled with the fruit of righteousness that comes through Jesus Christ – to the glory and praise of God.

Again in Ephesians 1:17–19 and 3:16–19 he writes:

> I keep asking that the God of our Lord Jesus Christ, the glorious Father, may give you the Spirit of wisdom and revelation, so that you may know him better. I pray also that the eyes of your heart may be enlightened in order that you may know the hope to which he has called you, the riches of his glorious inheritance in the saints, and his incomparably great power for us who believe… I pray that out of his glorious riches he may strengthen you with power through his Spirit in your inner being, so that Christ may dwell in your hearts through faith. And I pray that you, being rooted and established in love, may have power, together with all the saints, to grasp how wide and long and high and deep is the love of Christ, and to know this love that surpasses knowledge – that you may be filled to the measure of all the fullness of God.

Praying together with my mentorees has regularly been the highlight of my mentoring sessions. Christian leaders are more often than not in the role of praying for others, and yearn for those moments when someone will pray for them about the issues that really matter. And some of the most powerful moments of prayer may occur when a mentoree has the opportunity to speak out their private thoughts to the Lord in the presence of someone they trust.

James, a local church pastor, was father to three young children, the eldest of whom was giving James a very hard time as a parent. James would become so wound up by the boy's behaviour that he would use foul language and at times lash out physically. I encouraged him to unpack what was going on in those episodes and search for where God was in all of it. James started to explore his relationship with his father, how that had affected his own capacity as a parent, and how it had impacted on his view of God. James tried several strategies in an attempt to control his anger. But it was when he was finally able to address the issues in prayer during a mentoring session that the decisive breakthrough came. Amid his tears of confession and repentance, I had the opportunity to affirm forgiveness and witness a moment of deep healing.

Scripture

The value of appropriately bringing relevant biblical material to bear on issues presented in mentoring cannot be overestimated. The written word of God provides an objective standard by which subjective impressions, personal reasoning and the opinions of other people can be assessed. Over and over again in my experience, God's word has proven to be true: it is a lamp to our feet and a light to our path.[76] Eugene Peterson's translation of 2 Timothy 3:16–17 puts it well:

> Every part of Scripture is God-breathed and useful one way or another – showing us truth, exposing our rebellion, correcting our mistakes, training us to live God's way. Through the Word we are put together and shaped up for the tasks God has for us.

However, I have seen the Bible used in ways that are not at all helpful. The Bible is not a club with which to beat people over the head. It can actually be damaging to apply biblical texts to complex life issues in a simplistic, uncritical fashion. I recall meeting with Peter, who was struggling with depression and on the verge of burnout. He had been told by one of his advisors that depression must be strongly resisted, for the Bible commands us to 'rejoice in the Lord always'. Burnout too, he was told, could easily be overcome by claiming the verse, 'I can do all things through Christ who strengthens me.' Needless to say, this use of the Bible had in fact made Peter's situation worse than ever. Able mentors ensure that consideration of passages from scripture is attended by sound theological reflection in order to ensure an adequate method of interpretation that avoids shallow 'proof-texting'.

The Christian scriptures are a means by which the Holy Spirit brings about personal transformation in the lives of believers, but this process is not automatic and not necessarily rapid. A cursory scan of a few verses every now and then is unlikely to bring about a deep-rooted life in God. As Dietrich Bonhoeffer writes:

> It is never sufficient simply to have read God's Word.
> It must penetrate deep within us; dwell in us like the
> Holy of Holies in the Sanctuary.[77]

Lectio divina is one way of letting the Bible penetrate deeply that I have found helpful within mentoring. This four-stage exercise is preceded by a time of preparation in a quiet place, getting still and becoming aware of the presence of God. Before commencing, pray that God will speak to you through his word.

Stage one is called *lectio*, in which a section of the Bible is read slowly and repeatedly. Some people like to read aloud at this point to assist their concentration. Allow your attention to focus on a particular word or phrase to which the Holy Spirit may be alerting you. Stage two is called *meditatio*, in which you reflect on the word or phrase you have identified. This involves mulling over the words, getting the 'flavour' of them, perhaps putting yourself back into the situation to feel the impact of those words and considering what they might mean for you in your present circumstances. Stage three is called *oratio*, in which you pray, offering yourself to God in the light of his word, identifying what you wish to do in response. Stage four is called *contemplatio*, in which you rest in God, waiting for him to act in response to your prayer, yielding yourself to the work of the Spirit in your soul.

The progression of *lectio divina* takes the participant from reading with the eyes to reflecting with the mind; from reflecting with the mind to praying with the heart; from praying with the heart to resting with the soul. For the purposes of mentoring, the genius of *lectio divina* is in the final stage. Typically, Christian leaders I have mentored have the most experience with the first two stages of *lectio divina* which engage the eyes and the head. Some have had a little experience of the third stage, although close investigation often reveals that deep prayers of the heart in response to scripture are less frequent than the person desires. I have found very few mentorees regularly practise resting in God, allowing his grace, mediated through his word, to bring inner transformation and renewal. Most find this way of opening up to the work of the Spirit both liberating and refreshing.

Spiritual gifts

Spiritual gifts are given to God's people for the benefit of others. They are tools of ministry that help us get the job done. Spiritual gifts of insight – wisdom, words of knowledge and prophecy – are especially helpful for getting the job of mentoring done. These and all other pertinent gifts are to be employed freely for the blessing and benefit of the mentoree. The only reservations are that spiritual gifts never be used to short-circuit a necessary process for the mentoree, or to impress or exert undue influence.

Conversational methods

Conversations are an excellent basic method for mentoring sessions. Conversations seem such an ordinary, routine form of interaction that we may forget that where two or three gather, Christ is there in the middle of that conversation. Where clever methods may fail to touch the heart, a deep and meaningful conversation can be the tipping point for deep change. Mentors ask good questions to encourage disclosure, and employ good listening skills in order to give helpful feedback in their replies.

Asking good questions

At the beginning of this book I divulged one of my favourite questions: 'How's your soul?' I use this question like a playful nudge to throw unsuspecting mentorees off balance. I know perfectly well that it is a very difficult question that probably has no simple answer. Peter Block says that 'transformation comes more from pursuing profound questions than seeking practical answers.'[78] So the point of asking the question is not to get a satisfactory answer but to stimulate thoughtful reflection. I have other favourite questions which come from the Ignatian tradition, such as these: Who am I? Where am I? How am I? What is your greatest consolation? What is your greatest desolation?

Yet not all questions are helpful in mentoring. Some questions put the other person on the defensive and may be interpreted as aggressive or implying something negative. Good questions have the opposite effect. The best questions have the capacity to achieve a number of things of considerable value. First, they provoke curiosity, causing the other person to wonder. Second, they serve to identify deeper issues. Third, they gently challenge assumptions. Fourth, they may lead a person to confront personal fears. Fifth, they prepare the way for revelation from the Holy Spirit.

Good mentoring questions usually have the following features: they are easily understood, are not complex, require thought, do not allow for one-word answers, yet can be answered over time, and encourage self-disclosure. Statements represent conclusions, and as such tend to conclude conversations. There is certainly a place for statements, but earlier on in a conversation questions allow more space for the interaction to keep moving. It is helpful for a mentor to build up the skill of reframing statements as questions. To quote Peter Block once again:

> When we look for tools and techniques, which are part of the How? question, we pre-empt other kinds of learning. In a sense, if we want to know what really works, we must carefully decide which are the right questions for this moment. Picking the right question is the beginning of action on what matters, and this is what works. This is how we name the debate, by the questions we pursue, for all these questions are action steps. Good questions work on us, we don't work on them. They are not a project to be completed but a doorway opening onto a greater depth of understanding, action that will take into being more fully alive.[79]

No list of standard questions can take the place of carefully crafted enquiries that are specially constructed for the individual concerned. The following points are merely illustrative of ways in which a mentor might open up matters for exploration:

- When was your last full day off and how did you spend it?
- What memories give you strength?
- What do you see for yourself when you look ten years ahead?
- What have you done this week that will make a difference in five years' time?
- What ways of approaching God are most fruitful for you?
- Where has God been present in the events of today?
- Where was he working for your good?
- How is your discipling of others helping you to grow?
- How does your professional ministry performance impact

your personal spirituality?

- How do you satisfy the need to create something?
- What have you learned about yourself recently?
- Who do you need to forgive, and who owes you an apology?
- What are you reading at the moment?
- What makes you feel powerful/powerless? How do you respond to that feeling?
- Do people have expectations of you that make you uncomfortable?
- What is the hardest thing for you to be honest about?
- What grief/loss have you experienced recently and how are you dealing with that?
- How do family members other than your partner know that they are important to you?
- Who do you spend time with who enjoys your company but does not need you?
- Which of your relationships is most at risk of becoming unhealthy?
- How are you developing friendships with people who are not yet Christians?[80]

Another set of questions that you and your mentoree might agree should become a regular feature of your sessions together are those that have to do with accountability. The best collection of accountability questions I have found anywhere is at the back of Neil Cole's *Cultivating a Life for God*.[81] He has Wesley's small group questions, plus those from Richard Foster's Renovaré groups, Chuck Swindoll's pastors' groups and a host of others.

Whatever questions you ask as a mentor, it is vital that you do not allow yourself to become the Grand Inquisitor. Ask questions from alongside, not from above; ask them as a friend would, not as an adversary. Questions allow mentors to raise serious matters in a non-threatening, even light-hearted way. Have fun with them!

Listening actively

To truly hear what a mentoree is trying to communicate takes focused, active listening, since their words may not be adequate to their thought. There are at least eleven discrete skills associated with active listening, although real experts may identify more. The ones I try to use are these:

- *Paying attention:* Acknowledging what is being said by providing verbal and non-verbal indications of awareness of the other. Examples are keeping eye contact, nodding, and making small inarticulate sounds (such as 'uh huh').
- *Clarification:* This is checking perceptions, finding out if the listener's interpretations and perceptions are valid and accurate.
- *Probing:* This involves very brief, simple questioning in a supportive way that requests more information or that attempts to clear up confusion.
- *Support:* Showing warmth and caring in one's own individual way. This may involve body language, a gesture or a small kindness like offering water or a tissue.
- *Silence:* Being quiet and giving the other time to think as well as to talk.
- *Immediacy:* Articulating what the listener perceives is going on in that very moment.
- *Reflecting:* Mirroring in one's facial expression the feelings, experiences, or content that has been heard or perceived through cues from the speaker.
- *Restating:* Indicating understanding of the speaker's basic verbal message by paraphrasing what they have said.
- *Interpreting:* Offering a tentative view about the meaning and significance of the speaker's statements and feelings.
- *Giving feedback:* Sharing perceptions of the other's ideas or feelings and disclosing relevant personal information.
- *Summarizing:* Providing a focus by synthesizing the elements of what has been said into a simplified form.

These skills, like those of self-expression, can be learned, practised, and mastered. Our society places much more attention on the spoken side of the communication equation, but if you think about who influences you, are they good talkers or good listeners? As we come to understand ourselves and our relationships with others better, we rediscover that communication is not just saying words; it is creating true understanding. Active listening is an important skill in that process.

Replying

Mentors give helpful feedback, bringing affirmation, encouragement and support as well as constructive confrontation and challenge as appropriate to the situation. At times they wait and refrain from replying until the mentoree has finished what they have to say. The real skill lies in being able to identify the appropriate response in a given situation; a skill that is only developed through experience.

A common error is to reply in a way that defuses an emotionally charged moment, or minimizes a confession just made. It is a real temptation to overcome awkwardness by making a reply that provides an easy, painless way out of a difficult moment. However, these difficult, awkward moments are typically critical moments of potential breakthrough for the mentoree, so it is vital that the mentor be secure enough to remain in that moment and wait for what the Spirit of God may do and how the mentoree will respond.

There comes a time for a mentor to share their point of view. It is wise not to be hasty about this, yet one does not need to be unnecessarily evasive. Within Christian mentoring we affirm the reality of normative morality. Mentorees certainly do not want judgment in the sense of condemnation, but they are very interested in judgment in the sense of the astute discernment of someone they trust. Neuhaus makes the point:

> Not infrequently people want a judgment about whether they did right or wrong, and that is not

necessarily wrong. They should not be dismissed as moralistic, uptight, inhibited folk who need to be 'freed up.' They may not be helped by turning the question back on them. These good people came for informed counsel, not simply to be thrown back upon their own confusions. They assume [we] possess a discernment that is worth taking into account in what will, after all, finally be their decision about the matter.[82]

The replies mentors make are most helpful when they combine challenge and support – truth and grace – in the correct proportions according to the circumstances. Challenge is a matter of bringing the truth, as we see it, to bear on the situation. Support expresses grace so that confrontation with the truth does not become unbearable. According to Larry Daloz, the dynamics of support and challenge may be variously combined to produce stasis, retreat, confirmation or growth. You can picture it this way:[83]

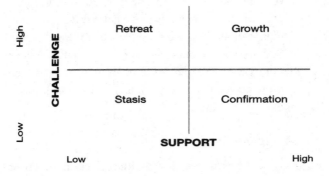

Without challenge, nothing changes except perhaps the level of comfort the mentoree has in the present situation. Without support, the only change that might occur is the withdrawal of the mentoree into their shell or the end of the mentoring relationship. It is only with the combined application of support and challenge that growth occurs. Mentors usually find one or the other of these modes of reply most natural. They must take care not to overplay their strong suit so as to avoid the negative effects of a lopsided interaction with their mentorees.

Written methods

Journalling

If a mentoree is literate, then journalling is certain to be a helpful method. However, this is true only so long as journalling is understood as a very broad category of recording life-significant matters. Each person needs to discover in what ways journalling is appropriate for them and what style they want to adopt. Some write a great deal, others very little, some frequently others infrequently. Some write in point form, others in poetry, still others write nothing at all – they just draw pictures or diagrams.

Ken Gire says, 'The purpose of a journal is to help us live reflectively.'[84] Used as a basis for reflection, a journal helps to show who we were and where we've been on our pilgrimage. It helps to show us where we are going and what is driving us there. It helps us to understand how we should change if the direction of our lives is dangerous to ourselves or others. Finally, it helps us to ponder our varied experiences in order to learn from them so we may grow personally and spiritually and so our ministry may become more credible.

Critical incident report

A critical incident report is a short written piece in which the mentoree reflects on a specific experience. These can help a mentoree to unpack what was going on in the midst of an intense period of their lives when their perception was distracted into dealing with the most urgent matters. Guided reflection on such incidents can bring significant insight.

Spiritual autobiography

Constructing a time line of the mentoree's spiritual autobiography can bring about breakthroughs in understanding. Consider how God has worked from the earliest period of the person's life, what divine contacts have been provided, what character tests have been encountered and what ensued, moments of revelation, periods of negative formation and so on.[85]

Conceptual methods

A mentor brings independent thinking to the relationship. He or she can offer their objective perspective as an observer, or advance an alternative view based on their experience. Mentors may also bring case studies to the attention of the mentoree to help them to think through issues they are going through using another lens. To help generate new options for the mentoree to consider when working through difficult issues, mentors can use thinking techniques such as these.[86]

Brainstorming for generating new possibilities

A brainstorming session may be used for generating a large number of new ideas and solutions. It should not be used for analysis or for decision making. Of course, you will need to analyse and judge the ideas later, but this is done afterwards and the analysis process does not involve brainstorming techniques.

To get the best out of brainstorming, it is important to clearly define the problem or opportunity for which you want to create ideas. You will have no fixed perceptions about the area and can often discover new ideas precisely because you didn't follow the normal path of thinking.

Lateral thinking for problem-solving

The process of lateral thinking refers to the generation of novel solutions to problems. The point of lateral thinking is that many problems require a different perspective to be solved successfully. Four critical factors are associated with lateral thinking. The first is to recognize the dominant ideas that polarize the perception of a problem. Second, this way of thinking searches for different ways of looking at things. Third, lateral thinking involves relaxing rigid control of thinking; free association can assist this part of the process.

Finally, lateral thinking uses chance to encourage other ideas. This last factor has to do with the fact that lateral thinking involves low-probability ideas which are unlikely to occur in the normal course of events. Lateral thinking is relevant to the stimulation of creativity and is most readily exercised in low-arousal states. The best time of day for such thinking is usually the early morning, when the mind is rested but not yet aroused or anxious.

Six Hat thinking for complex decision-making

In this way of thinking, there are six metaphorical hats, each of them coded by a colour – white, red, black, yellow, green and blue. The thinker puts on one of these hats at a time to indicate the type of thinking being used. As a new hat is put on it is essential to take off the previous hat, signifying that only one type of thinking is being employed at each moment. The hats are not to be used to categorize individuals, even though their behaviour may seem to invite this. When this exercise is used in a mentoring session, both mentor and mentoree wear the same hat at the same time. The types of thinking, or 'hats', may be described as follows.

- *White Hat thinking* is factual and logical – white being the colour of a sheet of paper on which data is recorded. Look at the information you have, and see what you can learn from it. Look for gaps in your knowledge, and try to either fill them through further research or take account of them as acknowledged variables. This separates in our mind what is fact and what is interpretation or opinion.
- *Red Hat thinking* gets us in touch with the non-rational

part of our responses. Look at problems using intuition, gut reaction, and emotion. Also try to think how other people will react emotionally. Try to understand the responses of people who do not fully know your reasoning.

- *Black Hat thinking* covers all the negative aspects of an issue. Look at things cautiously and defensively. Try to see why something might not work – what the barriers might be. This is important because it highlights the weak points in any given situation or plan. It allows you to eliminate them, alter them, or prepare contingency plans to counter them. Take care that Black-Hat thinking does not become paranoid!

- *Yellow Hat thinking* accentuates the positive – yellow being the colour of sunshine, brightness and happiness. The yellow hat helps you to think of the best possible outcomes. It is the optimistic viewpoint that helps you to see all the benefits of the decision and the value in it. Yellow Hat thinking helps you to keep going when everything looks gloomy and difficult. It ranges from practicality and logic to hopes, dreams and visions.

- *Green Hat thinking* is fertile and constructive. It stimulates creativity, searching for alternatives, going beyond the known, the obvious and the satisfactory. It is a free-wheeling way of thinking, in which there is little criticism of ideas. It may also involve the question of personal growth: what you are personally going to do about a situation or issue.

- *Blue Hat thinking* reflects on and controls the decision-making process; it organizes the thinking itself. It involves taking a step back to consider what kind of thinking is needed to further explore the situation or issue. When ideas are running dry, Blue Hat thinking may indicate the need for more Green Hat thinking. If a new threat emerges, Blue Hat thinking will steer the process towards Black Hat thinking, and so on. Blue Hat thinking is used to summarize, to provide overview and to articulate conclusions.

Six Hat thinking is a good technique for looking at the effects of a decision from a number of different points of view. It allows necessary emotion and scepticism to be brought into what would otherwise be purely rational decisions. It opens up the opportunity for creativity within decision making. The technique also helps, for example, persistently pessimistic people to be positive and creative.

Mind mapping for clarifying confused thinking

Mind maps are designed to get out on one piece of paper a representation of the things that are filling your mentoree's mind at any particular moment. They are most useful when the mentoree says, 'I don't know where to start.' They are quick to make and, because of their visual quality, easy to remember and review. The non-linear nature of mind maps makes it easy to link and cross-reference different elements of the map.

Start from the centre of the page with a circle that contains the name of your mentoree and the date. Work outwards using key words or, wherever possible, an image to depict what is on the mind of the mentoree. Make the centre a clear and strong visual image that depicts the general theme of the map. Create sub-centres for sub-themes. Put key words on lines to reinforce the structure of notes. Use colour to depict themes and associations and to make things stand out.

Anything that stands out on the page will stand out in your mind. Use arrows, icons or other visual aids to show links between different elements. Don't get stuck in one area. If you dry up in one area go to another branch. Put ideas down as they occur, wherever they fit. Don't judge or hold back. Be creative, as creativity aids memory. Have fun!

Profiling and planning methods

There is a vast range of profiling exercises available to mentors. Some are readily accessed on the World Wide Web[87] while others require special training and licensing. At one end of the scale are simple, lightweight diagnostic tools that identify the mentoree's learning style or favoured mode of conflict resolution or their 'wellness quotient' or something similar. At the other end are sophisticated psychometric instruments like the Myers Briggs Temperament Instrument, the DiSC Profile System, the Servant Leadership Profile, the Belbin Team Role Questionnaire and the SIMA profile, just to name a few. Very upmarket, technical profiling systems also exist, but in my opinion their usefulness lies beyond the scope of mentoring and they are best left to psychology professionals.

While not strictly profiling tools, exercises such as Covey's Personal Mission Statement[88] exercise, the GROW coaching model[89] and various project planning tools may be helpful. Providing a structured process, they help mentorees move beyond diagnosis to put goals and actions in place. My enthusiasm for these exercises is not as great as it once was. I still think they have a place, but should be employed judiciously. They can create an illusion of progress when all that is happening is playing games for amusement.

In the field

As a child I generally enjoyed school, but the time in the classroom did get monotonous at times. I can only imagine how tedious it must have been for the teacher to put up with all of us cooped up together week after week, month after month. Field trips were a special highlight. They got us out of the familiar context of the school and allowed us to learn in a different way. The things we did together on these days became fuel for many interesting lessons after we got back into our normal routine. Mentoring sessions do not have to be all the same. Getting out into the field together can breathe fresh life into any routine. A little variety can be introduced in one or more of these ways.

Changing location

A different physical context can open up new ways of relating and new topics of conversation. This might simply mean meeting in a different place. It might also involve planning a specific field trip to take in not only a new location but also a whole new experience together. One of my mentorees told me of a favourite place he used to visit for holidays as a child. It was only an hour and a half from where we normally met, so we arranged to go there for our next session. This led to a crucial conversation about his early experiences of God's presence in that place, and a powerful recovery of his sense of calling to ministry.

Doing ministry together

Some mentors who have ministry opportunities in various locations take a mentoree along when they speak somewhere. This could be simply a matter of observing the mentor, and later reflecting on what was observed, or may involve giving the mentoree a particular role; for example, providing prayer support or taking part in an interview or telling their story. Since I have started teaching about mentoring, I like to involve one of my past or present mentorees in the teaching sessions. As students ask my mentoree about what I'm really like as a mentor, I learn a great deal!

One of my hobbies is to play guitar, and I sometimes lead singing for worship in my own church. On a few occasions, mentorees who have been invited to speak at various functions have had me tag along as their musician. We have great fun together and also have the opportunity to learn things about each other that we could never find out through our regular sessions.

Providing assistance and making introductions

Where a mentor has particular skills or experience that could be useful to the mentoree, this may be imparted in a way that allows for later reflection with the mentor. A mentor might also help a mentoree by providing practical assistance, but this should be carefully done so that it does not produce obligation or breed dependence.

A potentially very valuable resource that mentors might choose to share with their mentorees is their relational network. Great care should be exercised if the mentor should choose to open doors, make introductions, or direct the mentoree towards possible sponsors. In the long run, mentorees are not helped by being given shortcuts into positions for which they are not properly prepared through experience and hard work.

These are only a few of the methods that might be used in mentoring. I am reminded of my Uncle Cliff, who had the most amazing workshop at the end of his garden. He would take me in there when I was small and allow me to watch him work. His array of tools was vast beyond my comprehension. It seemed to me that he had a tool for every job that could ever possibly exist! And yet, on one occasion I remember clearly, he needed to do something that required a tool that he did not have. To my great admiration, he took the cover from his metal lathe and made the tool he needed. For all I know, he might have invented a brand new kind of tool right there on the spot. That is the sort of creativity that I encourage you to develop in your mentoring. By all means gather together a rich toolbox of methods. But never let your work of mentoring be limited by the methods presently at your disposal. Create new methods as you go, always guided by what is required to identify and promote the work of the Holy Spirit in your mentoree's life.

Chapter 9

Challenges in Mentoring

In recent years I have had the privilege of running courses and holding seminars on mentoring in Asia, Africa and Europe as well as in my home country of Australia. The relevance of mentoring across a very broad range of cultures and traditions has served to increase my conviction that this is a key idea for our time. One of the best things about teaching on mentoring in such a variety of settings is hearing the superb questions that come from seminar participants. The vast majority are captured by the concept and enthusiastically start thinking of ways to apply mentoring in their contexts. Then I'll see a furrowed brow and a raised hand. 'Yes, but what about...' These are the moments I love best. Someone with a willing heart and a keen mind is about to stretch the whole group to think carefully about the practical implications of implementing mentoring. In this final chapter I will briefly examine a few of the special challenges that we have grappled with together.

Overcoming physical distance

Mentoring relationships arise in a variety of ways. The partners may connect because they live in the same city and move in the same circles. A local connection like this certainly makes arranging and conducting mentoring sessions much easier, and some of the practical suggestions I have made about mentoring sessions in Chapter 4 and Chapter 8 presume that mentoring partners can meet face-to-face. But mentoring relationships do not always come from local connections. They can also arise out of a range of circumstances that have little to do with locality. For example, a non-routine encounter when one of the parties is out of their normal context, or correspondence over an article someone has written, or meeting in a chat room online all give rise to connections that may develop into mentoring relationships.

Furthermore, when mentoring Christian leaders it is likely that at some point vocational mobility will put distance between partners who once lived close by. At that point they must decide whether to conclude their mentoring relationship or find ways to overcome the inconvenience of physical distance. Most of us know a little about maintaining relationships over distance with family and friends with whom we do not wish to lose contact. The methods of staying in touch are not especially different for mentoring, although they do require a little more structure and planning.

Where possible, I recommend occasional face-to-face contact backed up by other forms of remote contact in between those meetings. One of my mentorees, with whom I meet monthly, lives three hours' drive away. In the first two months we meet by phone. In the third month, I drive one hour and he drives two to meet with each other at a coffee shop. Each form of contact has its advantages and they complement each other well. However, at present I mentor several Christian leaders whom I see very infrequently because they live overseas. So how do we manage it? The first challenge is to synchronize diaries across different time zones. It only takes one or two embarrassing mistakes to straighten out our calculations!

Skype, a web-based telephony system, is the favourite form of contact for most of my mentorees who have internet access with sufficient bandwidth to avoid the worst lagging. With small webcams in place, it is an inexpensive form of video conferencing. The second-best option is the telephone, partly because of the expense, but also because it is not possible to pick up the visual cues of facial expression and body language. I have found that both Skype and telephone conversations tend to be more intense than those conducted face-to-face, perhaps because we feel more keenly the pressure of time.

Generations past have not had the benefit of such sophisticated ways of staying in touch and still today in many parts of the world electronic communication is either not available or prohibitively expensive. This was the case for a group of senior church leaders in the Philippines with whom I was discussing mentoring. They wanted to provide mentoring for hundreds of pastors in tiny villages all over their far-flung nation of islands. Their solution was the old-fashioned letter.

As we shall see below, for people like Madame Guyon, John Wesley and C. S. Lewis, correspondence written with physical pen and paper worked just fine for mentoring. This longhand process may be slower than one which employs electronic communication, but that does not necessarily mean it will be any less effective. We need only turn to the Pastoral Epistles to see how Paul overcame physical distance to effectively mentor Timothy and Titus by letter.

The gender divide

The personal and deep relational element, so pivotal to mentoring, raises the difficult question of whether or not it is wise to establish mentoring relationships between males and females. I call it a difficult question, although for some leaders, particularly males and particularly in Asia and Africa, the question is not difficult at all: it is simply not to be even contemplated! Yet for women emerging into the male-dominated world of Christian leadership who are searching for a mentor, there are few female candidates. The refusal of males to promote the work of God's Spirit in their lives is a factor contributing to the ongoing gender imbalance in Christian leadership.

Mentoring literature is divided on the issue of mentoring between males and females. Biehl strongly counsels against it, saying that 'mentoring relationships get deep enough, fast enough that the love individuals give and receive can easily be reinterpreted into sexual dimensions.'[90] Kraft asks, 'Who but another woman can fully understand all the differing aspects of pregnancy and childbearing, postpartum blues and PMS?'[91] Murray and Owen argue both sides of the debate, listing pitfalls and advantages.[92] Mallison is quietly supportive, citing biblical examples of Eunice and Lois mentoring Timothy and Priscilla (with her husband) mentoring Apollos.[93] Prescott and Marshall present several positive examples of Christian mentoring between men and women.[94] Shea is strongly supportive as is Pue, the International Director of Arrow Leadership.[95]

It is a fact that Jesus did not draw women into his mentoring circle of the Twelve. How are we to understand the significance of this? Is it to be taken as the final word on the matter, proving that men should not mentor women? Perhaps it's not quite that open-and-shut. We might also bear in mind that Jesus was clearly concerned to provide the women among his wider group of disciples with some level of teaching and spiritual counsel, as shown by his interaction with Mary the sister of Martha and Lazarus.[96] This is all the more significant when we take into account that such behaviour was radically counter-cultural for Jesus' historical and cultural context.

In the early centuries of the church, the Celts had no difficulty mentoring members of the opposite sex. Brigid of Kildare and Hild of Whitby are just two of the most notable of the female saints who mentored males.[97] In the late sixteenth century Teresa of Avila conducted a most powerful mentoring relationship with St John of the Cross. A hundred years later, Madame Guyon mentored François Fénelon by means of a series of letters. Correspondence was also used by John Wesley in his mentoring which included several women. One of these was Ann Bolton, whom Wesley called 'Nancy', and in whom he took a personal interest. Over a period of 29 years he wrote her 130 letters of spiritual guidance.[98] Likewise, in the twentieth century, correspondence was used by Baron Friedrich von Hugel in his mentoring of Evelyn Underhill, and by C. S. Lewis, who wrote over 100 letters to the 'American Lady', Mary Shelburne, between 1950 and 1963.

The principal objection to male/female mentoring relationships is that it creates an environment that could foster inappropriate sexual attraction. For me personally, this is a powerful argument, but not altogether conclusive. I recognize that, as a heterosexual male, I am vulnerable to sexual temptation in certain of my relationships with women. However, with this awareness I do not avoid relationships with every woman I find attractive but construct ways to prudently manage those relationships. It might be said that Guyon, Wesley, von Hugel and Lewis all used correspondence as a way of constructing their mentoring relationships so as to eliminate the element of sexual attraction. Quite apart from the fact that letter writing can be very romantic indeed, one must also acknowledge that in each of these cases, the people involved were separated by significant distances and had no other means apart from correspondence by which to carry on their mentoring.

Other, less powerful, objections to mentoring relationships between men and women also exist: that they may become a source of gossip; that men don't fully understand women and vice versa; and that they don't work because of cultural barriers between the sexes. My responses to these are: we should never allow ourselves to be controlled by fear of the false opinions of others; no human being fully understands another and, in any case, mentoring does not rely on such knowledge; and cultural sensibilities, while worthy of genuine respect, are not the final arbiter of wisdom.

Nevertheless, I am cautious. Of all the Christian leaders I mentor, a small proportion of them are female. In an initial conversation with a potential female mentoree I am particularly alert to signals that misunderstandings or role confusion may develop. If uncertain, I will refer the person to a female mentor. In cases when we proceed, I am careful to conduct the relationship in a way that is open and transparent, especially to her husband and my wife. Our sessions are conducted where we can be seen and interrupted at any time. As with all my mentorees, I encourage her to also have informal mentoring relationships alongside our structured, formal one. We do not delve far into intimate matters of marriage and sexuality; once flagged, these are referred to one of her informal mentors.

My conclusion is this: establishing mentoring relationships between men and women is not morally wrong, but may or may not be wise. Each situation should be judged on the basis of the self-awareness and emotional maturity of the people concerned, and with an eye to cultural sensitivity.

Cross-cultural mentoring

Our cities are becoming more and more multi-cultural. The church is running to catch up and so must our structures for developing Christian leaders. It may be more comfortable to form a mentoring relationship with someone from the same cultural background, but this is a comfort we cannot afford. Leaders from ethnic minorities must be able to find suitable mentors from outside their cultural group. Quite apart from the exigencies of our increasingly multi-cultural context, there is great benefit in embracing cross-cultural mentoring. Each culture has its strengths, and we are all better off if we can share them with each other, learning how to develop the special capacities of other cultures.

Cross-cultural mentoring requires awareness of and sensitivity to cultural differences. For instance, simply how the word 'mentor' is culturally understood could alter the very essence of the relationship. In some cultures, the word 'mentor' is closely related to the word 'teacher'. If, in that culture, teachers expect to initiate all contact with students and control the process of learning, the implications for mentoring are profound. Someone from that culture may find it inappropriate, or a sign of weakness, to seek a mentor.

Mentors working across cultures need to bear in mind that unidentified cultural factors might preclude an effective mentoring relationship. At the same time, certain cultural differences, once they are identified and explored, can produce highly advantageous, synergistic outcomes in mentoring. Let me offer three measures I learned from Lois Zachary that may be helpful in this regard.[99]

First, do your best to become culturally self-aware. You are not 'normal' while others are 'strange'. I recall the first time I went overseas, stepped into another culture and realized that I spoke English with an accent! The thought had never occurred to me before. Becoming culturally self-aware is like that. Through exposure to another culture you come to appreciate your own inclinations to think, feel and act in ways that are culturally influenced. These inclinations are cultural orientations.

Second, it is necessary to gain a working knowledge and appreciation of the cultural orientations of the person you are seeking to mentor. This does not necessarily mean learning a new language, but your awareness will be greatly helped by spending time in a social context that expresses that culture. This might be found in a certain part of town, or just by visiting the home of a family from that culture.

Third, good cross-cultural mentors constantly improve their communication skills, avoiding regionally specific illustrations and local idioms, and checking regularly to see if they are making sense. This is not as easy as one might imagine, and has proven to be a challenge to me even in the writing of this book.

Though these three measures sound very simple, culture is such a vast and slippery reality that it is difficult to know where to begin to identify cultural differences. Standing within our own culture, we lack the perspective required to see differences. We don't know what we don't know. Phillipe Rosinski has constructed a most helpful tool for this purpose called the Cultural Orientations Framework.[100] To get the most out of his model, you really need to read his book, but I will give a short summary.

Rosinski presents seven broad categories of cultural orientation: sense of power and responsibility; time management approaches; definitions of identity and purpose; organizational arrangements; notions of territory and boundaries; communication patterns; and modes of thinking. Each of these categories has specific dimensions which serve to describe alternative cultural orientations:

Categories	Dimensions
Sense of power and responsibility	*Control:* people can forge the life they want. *Harmony:* strive for balance and harmony with nature. *Humility:* accept inevitable natural limitations.
Time management approaches	*Scarce:* time is scarce; manage it carefully! *Plentiful:* time is abundant; relax!
	Monochronic: one activity/ relationship at a time. *Polychronic:* multiple tasks/ relationships simultaneously.
	Past: learn from the past; the present is a repetition of the past. *Present:* focus on the here and now. *Future:* bias toward far-reaching vision.
Definitions of identity and purpose	*Being:* stress living itself, developing talents, relationships. *Doing:* focus on accomplishments.
	Individualistic: emphasize your own attributes and projects. *Collectivistic:* emphasize affiliation with a group.
Organizational arrangements	*Hierarchy:* organizations must be stratified to function properly. *Equality:* people are equals who play different roles.
	Universalist: all cases should be treated the same for consistency. *Particularist:* emphasize special circumstances, tailored solutions.
	Stability: value a static and orderly environment. *Change:* value a dynamic and flexible environment.
	Competitive: success and progress through competitive stimulation. *Collaborative:* success and progress through mutual support.

Notions of territory and boundaries	*Protective:* keep personal life private (mental boundary), minimize intrusions into personal space (physical boundary). *Sharing:* build closer relationships by sharing psychological and physical domains.
Communication patterns	*High context:* rely on implicit communication – gestures, posture. *Low context:* rely on explicit communication – actual words.
	Direct: get your point across clearly at risk of offending or hurting. *Indirect:* maintain cordial relationship at risk of misunderstanding.
	Affective: display emotions and warmth when communicating. *Neutral:* stress conciseness, precision and detachment.
	Formal: Observe strict protocols and rituals. *Informal:* Favour familiarity and spontaneity.
Modes of thinking	*Deductive:* emphasize concepts, theories and general principles. *Inductive:* start with experiences, concrete situations and cases.
	Analytical: dissect a problem into smaller chunks. *Systemic:* explore connections between elements; focus on the whole.

When mentoring cross-culturally, this framework helps you to know what to look for to map cultural differences. Given this perspective, areas of potential misunderstanding may be turned into assets as the partners discover the strengths of alternative approaches.

Psychological pitfalls

I am not a psychologist, nor have I studied psychology or counselling. This is made very clear to my mentorees and I am quick to refer them for professional help when they need it. Mentors can do a great deal of damage when they play at being psychologist. They are much better off to stick to their core business of promoting the work of the Holy Spirit in another's life and to leave sorting out complex psychological problems to those who really know what they are doing. But I have learned the hard way that even when I stay within my area of expertise and refer matters that go beyond me, I am not excused, as a mentor, from having to deal with some important psychological pathology.

Transference

I had been mentoring Wes for about three months when I noticed a sudden, negative change in his attitude towards me. Our sessions became quite frosty, but Wes did not acknowledge what I was sensing. Looking back, I'm not sure how we managed to keep going through that troublesome period. Several months later, things were suddenly resolved, and I learned what had been going on. Wes had suffered spiritual abuse from a spiritual authority figure early on in his Christian life and had carried this burden with him for years without realizing it. Once he came to regard me as a spiritual authority figure, all the bitterness and resentment he felt towards his abuser were suddenly applied to me. What broke the cycle was a chance meeting Wes had with his abuser. It completely unnerved him, but it did serve to alert him to the fact that I was not the one who had hurt him. The conversations we had about this were extremely productive. I'm so glad we toughed it out through those difficult months, because Wes might otherwise not have resolved a serious barrier to his spiritual development. The thing we were dealing with is called negative transference.

Perhaps even more detrimental to a mentoring relationship are cases of positive transference, where a mentoree transfers positive attitudes they have had towards someone else, or even an ideal, fantasy person, on to the mentor. If mentorees start to give you effusive, over-the-top affirmation, the chances are transference is going on. The first thing to do is get your ego out of the way. You must be clear in your own mind: this is not real. However, it is not best to directly confront positive transference, no matter how uncomfortable it may make you feel. Unfortunately, people can become quite hostile if their fantasy bubble is popped peremptorily. Positive transference inevitably becomes negative before it is resolved. The best approach is to receive the transference without rebuttal, and channel it constructively over time. Transference can provide valuable information about a person's needs. You can limit idealization through a process of progressive transparency, revealing more about yourself as the relationship grows.

Projection

Projection is an unconscious process by which a person takes negative things about themselves and imagines that they are present in other people. It is a defence mechanism that denies awful, unbearable truths about oneself, allowing the associated opprobrium to be directed elsewhere. For example, someone who is highly concerned that the young people at church are sexually promiscuous may, in fact, be grappling with matters of their own sexuality.

When mentors are not familiar with the context of their mentoree's family, ministry and community, it can be difficult to pick up when projection is occurring. All you have to go on is the mentoree's word about the concerning things they see in people all around them. When concerns about the vices of other people are expressed strongly or repeatedly, it is worth asking some questions of the mentoree to find out if other people share the same concerns. Direct questioning on whether the issue at hand is a problem for the mentoree is unlikely to be productive. That is the nature of denial which lies at the heart of projection. Mentors must use indirect methods of disclosure, feedback and reflection to lead the mentoree towards a better knowledge of themselves and how the Holy Spirit is working within them.

Dependence and co-dependence

Many mentors get into this form of ministry because they enjoy helping others. That may be a noble motivation, but to such people I have one clear message: beware perpetual rescuing! Sometimes a mentor might step in to save the mentoree from situations that are beyond them, but these are the rare exceptions. Repeated rescuing only reinforces irresponsible behaviour. In fact, the rescuing is itself irresponsible. Psychologists have a name for that sort of behaviour. It is called co-dependence, because it assists someone else to keep doing something which is harmful to them.

Mentorees must learn to deal with the reality that there are consequences to their actions – both positive ones and negative ones. They can gain significant learning through reflection on their failures as well as their successes. This reflection is an important way of averting the dependency factor, as it develops insights of self-understanding. When reflection on failure is handled well, it will lead to frank ownership of problematic behaviour and the emotions that ensue. Then the mentoree will be motivated and ready to set goals and formulate action steps to modify or manage the relevant personal issues. While it may feel like you're being uncaring to let a mentoree flounder in their own mistakes, there are good reasons to avoid building up habits of dependency in them and habits of co-dependency in yourself. Good mentors help mentorees take responsibility for their own lives.

The limitations of mentoring

According to The Uncommon Individual Foundation, an organization devoted to mentoring research and training, mentoring is the *third* most powerful relationship for influencing human behaviour, after marriage and the extended family. Even that apparently modest statement may be claiming too much for mentoring. Although I am a most enthusiastic advocate of the value of mentoring, I freely concede that there are so many other factors operating in the lives of mentorees that it is unrealistic to advance this process as the universal tool to fix every problem. So that mentoring should not disappoint those expecting a panacea, it is important to state its limitations.

Mentoring is limited in three ways. First of all, it is limited by the people involved. Mentors are not perfect. They sometimes miss things, make false assumptions and allow mentorees to head off on wild goose chases. At their worst, mentors can be dominating or misleading. Mentorees, likewise, can limit the effectiveness of mentoring by not engaging in the process wholeheartedly or using it as a cover for seeking their own agenda rather than God's. These limitations are real, but they may be recognized and corrected. In spite of human weakness, mentoring is found to be valuable in the overwhelming majority of cases. This is precisely because its effectiveness relies on the power of the Holy Spirit rather than human cleverness. We do not discard good tools when they are misused, and mentoring remains an excellent, accessible tool for developing disciples of Jesus, especially leaders.

Second, mentoring is limited by opposing forces. These forces are spiritual, cultural and organizational. Opposing spiritual forces are with us always, and we might expect that they would stand in the way of anything that seeks to further God's agenda. This limitation begs for a fight. Cultural opposition is not nearly as strong as one might think. All over the world, Christian leaders are crying out for companions who will walk the journey with them. What cultural limitations do exist may be overcome by finding the right language to present this timeless, universally relevant biblical model of ongoing discipleship. Organizational opposition, the toxicity discussed in Chapter 3, is a real threat. If mentoring for Christian leaders is not an intrinsic part of the power structures, as I insist it should not be, then it will have a hard time gaining acceptance and validation from those structures. Perhaps such validation is not necessary;

perhaps mentoring will grow up as a grass-roots movement without official sponsorship. I hope and pray that this happens, but the jury is still out on this one.

Third, mentoring is limited by the nature of the process itself in that it lacks significant dimensions of scholarship, praxis and community. Mentoring is not designed to provide education but to weave knowledge into life according to the Holy Spirit's blueprint. Even then, mentorees may enjoy brilliant sessions with their mentor, but without a practical field of mission in which to apply the insights gained, no real progress can be made. Furthermore, the work of the Holy Spirit in an individual cannot be fully understood in isolation from his work with the whole of God's people. Christian leaders need to work out their apprenticeship to Christ in the context of community in order to appreciate God's agenda for their lives in the light of his larger agenda for the kingdom.

These limitations are not flaws in the mentoring model. Rather, they are realities that encourage us to rely on the power of the Holy Spirit rather than our own skill, to press ahead with determination in the face of resistance, and to view mentoring as one essential element in developing Christian leaders alongside formal training, practical involvement in mission and participation in community.

Taking the challenge

As part of our response to Christ's call to mission, we face the significant challenge of not only producing but also sustaining a diverse range of leaders to spearhead our efforts for the kingdom of God. We simply cannot afford to keep suffering the kind of losses and debilitation among Christian leaders as is presently the case, particularly among those who are most intent on transformational change in churches, in Christian organizations and in society generally. In this book I have presented mentoring as a well-adapted means of taking up the challenge to develop and sustain Christian leaders, helping them to flourish and keeping them in good shape by identifying and promoting the work of the Holy Spirit in their lives.

From a personal perspective, I find mentoring so enjoyable and satisfying that it is natural for me to recommend it to others, even though it is hard at times. There is no getting around the fact that to engage in mentoring as a giver or a receiver or in a mutual partnership is difficult. It confronts us with the uncomfortable contrast between our agenda and God's agenda, putting a finger right on things that must change if we are to press on in God. Not least of these is the need for mature Christian leaders to invest selflessly in the next generation for the sake of the kingdom, rather than investing only in those things that will bring a return for their own projects and reputation.

As challenging as mentoring is, I insist that it is a challenge to be taken up with determination, delight and confidence:

Let mentoring be taken up with *determination* in the light of the urgency of the need. May those called to this ministry give it their very best so that we will have the healthy leaders we need to grasp the missional opportunities that are opening up before us in the twenty-first century.

Let mentoring be taken up with *delight* because of its enormous potential for good. May both mentors and mentorees be inspired by the realistic prospect of the work of the Holy Spirit moving forward in their lives.

Let mentoring be taken up with *confidence* in view of the power of the Spirit. May we be bold enough to step out in faith that God will use us, and may God be pleased to do what he has done through the centuries, pouring out his grace through ordinary people who are surrendered to his purposes.

Appendix 1

Surprised by Pain

Christian leadership in Australia is in trouble. The level of pain and distress present in the lives of Christian leaders today is at epidemic proportions. It is well documented that there are at least as many ex-pastors as there are pastors presently ministering. The additional bad news is that a significant proportion of those who are still involved in Christian leadership are not doing very well.

Let me backtrack three years to give you the background and recent personal experience which leads me to make the above statements. Since concluding a twenty-four-year ministry as Principal of ACoM (Australian College of Ministries; a Churches of Christ theological college) three years ago, I have engaged in a combination of ministries. Initially this involved a two-day-per-week local church Associate Ministry, itinerant preaching and teaching, and mentoring a few Christian leaders. Most of my mentorees were graduates of the college where I had been. Since then an evolution has taken place which led to me asking to be relieved of my local church responsibilities (except for regular preaching and mentoring of the ministry team of that church) and increasing my mentoring role.

A significant indication of what was about to happen occurred just prior to the conclusion of my time at ACoM. I had introduced an overseas visiting lecturer at a combined Doctor of Ministry, Master of Theology and Bachelor of Theology class and stayed to listen to the first morning of lectures. One of the ministers enrolled in the Doctor of Ministry programme asked if he could have lunch with me. I knew him casually. He is the Senior Pastor of a church which now has thousands of people worshipping each weekend. He asked me if I would mentor him and his wife. I was dumbfounded until he explained that he already had a coach (to help him with what he did in ministry) but he was asking me to swing alongside in order to support them for 'who they are' in life and ministry.

He indicated briefly that he had recently experienced quite a 'flat spot' during which he had lost some of his motivation and found himself sitting in meetings wishing they were over, whereas normally he would have been enthusiastic about the issues of the meeting. With some hesitancy I agreed to meet them twice and then assess if it was worthwhile to go on. It was then decided to continue with the mentoring. These people met with a peer group of other senior pastors of large churches in that city, mostly Pentecostal/Charismatic, and they had mentioned in that group what we were doing. Four other couples then asked if they also could be involved in mentoring. I was asked, 'Would you be prepared to do that?'

Cut forward three years till the present and I am now mentoring over eighty Christian leaders from a wide range of churches and Christian ministries across all States of Australia. I have only ever asked one leader if they would like me to mentor them. The others have learned of my availability by word of mouth. I have given preference to people who I discern to be or are becoming 'transformational leaders'. The range of ministries of those whom I mentor includes theological college students, church planters, emerging church leaders, para-church leaders, associate pastors, senior pastors, denominational leaders, and Pentecostal network leaders. Approximately half are within denominational churches and structures, and half are within Pentecostal and Charismatic networks.

From the relatively brief time of three years of close contact with these leaders I have developed a great respect for the commitment, giftedness and integrity of Christian leaders in all branches of Christianity. Concurrently I have developed a deep level of concern for the general well-being and therefore the future ministry of a significant proportion of these leaders. Approximately two out of three contacts involve discussion which has the capacity to take the person or couple out of ministry. Approximately one in three of these leaders has needed to take medication for depression and/or anxiety during the time that I have been mentoring them. My impression is that this is probably a little higher than in the general population.

Considering that we have quality people with respect to commitment, giftedness and integrity in Christian leadership roles in Australia, there is a clear indication that the role of minister or pastor is very difficult today. If there is any bias in the group which I mentor compared with other Christian leaders in Australia, my assessment is that my mentorees tend to be towards the effectiveness end of any continuum assessing 'success' rather than the ineffectiveness end. My heart and my mind therefore wonder how quietly desperate many other leaders may be. I will address some factors which I have recently come to see as contributing to the role's difficulties.

The cultural context of ministry

General community issues

Within Australia, as within most Western nations, Christianity has been gradually declining. This has placed great pressures on Christian leaders to 'grow' their ministry or church, encouraged by the 'church growth' movement. Many of the major cultural thrusts in Australia are evident in our churches. Consumerism has led to people seeking the church which offers them and their family the best programmes for children and youth, the best worship with the best musicians and preachers. People will readily change churches if they think there is a better one.

Related to this is the performance ethic which places great emphasis on how well a particular ministry delivers results, with great emphasis on the wide range of skills required, such as vision, management, communication, team-building, motivation and so on. When factors such as these are combined with the marginalizing of Christianity, and therefore churches, within Australian culture and the related decline in prestige of ministry and trust in ministers, it is not difficult to imagine the reluctance of people to take up ministry leadership roles and the pressures involved.

Christianity/church-based issues

The two primary issues faced in the last ten years as a result of the gradual diminishing of Christianity in Australia are the interrelated needs for churches to become more missional and have more effective leadership. The need for more outward-focused, incarnational churches has at the same time helped to define the kind of ministry leaders needed and put increasing pressure on ministry leaders to be transformational and effective as change agents.

The urgent and important need for more incarnational, other-centred, missional expressions of church emanating from the essential nature of God/Jesus, requires leadership which is able to either forge new paradigms of Christian community (church planting and new missional expressions) or transform established ones. Both of these roles are very difficult and therefore stressful.

The pressures of church planting and transformation of existing congregations are added to by the fact that several of the larger churches or more effective church networks have now embraced the model of cloning new congregations. Thus a strong, well-resourced congregation can spring up overnight anywhere. This is not meant to be critical of this model, as it evidently is working well, but it puts added pressure on existing congregations and church plants in the area. To some extent, within Christianity, the general trend in our society is being replicated in that the really strong churches (and I thank God for them) are getting stronger, while even churches which have previously been doing quite well are experiencing stagnation or decline because they cannot compete effectively.

Within established churches there is often a clash of cultures between those who have a 'congregational' governance approach and those who are seeking to be more 'entrepreneurial' in their leadership, while hopefully remaining accountable for policy and direction to elders and/or congregation. This clash of models has led many younger leaders or potential leaders to be unwilling to become involved in what they see as essentially outdated governance and leadership models.

There is therefore, at least in the denominations, a dearth of people able and willing to be involved in the 'Senior Pastor' role, while in the more Pentecostal/Charismatic churches and networks the strong emphasis on church growth and success factors means that although more people aspire, it is very difficult to be successful. My recent experience in mentoring several senior pastors of Pentecostal churches is that most of their networking and support is about what leaders do, rather than who they are. Denominational leadership is often trying to alter the culture within the denomination to one of mission, so that at this time a considerable proportion of their efforts and resources are focused there.

In general, training for ministry emphasizes knowledge and skills areas rather than the 'being' of the ministry leaders. Most colleges do have some emphases on spiritual formation, but it is not the main thing.

The vital role of mentoring

I believe *who we are* is the basis for, and fuel of, *what we do*. This needs not only to be the foundational value and practice of colleges and churches, but should also be inculcated into leaders as a lifelong learning priority. It is when leaders are under pressure that their credentials for ongoing Christian leadership are most evident. Since the pressures are strong, if the Christian character is not developed and developing, then personhood and leadership can unravel. At one and the same time I regret both the tensions within churches, and the struggle of the present leaders to cope with those tensions.

However, I believe it will be effective leaders who are accountable, visionary, entrepreneurial servants, who will be able to be pioneering and/or transformational in ways which allow missionality to become the essence of church. Hopefully these leaders will be able to be empowering, probably along with a team, and even integrative for both the established and the emerging church.

The key issue for these leaders is the development of Christian character through Christian spirituality. This is a deep and usually a long relational journey. It will progressively result in the leader being personally secure in who he/she is in God, with a lessening need to prove worth through performance. Thus the motivation for leadership will be kingdom-of-God based, rather than personal-insecurity based. This deep change in the mainspring will mean different relationship capacity, greater capacity to express the fruit of the Spirit, more medium- and long-term resilience, and greater congruence of means and ends.

Peter McHugh, who I have the privilege of mentoring, has just written personally and powerfully about this in his book *A Voyage of Mercy* (The Hanerda Trust, 2006).

The supports Christian leaders urgently need

One way which I am sure will help is to have networks, denominations and leaders recognize the pivotal role the 'who you are' kind of mentoring can and should have. I believe that a network of mentors needs to be intentionally and strategically further developed across Australia, and across Christian traditions. A key feature of this mentoring is the persona of the mentor. He/she should be a person of Christian leadership experience who has been able to stay healthy personally, and positive and optimistic, not only about the kingdom of God but also about its many and varied expressions here in Australia. I believe there are men and women who are in the 'convergence' stage of their ministry leadership lives who can be encouraged to be mentors. These people need to be good listeners who are 'safe' because of their empathy, confidentiality and non-involvement in any structures which directly relate to the leader's security in their ministry.

In addition to mentoring, I believe Christian leaders need to:

- Have a coach for what they do. The coach is someone who is in the same type of ministry and has more experience and/or has taken a church or organization through the stage or dilemmas that presently face the leader.
- Be involved regularly in a 'Peer Support Group' of Christian leaders. These groups would major on sharing honestly and praying together. One-upmanship or competitiveness cannot be a part of these groups. In fact it would be good if they were based on a twelve-step programme, similar to Alcoholics Anonymous, where each leader 'confesses' (not as a sin), 'I am a pastor.'

What does mentoring involve?

I have embraced what might be described as a relational model for mentoring. When people meet with me for mentoring I ask them seriously, *'How are you going?'* That question could absorb us for the next three hours. I have learned something about mentoring by doing it. Early in my endeavours, one of my mentorees gave me two books to read on the subject. I read them avidly and learned a great deal. However, I have basically developed the model of mentoring which I follow by asking the above question and listening intently to the issues people raise. There is now a straightforward template which operates as a minimalist structure to the mentoring. Each of the factors is interrelated and if I were to diagrammatize the configuration of the factors, it would be like this:

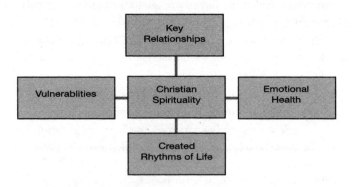

Christian spirituality

The straightforward question here is, *'How are you and God doing?'* I have come to listen for passion rather than process; to ask if the person seeks an intimate relationship with God as diligently as the seeking for food and drink on a regular basis. Christian spirituality comes out of spiritual hunger. We can then go on to talk about the means whereby spirituality can be attained or partially attained, such as scripture, prayer and meditation, Christian community and so on. But this is about a relationship rather than a process.

The reason that I would place this at the centre of the process is that the other four are derivations of Christian spirituality. For example, the fruit of the Spirit expressed in Galatians 5:22–23 – love, joy, peace, patience, goodness, faithfulness, gentleness, self-control – are the key qualities of good relationships and sound emotional health. Peterson in *The Message* brings out the relational and emotional health colours of the fruit of the Spirit when he translates the passage in this way:

> But what happens when we live God's way? He brings gifts into our lives, much the same way that fruit appears in an orchard – things like affection for others, exuberance about life, serenity. We develop a willingness to stick with things, a sense

of compassion in the heart, and a conviction that a basic holiness permeates things and people. We find ourselves involved in loyal commitments, not needing to force our way in life, able to marshal and direct our energies wisely.

Similarly, what I have called 'created rhythms of life' are often strongly related to issues of discipline or self-control, which is a fruit of the Spirit, and therefore plays into the issue of Christian maturity or spirituality. Key vulnerabilities often arise as compensations for the pressures of ministry. They are often immature, self-centred responses to woundedness resulting from conflict and so on – the Christian answer to which is healing.

Key relationships

Other than spirituality, which is essentially a relationship, human relationships have more power for help or harm than any other part of life. *'According to the opportunity, so is the responsibility'* is a biblical concept. Those closest to us, those with whom we spend the most time, are not only most likely to influence and be influenced by us, but are also the key stewardships of our lives and our ministries! The key capacities for relationships are the fruit of the Spirit listed above. When most people chart or reflect upon the most powerful influences in their lives, they invariably settle on relationships with key people.

Emotional health

Again the interrelationship between spirituality, relationships and emotional health is profound. It is crucial that we replace whatever we have expended emotionally. We need to regularly be involved in whatever will replenish our emotional tank. Even the most motivated and energetic leader will not be inexhaustible emotionally. There will be differences to some extent in what replenishes us, but emotional health will have a strong interrelationship with love and grace from key relationships and the renewal of heart and mind from Christian spirituality.

Emotional resources are closely related to the biblical concept of the heart, the Greek word for which is *kardia*, meaning 'the seat of feeling, impulse, and affective desire'. This is translated by Peterson in *The Message* as 'passion'. One example is found in Matthew 22:37: *'Love the Lord your God with all your passion.'* The emotional resources of the heart can be seen as an integral and central part of who we are.

Part of my role as mentor is to help mentorees to be more attentive to their own emotional needs. Part of the problem lies in the fact that not only do they not fully appreciate the possible difficulties, but the Boards and other authority structures to which they are accountable do not seem to appreciate the dilemma. In the past decades when ministry was being equated with the 'professions', the conditions of work for those in ministry have gradually been amended through the concept that ministry as a profession should provide employment conditions commensurate with other work which normally requires Higher Education qualifications.

However, for at least the last ten years, the 'heart' of ministry leaders has been to see their role as closer to a 'vocation' involving a strong calling, rather than a profession with employee entitlements because of training and qualification. I applaud this change, but we have slipped into an area of oversight of emotional well-being which can be very damaging for individuals, families and churches.

Created rhythms of life

God has created us according to a basic principle: 'Stop well and you will go well.' In particular for Christians this is: 'Stop well with God and you will go well.' An obvious example of this created rhythm of God is sleep. It makes a great deal of difference to the quality of the next day if we have not slept well or for long enough. It is therefore a stewardship of life that we manage the approximately one third of our lives when we sleep. But there are many other created rhythms of life.

Eugene Peterson has written very eloquently and

persuasively concerning the godly rhythm of 'sabbath' (Eugene H. Peterson, *Working the Angles: The Shape of Pastoral Integrity*, Eerdmans, 1998). He emphasizes the 'pray' and 'play' nature of having a weekly sabbatical. Most of the people I am in contact with have put this in place and observe it regularly. What has not been widely recognized is that the scripture outlines not only the seven-day rhythm with one day as sabbatical but also the seven-year rhythm with one year as sabbatical (Exodus 23:10–11; Leviticus 25:1–7). The vital resources of productive land require that there be a fallow year in order to allow it to keep producing for the long term. The sabbatical year also freed the landowner from the day-to-day responsibilities of producing and harvesting crops, which would therefore also bring refreshment for the future of their vocation. The Babylonian exile of seventy years is even expressed as allowing for seventy years of fallow to make up for what the Israelites had neglected to do for many years (2 Chronicles 36:20–21).

My suggestion is that we consider it normative for ministry leaders who are vocational in their approach to ministry to be granted, in addition to one day of rest per week, the equivalent of the sabbatical year. For the Australian context, I believe this one-in-seven sabbatical leave should be allocated between holidays and long-service leave (play), and special leave (pray); that is, an average of four weeks of annual leave plus one week of long-service leave plus two and a half weeks of special leave per year. Other contexts may require different proportions of leave. However, for Christian leaders anywhere in the Western world, it is probably best arranged that special leave be taken approximately every three or four years and long-service leave every ten years. It is important to convey that special leave is not to be regarded as holidays but as the opportunity to be refreshed and refuelled vocationally and spiritually for the next three or four years of ministry.

It is interesting to note that the scriptural principle of sabbatical became accepted a long time ago within church-run education centres and has become accepted practice in Higher Education, which is predominantly secular, while the churches have not recognized its application to ministry. The ministry leader would normally be required to submit a proposal to his/her Board for approval. A wide range of ways of effectively using this time could be invoked; from retreating through to undertaking formal professional development, or being exposed to the ways other ministries and churches operate. The necessity is that the person is not responsible for a period of time for their normal, emotionally draining, responsibilities.

Vulnerabilities

I only added this emphasis after listening to ministry leaders' stories and situations for about eighteen months. It had gradually occurred to me that one of the major potentially valuable roles that mentoring can have is that of gentle accountability. People were talking with me about what tended to be thinking and behaviour patterns which arose primarily when they were under pressure. It is when we are under pressure that there is an increased risk that our thinking and behaviour patterns will potentially undermine our leadership opportunities and capacities for the future. Negative 'self talk' can lead to leaders seeking consolation in behaviours which may be addictive and destructive to relationships and generally to quality of life.

One way in which I introduce this theme to mentoring is to ask the question: 'If Satan was going to take you out of ministry, from your experience, how would he be likely to do it? Would it be OK if each time we talk I ask you how you are going in these areas?' This gentle accountability can be a constructive restraint to these behaviours. But an important part of mentoring is to address these issues directly with absolute confidentiality.

It is interesting that although each mentoree will have a unique combination of vulnerabilities and responses, there tends to be a great deal of repetition of certain issues. In one sense we are all keeping the same secrets from one another.

In general, the process is as follows: the stresses of leadership – such as criticism, people leaving the church, and lack of effective boundaries – lead to very negative self talk. For example, the leader may say to themselves, 'I am a failure as a leader.' This in turn leads to compensatory behaviour of a self-indulgent and/or addictive nature. Examples are pornography, gluttony, and overconsumption of alcohol.

As you have read the above you may be wondering why I have not included a specific emphasis on the cognitive area of our lives. The way we think is very important with respect to quality of life and is relevant to Christian leadership effectiveness. It may be in the near future that I will add this as a sixth emphasis. My reluctance to do so arises simply from the desire to not have the mentoring times be predominated by doctrinal or theological discussions.

I mentor people with quite a wide range of theological positions, although most would fall within the Evangelical/Charismatic part of the spectrum. The reluctance I have is undergirded by my observation that rarely is theology or doctrinal difference an important contributor to the stresses and strains of Christian leadership. Every now and then it is because the belief system has led to attitudes and/or relational issues which are detracting from the quality of life and ministry. If so, we address the issues thoroughly.

I do encourage leaders to read avidly and widely and quite regularly recommend reading for devotional and/or skills purposes. It is also important for all of us to keep our minds stimulated and active so that our thinking processes are alert and well developed. Reading for relaxation and fun purposes is also potentially extremely valuable in the 'play' part of a leader's life.

I emphasize that the above headings have not been developed in a system and are not comprehensive. They are the key areas that people have talked about when I ask them 'How are you going?' The normal mentoring session lasts between two and three hours, with the latter part of the time spent checking any of the five areas which have not been directly addressed by the mentoree's response to my first question.

Giving Christian leaders a wider perspective

One of my real surprises as I have become a mentor to a wider range of leaders is how helpful and important it is for them to be able to see the bigger picture accurately. They are able, therefore, to know that they are not the only one experiencing the issues they are sharing, and perhaps able to perceive much wider and deeper dynamics at work than those present in their ministry.

I move around Australia regularly and am involved in deep and intimate conversations with a wide range of leaders: from church planters to senior pastors of mega-churches; from emerging-church leaders to denominational leaders; from those involved in strongly structured hierarchical denominations to those in Charismatic/Pentecostal networks; from student ministers to people who have been leaders for about forty years; from those whose ministries are within large corporate structures to those who are almost a lone presence and voice amongst the poor and powerless of our society.

As a result I am also asked to preach, teach and consult with the leaders of a much wider range of churches than when I was ministering in a denominational theological college. I have been on a very steep learning curve which I believe will continue for some time yet. I want to document some of my current observations, understandings, analyses, joys, concerns and tentative predictions. Many of my statements are generalizations and are therefore not to be regarded with the same reliability as well-designed research or survey work and will also inevitably have many individual exceptions.

My overall outlook for the future is relatively positive and hopeful despite the fact that Australian Christianity has been in the doldrums, and numbers have generally been in decline for at least two decades. My understanding is that relatively early publication of the general trends from the latest National Church Survey indicates that the general picture is probably fairly stagnant in many overall numerical assessment areas, but that there is a quite detectable change in some of the key qualitative areas of Christian church life and witness – for example, indicative of intrinsic indicators of commitment to following a radical discipline of Jesus' lifestyle and set of values. I believe that God has begun doing some things which will blossom very positively into a regeneration of the vitality and place of Jesus in individual, church, local community and national life.

There are negatives and some positives in the present situation in which Christians and Christianity are marginalized formally and informally from most community decision making, and even from the debate about values. The positives have to do with the fact that to be a card-carrying Christian does require a willingness to be in the minority and still be committed, as well as bringing the challenge to 'make sense' to the wider community in order to earn the right to be listened to.

The churches which are doing really well in several key areas of Christian community life and witness tend to be the mega-churches – those with over 2,000 weekly worship attenders. They are managing to attract young people and young adults to services of worship, youth events and small groups, in a way which is not happening in most smaller churches. My impression is that most of these churches are still growing. Almost all of these mega-churches fall into the general category of Charismatic/Pentecostal network churches.

These churches are also quite effective in mission and would typically have several hundred baptisms per year. They are invariably led by senior pastors and lead pastors who have an incredibly high level of commitment and giftedness across a wide spectrum of abilities. Although they have a wide range of ministries, including ministries to the poor and powerless, most of these take place in or around their very well-resourced properties.

These churches tend to be weekend-event centred and have the facilities and talent to present very professionally and with excellence. As I mentor in some of these churches, I encounter a team of relatively young, innovative, intelligent and successful people who have committed their lives to energetically and skilfully ministering in a church which has a big vision and demands a great deal in a positive way of those who lead.

At the other end of the church-numbers spectrum are the many informal get-togethers of those who are categorized as part of the 'emerging church'. If we accept for Australia what George Barna says of these people in America, they are mainly really committed Christians who for one reason or another have decided not to continue to be committed to and attend a congregation of an 'established' church. My general impression is that as a total part of Christianity in Australia this 'emerging church' segment is still growing and may be burgeoning.

My sense is that from a numerical perspective each extreme end of the churches continuum is doing quite well. It is the churches between fifty and 1,500 which are presently experiencing the major part of the problems.

In some ways these churches and their leadership are being 'squeezed' from both sides. People, because of their tendency towards consumerism, are gravitating towards the best preaching, facilities, children's programme, youth programme, worship and so on in their geographic area. These churches are also multiplying their congregations, rather than church planting, and in many situations bring all of the resources of the mother church alongside the additional congregation. More than one situation which has come to my notice recently has involved a mega-church starting a new congregation with more than 500 people, with worship, preaching and so on being provided at the same standard as for the mother congregation. You can imagine the discouragement this can be to the leaders of the churches within five kilometres of the new congregation as people see if this new congregation would meet their needs more effectively.

Churches in the middle of the size spectrum which are seeking to attract people from the community and/or Christians from other churches on the basis of the excellence of presentation, programme, personnel or facilities are feeling/experiencing stress, relative failure and discouragement. This is going to be felt more intensely if these churches are also losing people to the informality, spontaneity, warmth and frontline missionality of the emerging church. These feelings of discouragement will be reinforced if those leaving are overtly critical of the established church and its supposed introspection and institutionalization.

A part of the present situation is that both ends of the spectrum which seem to be doing quite well have the seeds of difficulty within them which may grow to significance. Within our society there are now well-documented critiques of consumerism, individualism, sensuality and materialism as non-constructive preoccupations. (Clive Hamilton at The Australia Institute and Richard Eckersley at the Australian National University are two who offer such critiques.) There is beginning to be an acceptance that there can be deeper meaning in life accomplished through spirituality, community and relationships. The idea that more or bigger is essentially better is being challenged. I am sure that the model of most of the mega-churches will thrive for a considerable time yet, but wonder whether it is going to be the predominant model fifteen to twenty years in the future.

The emerging church also has within it, I believe, the seeds of future difficulty. The emphasis is so much on lack of structure, informality, spontaneity, grass-roots leadership, that groups are beginning to rise and fall at quite a rapid rate. There seems often to be a lack of committed leadership and little resourcing for fulfilment of a vision or an accepted mission.

My wife and I were involved several years ago in an emerging-church-style home church. Our mission was to get to know our geographical neighbours and be able to effectively witness to them. We disbanded after three years because most of us, including me, were too busy in our work to spend time and emotional energy getting to know our neighbours. All of the families are now back worshipping in established churches, including the family whose children were going into teenage years and who were looking for a good youth group for them to attend.

Concurrently there are the seeds of hope and health in an increasing number of the middle churches. Recently I sat in the office of Peter McHugh, Senior Pastor of Whitehorse Christian City Church in Melbourne. He had recently experienced, through addressing some trauma in his life and the church, a greatly deepened sense of security in God which had led even his wife to say to me that her husband is a different person, particularly when he is under pressure.

He expressed to me that he would now be a different leader, and that the church could be a different church. When I asked him what he meant by that, he indicated that 'incarnation' would be the key. He said he would go back to his initial training in the helping profession of social work, and help the people to live lives of love and grace with those around them. There is therefore what I believe is a movement of God in the middle churches, and possibly also in some of the mega-churches, to engage more intentionally with the people, particularly the hurting people – both up-and-out and down-and-out – in compassionate, caring and redemptive ways. Concurrently there is also a move in some of the emerging-church groups to consider re-linking with the established church for some resourcing and leadership, provided it is non-controlling, empowering leadership.

Therefore my hope is that there is coming a rapprochement, sometimes out of near desperation, between the missionally oriented, multi-sited, empoweringly led established churches and the newer emerging groups. This is, I believe, a powerful model for the future within Australia. Part of my mentoring is therefore helping leaders to see where they and their church are in the wider picture and what God seems to be doing for the medium- and longer-term future, and to implore them to hang in there in the present very difficult times of change.

God is at work.

Keith Farmer
13 November 2007

Appendix 2

A Sample Annual Summary

In Chapter 4 I indicated that I would provide this sample annual summary to give an idea of how such feedback to mentorees might be constructed. This is based on an actual summary, but the names and places have been altered.

Fred, this summary is meant as a snapshot of the way I see you and what you have told me about your life this year, and a brief indicator of some ways forward for you. It's bound to be incomplete and, in places, missing the mark. Weigh it carefully.

Personal development

Spirituality

Your relationship with God has, understandably, centred on this year's changes. You have prayed for and experienced his guidance and provision in the move to Newtown, getting a house, finding your wife's job and adjusting to a new ministry. You have 'chased God' for the power of the Spirit in your preaching. Prayer has largely been about what to do – the servant taking orders, receiving resources and getting organized for the task. Then last month you spoke about relating to God as Father. Music to my ears. I recommend you pursue this line. There is much blessing in it for God as well as for you.

Family

I think you had great hopes that by starting in a new situation you would be able to structure your work differently so that your wife and the kids got more of your time. But it's not that easy, is it? You're still the same person and you still respond to ministry demands, perhaps even more so in a bigger church. The impact of your ministry at home is already considerable. That will increase as the children grow and become more aware of what's going on. Better get some boundaries in place very soon.

Emotions

You are a remarkably stable person, which is one of the reasons you make such a good pastor. But do you remember your disappointment and sadness last Easter? Your wife got quite concerned about you. That was a mild depression, and I think it was a learning time for you. As a pastor you are in a loss-prone business. It's a vocational hazard. You are very strong emotionally, but not invulnerable. When you are down you're liable to end up in the 'dirt', like last April. Know when to go easy on yourself.

A few times you have mentioned feeling manipulated, and how you dislike that feeling. It would be helpful for your emotional health to develop some strategies for dealing with manipulative people and other factors that stir you up emotionally. They can evoke the 'dark side' if you're not careful. Back in March you saw these as pressure points from the days at your old church which might continue to affect you in Newtown. Of course, dark-side pressures are still with you. Take precautions!

Identity

Earlier in the year you were asking God the question, 'Who am I?' You came up with the partial answer of being 'called to be oil'. You like fixing things and you like resolving conflicts. You are motivated and able to bring order out of chaos. These were good insights, but very different from the more recent ones that had to do with you finding your identity in God and being less concerned with performance in ministry. You're coming at the question from two angles – being and doing. Both are helpful for figuring out what God has in mind for you.

Vocational development

Leaving your old church

My hat is off to you on this one. You did a great job of handling the issues. You communicated to the congregation in a clear and caring way about your decision to leave and how you regarded them. You worked conscientiously within the denominational system, involving the area superintendent, and getting a moderator appointed. You worked with the key leaders, helping them make plans for the future and expressing confidence in their ability to see it through. You released people into ministry and encouraged the development of the prophetic, which you discerned was pivotal for the church's survival after your departure. And, finally, you continued to love the people and work hard even when your thoughts were tending more and more towards Newtown. You should write it up as a case study for ministry students.

Preparing for Newtown

Earlier in the year Newtown was, in your mind, something pretty close to the perfect church. Then a few worries crept in. It was hard trying to get clarity about responsibilities and terms, you became concerned about how the team dynamics would work, adjusting to a new organizational culture, unrealistic expectations, lack of support for postgraduate study, and not being made an elder from the outset.

Being utterly convinced that God had called you to Newtown, you were sure it would all work out okay. Your intuitive grasp of God's call was, I believe, well founded. But did you use it as a broom to sweep the negative issues under the carpet? Would it have made a difference if you'd looked more closely at them before you arrived? My observation is that you sustained the vision by minimizing the difficulties. This was unwise and unnecessary, since the vision was clearly from God.

Arriving at Newtown

Now you have landed in a great church – which also has quite a few problems, some of which you did not anticipate. You are having to change gear from a traditional model of ministry to a 'new church' entrepreneurial one. You have to walk the line between being influenced and being an influencer, resisting the affluent secularism of Newtown and raising a prophetic voice.

You are dealing with a large set of adjustments, and I think you are handling them very well. You have good judgment, especially in regard to positioning yourself vis-à-vis the other major players in the leadership team. But it's a steep learning curve. Be careful not to take on responsibilities that will become a noose around your neck. New boys often get the jobs that others have failed to crack, and I reckon you're a sucker for a challenge.

General ministry issues

In the course of the year it's been good to chat through issues like remuneration, pastoral care, counselling, referral, preaching, further study and lots of other issues that arise in passing. You have a great capacity for thinking through these things in a clear and down-to-earth manner. I think you could be a great help to other young ministers who struggle with such issues and often end up confused.

The way forward

Get perspective, and relax. This year has brought great change. You'll feel the stress effects for about twelve months, and in the meantime you're on that steep learning curve and further change will occur. I have a feeling that new challenges will come at you from directions you do not expect. Use your journal to get perspective on all this. Be sure to review it regularly. Fred, you need time for you, as well as time for your wife and the kids Don't skimp on personal recreation and creativity.

Bibliography

Christian mentoring

Anderson, Keith R. and Randy D. Reese. *Spiritual Mentoring: A Guide for Seeking and Giving Direction.* Downers Grove: IVP, 1999.

Barry, William A. and William J. Connolly. *The Practice of Spiritual Direction.* New York: Seabury Press, 1982.

Biehl, Bobb. Mentoring: *Confidence in Finding a Mentor and Becoming One.* Nashville: Broadman & Holman, 1996.

Brazo, Carol. *Divine Secrets of Mentoring: Spiritual Growth Through Friendship.* Downers Grove: IVP, 2004.

Clinton, J. Robert and Richard Clinton. *The Mentor Handbook: Detailed Guidelines and Helps for Christian Mentors and Mentorees.* Altadena: Barnabas Resources, 1991.

Cole, Neil. *Cultivating a Life for God.* St Charles: ChurchSmart, 1999.

Collins, Gary R. *Christian Coaching: Helping Others Turn Potential into Reality.* Colorado Springs: NavPress, 2001.

Demarest, Bruce. *Soulguide: Following Jesus as a Spiritual Director.* Colorado Springs: NavPress, 2003.

Edwards, Tilden. *Spiritual Friend: Reclaiming the Gift of Spiritual Direction.* New York: Paulist Press, 1980.

Edwards, Tilden. *Spiritual Director, Spiritual Companion.* New York: Paulist Press, 2001.

Egeler, Daniel. *Mentoring Millennials: Shaping the Next Generation.* Colorado Springs: NavPress, 2003.

Elmore, Tim. *Mentoring: How to Invest Your Life in Others.* Indianapolis: Wesleyan Press, 1995.

Engstrom, Ted with Norman B. Rohrer. *The Fine Art of Mentoring: Passing on to Others What God has Given You.* Brentwood: Wolgemuth & Hyatt, 1989.

Hendricks, Howard and William Hendricks. *As Iron Sharpens Iron: Building Character in a Mentoring Relationship.* Chicago: Moody, 1995.

Horsfall, Tony. *Mentoring for Spiritual Growth: Sharing the Journey of Faith.* Abingdon: Bible Reading Fellowship, 2008.

Hughes, Bryn. *Discipling, Coaching, Mentoring: Discovering the Hallmarks of Jesus' Discipling.* Eastbourne: Kingsway, 2003.

Irwin, Lloyd. *Mentor Training Manual.* Sydney: Australian College of Ministries, 1999.

Jones, Timothy K. *Finding a Spiritual Friend: How Friends and Mentors Can Make Your Faith Grow.* Nashville: Upper Room Books, 1998.

Kraft, Vickie. *Women Mentoring Women.* Chicago: Moody Press, 1992.

Krallmann, Gunter. *Mentoring for Mission.* Hong Kong: Jensco, 1992.

Leech, Kenneth. *Soul Friend* (revised edn). New York: Harper, 2001.

Mallison, John. *Mentoring: To Develop Disciples and Leaders*. Adelaide: Openbook / Lidcombe: Scripture Union, 1998.

Maxwell, John C. and Jim Dornan. *Becoming a Person of Influence: How to Positively Impact the Lives of Others*. Nashville: Thomas Nelson, 1997.

May, Gerald G. *Care of Mind, Care of Spirit: Psychiatric Dimensions of Spiritual Direction*. San Francisco: HarperSanFrancisco, 1982.

Merton, Thomas. *Spiritual Direction and Meditation*. Collegeville: Liturgical Press, 1960.

Morneau, Robert F. *Spiritual Direction: Principles and Practices*. New York: Crossroad, 1992.

Otto, Donna. *The Gentle Art of Mentoring*. Eugene: Harvest, 1997.

Peterson, Eugene H. *The Contemplative Pastor: Returning to the Art of Spiritual Direction*. Carol Stream: Christianity Today/Dallas: Word, 1989.

Prescott, Ruth and Peter Marshall (eds). *Relating Faith in Public Life: Australian Mentoring Stories*. Adelaide: OpenBook Publishers, 2002.

Pue, Carson. *Mentoring Leaders: Wisdom for Developing Character, Calling, and Competency*. Grand Rapids: Baker, 2005.

Rice, Howard. *The Pastor as Spiritual Guide*. Nashville: Upper Room, 1998.

Robinson, Martin. 'Developing Soul Friends'. *Church Growth Digest*, July 1998.

Sanders, Martin. *The Power of Mentoring: Shaping People Who Will Shape the World*. Camp Hill: Christian Publications, 2005.

Sellner, Edward C. *Mentoring: The Ministry of Spiritual Kinship*. Notre Dame: Ave Maria, 1990.

Stanley, Paul D. and Robert J. Clinton. *Connecting: The Mentoring Relationships You Need to Succeed in Life*. Colorado Springs: NavPress, 1992.

Tamasy, Robert and Stoddard, David A. *The Heart of Mentoring: Ten Proven Principles for Developing People to their Fullest Potential*. Colorado Springs: NavPress, 2003.

Walling, Terry B. *Focussed Living Resource Kit*. Mt Gravatt East: Direction Ministry Resources, 1997.

Wright, Walter C. *Mentoring: The Promise of Relational Leadership*. Waynesboro: Authentic Media, 2005.

Secular mentoring

Biestek, Felix P. *The Casework Relationship*. London: Allen & Unwin, 1961.

Cohen, Norman H. *Mentoring Adult Learners: A Guide for Educators and Trainers*. Malabar: Krieger Publishing Company, 1995.

Daloz, Laurent A. *Effective Teaching and Mentoring*. San Francisco: Jossey-Bass, 1986.

de Bono, Edward. *How to Have a Beautiful Mind*. London: Vermilion, 2004.

Hay, Julie. *Transformational Mentoring*. London: McGraw Hill, 1995.

Kerry, Trevor and Ann Shelton Mayes (eds). *Issues in Mentoring*. London: Routlege, 1995.

Knowles, M. S. and H. F. Knowles. *How to Develop Better Leaders*. New York: Association Press, 1955.

Kram, Kathy E. *Mentoring at Work*. Lanham: University Press of America, 1988.

Lacey, Kathy. *Making Mentoring Happen: A Simple and Effective Guide*. Mona Vale: Business and Professional Publishing, 1999.

Lewis, Gareth. *The Mentoring Manager: Strategies for Fostering Talent and Spreading Knowledge*. London: Pitman, 1996.

Maldevez, Angi and Caroline Bodóczky. *Mentor Courses: A Resource Book for Trainer-Trainers*. Cambridge: Cambridge University Press, 1999.

Megginson, David and David Clutterbuck. *Mentoring in Action: A Practical Guide for Managers*. London: Kogan Page, 1995.

Murray, Margo with Marna A. Owen. *Beyond the Myths and Magic of Mentoring: How to Facilitate an Effective Mentoring Program*. San Francisco: Jossey-Bass, 1991.

Rosinski, Phillipe. *Coaching Across Cultures*. Boston: Nicholas Brealey Publishing, 2003.

Shea, Gordon F. *Mentoring: How to Develop Successful Mentor Behavior*. Menlo Park: Crisp, 1998.

Whitmore, John. *Coaching for Performance* (3rd edn). London: Nicholas Brealey Publishing, 2002.

Zachary, Lois J. *The Mentor's Guide: Facilitating Effective Learning Relationships*. San Francisco: Jossey-Bass, 2000.

Resources for mentoring Christian leaders

Anderson, Ray. *The Soul of Ministry, Forming Leaders for God's People*. Louisville: WJKP, 1997.

Brueggemann, Walter. *Cadences of Home*. Louisville, Kentucky: John Knox Press, 1997.

Cloud, Henry and John Townsend. *Boundaries: When to Say Yes, When to Say No to Take Control of Your Life*. Grand Rapids: Zondervan, 1996.

Cloud, Henry and John Townsend. *How People Grow: What the Bible Reveals about Personal Growth*. Sydney: Strand, 2001.

Coleman, Robert E. *The Master Plan of Evangelism*. Grand Rapids: Fleming H. Revell, 1993.

Covey, Stephen R. *The Seven Habits of Highly Effective People: Restoring the Character Ethic*. New York: Simon & Schuster, 1989.

Crabb, Larry. *Connecting: Healing for Ourselves and Our Relationships*. Nashville: Word, 1997.

England, Edward (ed.). *Keeping a Spiritual Journal*. Crowborough: Highland Press, 1988.

Foster, Richard J. *Celebration of Discipline: The Path to Spiritual Growth*. London: Hodder & Stoughton, 1985.

Foster, Richard J. *Money, Sex and Power: The Challenge of the Disciplined Life*. London: Hodder & Stoughton, 1986.

Gire, Ken. *Windows of the Soul: Experiencing God in New Ways*. Grand Rapids: Zondervan, 1996.

Hagberg, Janet O. *Real Power*. Salem: Sheffield Publishing, 1994.

Hagberg, Janet O. and Robert A. Guelich. *The Critical Journey: Stages in the Life of Faith*. Dallas: Word, 1989.

Hart, Archibald D. *Coping with Depression in the Ministry and Other Helping Professions*. Waco: Word, 1984.

Hart, Archibald D. *Thrilled to Death*. Nashville: Thomas Nelson, 2007.

Herrington, Jim, R., Robert Creech and Trisha Taylor. *The Leader's Journey: Accepting the Call to Personal and Congregational Transformation*. San Francisco: Jossey-Bass, 2003.

Houston, James. *Prayer: The Transforming Friendship: A Guide to the Spiritual Life*. Oxford: Lion, 1989.

Kelly, Thomas R. *A Testament of Devotion*. San Francisco: Harper & Row, 1996.

Larson, Craig Brian. *Pastoral Grit: The Strength to Stand and to Stay*. Minneapolis: Bethany House, 1998.

MacDonald, Gordon. *Ordering Your Private World*. London: Hodder & Stoughton, 1984.

McIntosh, Gary L. and Samuel D. Rima. *Overcoming the Dark Side of Leadership: The Paradox of Personal Dysfunction*. Grand Rapids: Baker, 1997.

Nouwen, Henri. *In the Name of Jesus: Reflections on Christian Leadership*. New York: Crossroad, 1989.

Nouwen, Henri. *Making All Things New: An Invitation to the Spiritual Life*. San Francisco: Harper & Row, 1981.

Ogden, Greg. *The New Reformation: Returning the Ministry to the People of God*. Grand Rapids: Zondervan, 1990.

Peterson, Eugene H. *Working the Angles: The Shape of Pastoral Integrity*. Grand Rapids: Eerdmans, 1987.

Peterson, Eugene H. *Subversive Spirituality*. Grand Rapids: Eerdmans, 1997.

Roberts, Robert C. *The Strengths of a Christian*. Philadelphia: Westminster, 1984.

Smith, Fred. 'Conducting a Spiritual Audit'. *Leadership Journal*, Winter 1998: pp. 41–6.

Steinke, Peter L. *Congregational Leadership in Anxious Times: Being Calm and Courageous No Matter What*. Herndon: The Alban Institute, 2006.

Willard, Dallas. *Renovation of the Heart*. Leicester: IVP, 2002.

Willard, Dallas. *The Spirit of the Disciplines: Understanding How God Changes Lives*. San Francisco: Harper & Row, 1990.

Index

Endnotes

1   Matthew 11:28–30 (*The Message*).

2   'Mentoree' is the term I use for the person receiving the primary benefit of a mentoring relationship. Parallel terms in other literature on mentoring are 'mentee', 'protégé', 'trainee' and 'apprentice'.

3   Eugene Peterson, *Working the Angles: The Shape of Pastoral Integrity*, Grand Rapids: Eerdmans, 1997, p. 6.

4   Eddie Gibbs, *Leadership Next: Changing Leaders in a Changing Culture*, Leicester: IVP, 2005, p. 190.

5   Martin Robinson, *Planting Mission-Shaped Churches Today*, Oxford: Monarch, 2006, p.124.

6   Christian Schwartz, *Natural Church Development: A Guide to Eight Essential Qualities of Healthy Churches*, Carol Stream: ChurchSmart Resources, 1996.

7   Andrew McCafferty, *Report on the Keith Farmer Mentoring Phenomenon*, Brisbane: Capacity Builders, 2007.

8   Kathy E. Kram, *Mentoring at Work*, Lanham: University Press of America, 1988, p. 149.

9   Paul D. Stanley and J. Robert Clinton, *Connecting: The Mentoring Relationships You Need to Succeed in Life*, Colorado Springs: NavPress, 1992, p. 33.

10 Bobb Biehl, *Mentoring: Confidence in Finding a Mentor and Becoming One*, Nashville: Broadman & Holman, 1996, p. 19.

11 Gunter Krallmann, *Mentoring for Mission*, Hong Kong: Jensco, 1992, p. 122.

12 John Mallison, *Mentoring to Develop Disciples & Leaders*, Adelaide: Open Book/Lidcome: Scripture Union, 1998, p. 8.

13 Anderson and Reese, *Spiritual Mentoring: A Guide for Seeking and Giving Direction*, Downers Grove: IVP, 1999, p. 12.

14 2 Timothy 1:7.

15 Eric Parsloe, *Coaching, Mentoring and Assessing: A Practical Guide to Developing Competence*, New York: Nichols Publishing, 1992.

16 Larry Crabb, *Connecting: Healing for Ourselves and Our Relationships*, Nashville: Word, 1997, pp. 199f.

17 Laurie Goldstein, 'Minister's Own Rules Sealed His Fate', *New York Times*, 19 November 2006.

18 Psalm 139:23–24.

19 1 Corinthians 3:6–9.

20 Howard Hendricks and William Hendricks, *As Iron Sharpens Iron: Building Character in a Mentoring Relationship*, Chicago: Moody, 1995, p. 137.

21 Ted Engstrom with Norman B. Rohrer, *The Fine Art of Mentoring: Passing on to Others What God has Given You*, Brentwood: Wolgemuth & Hyatt, 1989.

22 Julie Hay, in *Transformational Mentoring*, London: McGraw Hill, 1995, p. 38, suggests that Janus, the Roman god of doors, might have been a better choice than Homer's Mentor as a historical antecedent of what has become known as mentoring.

23 Gerard Kelly, *Get a Grip on the Future Without Losing Your Hold on the Past*, London: Monarch, 1999, p. 54.

24 Lois J. Zachary, *The Mentor's Guide*, San Francisco: Jossey-Bass, 2000, p. 161.

25 I am indebted to Mike Grechko, whose unpublished thesis from 2003 was most helpful for this section.

26 Günter Krallmann, *Mentoring for Mission*, Hong Kong: Jensco, 1992, pp. 52–3.

27 Helen Waddell (tr.), *The Desert Fathers*, New York: Random House, 1998, p. 68.

28 Basil, as quoted in Kenneth Leech, *Soul Friend*, New York: Harper, 1977, p. 41.

29 Edward C. Sellner, *Wisdom of the Celtic Saints*, Notre Dame: Ave Maria, 1993, p. 27.

30 Edward C. Sellner, *Wisdom of the Celtic Saints*, p. 73.

31 Aelred of Rievaulx, *Spiritual Friendship* (M. E. Laker, tr.), Collegeville: Cistercian Publications, 1989, p. 19.

32 Thomas à Kempis, *The Imitation of Christ*, Chicago: Moody, 1984, p. 18.

33 http://jmm.aaa.net.au/articles/8061.htm, accessed 12 October 2007.

34 At the Reform and Resurge Conference in Seattle in 2007 Mark Driscoll presented this summary of statistics from several research sources in the United States: 1,500 pastors leave the ministry each month due to moral failure, spiritual burnout, or contention in their churches; 50% of pastors' marriages end in divorce; 80% of pastors feel unqualified and discouraged in their role as pastors; 50% would leave the ministry if they could, but have no other way of making a living; 70% of pastors fight depression.

35 Peter Kaldor and Rod Bulpitt, *Burnout in Church Leaders*, Harboard: National Church Life Survey, 2001.

36 Personal correspondence, 11 April 2008.

37 Eddie Gibbs, *Church Next*, Leicester: IVP, 2000, p. 118.

38 R. H. Lauer, quoted in Paul and Libby Whetham, *Hard to be Holy*, Adelaide: Open Book, 2000, p. 16.

39 Paul and Libby Whetham, *Hard to be Holy*, p. 37.

40 On the subject of depression, see Archibald Hart, *Coping with Depression in the Ministry and Other Helping Professions*, Waco: Word, 1984. More recently, Hart has identified the growing problem of anhedonia, the loss of pleasure, due to addictive pleasure-seeking behaviours. See Archibald Hart, *Thrilled to Death*, Nashville: Thomas Nelson, 2007.

41 http://jmm.aaa.net.au/articles/8061.htm, accessed 12 October 2007.

42 Mike Pegg, *The Art of Mentoring*, Cirencester: Management Books, 1998, p. 7.

43 Bobb Biehl, *Mentoring: Confidence in Finding a Mentor and Becoming One*, ashville: Broadman & Holman, 1996, p. 5.

44 Lois Zachary, *The Mentor's Guide*, San Francisco: Jossey-Bass, 2000, p. 100.

45 John Mallison, *Mentoring to Develop Disciples and Leaders*, Adelaide: Openbook/Lidcombe: Scripture Union, 1998, p. 37.

46 Bruce Demarest, *Soulguide*, Colorado Springs: NavPress, 2003, pp. 173–7.

47 Richard J. Neuhaus, *Freedom For Ministry* (2nd edn), Eerdmans, 1992, p. 27.

48 Richard J. Neuhaus, *Freedom For Ministry* (2nd edn), p. 28.

49 Philippians 2:5; 1 Corinthians 11:1.

50 John 10:3–4.

51 Dallas Willard, *The Divine Conspiracy: Rediscovering Our Hidden Life in God*, Fount Paperbacks, 1998, p. 349.

52 Dallas Willard, *The Divine Conspiracy*, p. 351.

53 Matthew 28:19–20.

54 Hebrews 13:7; 12:2.

55 John 4:34; 5:19, 30; 6:38; 7:16, NIV.

56 Norman H. Cohen, *Mentoring Adult Learners: A Guide for Educators and Trainers*, Malabar: Krieger Publishing Company, 1995, pp. 3–5.

57 Adapted from Lois Zachary, *The Mentor's Guide*, San Francisco: Jossey-Bass, 2000, p. 105.

58 Carl Jung, 'On the Psychology of the Unconscious', an essay first published in German in 1943, found in English translation in R. F. C. Hull (tr.), *Two Essays on Analytical Psychology* (2nd edn), London: Routledge, 1966, p. 53.

59 Paul Hersey and Ken Blanchard, *Management of Organizational Behavior*, Englewood Cliffs: Prentice-Hall, 1988, p. 204. An alternative view was cogently expressed by Stephen Covey in *Seven Habits of Highly Effective People*, New York: Simon & Schuster, 1989, but his voice is still in the minority.

60 For more on this topic, see Janet Hagberg, *Real Power*, Salem: Sheffield Publishing, 1994.

61 2 Timothy 2:24–25.

62 Bobb Biehl, *Mentoring: Confidence in Finding a Mentor and Becoming One*, Nashville: Broadman & Holman, 1996, p. 101.

63 Peter Steinke, *Congregational Leadership in Anxious Times: Being Calm and Courageous No Matter What*, Herndon: Alban Institute, 2006, pp. 8–9.

64 Jim Herrington, R. Robert Creech and Trisha Taylor, *The Leader's Journey*, San Francisco: Jossey-Bass, 2003, p. 18.

65 Lawrence Crabb quoted in John Mallison, *Mentoring to Develop Disciples and Leaders*, Adelaide: Openbook/Lidcombe: Scripture Union, 1998, p. 50.

66 Gerald May, *Addiction and Grace*, San Francisco, Harper One, 1991, pp. 83–5.

67 Gerald May, *Addiction and Grace*, pp. 3–4.

68 Fred Smith, www.christianitytoday.com/bcl/areas/shepherding/articles/le-911-911094.html

69 Carl Jung, 'The Relations Between the Ego and the Unconscious', an essay first published in German in 1928, found in English in R. F. C. Hull (tr.), *Two Essays on Analytical Psychology* (2nd edn), London: Routledge, 1966, p. 155.

70 Henry Cloud and John Townsend, *How People Grow*, Sydney: Strand, 2001, p. 335.

71 Felix P. Biestek, *The Casework Relationship*, London: Allen & Unwin, 1961.

72 M. S. Knowles and H. F. Knowles, *How to Develop Better Leaders*, New York: Association Press, 1955, *passim*.

73 Walter Brueggemann, *Cadences of Home*, Louisville, Kentucky: John Knox Press, 1997, p. 29.

74 Originally conceived by Joseph Luft and Harry Ingham in 1955, an updated version is presented in 'The Johari Window: A Graphic Model of Awareness in Interpersonal Relations' in Joseph Luft, *Group Processes: An Introduction to Group Dynamics*, Palo Alto, CA: National Press Books, 1963, pp. 11–20.

75 John Mallison, *Mentoring to Develop Disciples and Leaders*, Adelaide: Openbook/Lidcombe: Scripture Union, 1998, p. 99.

76 Psalm 119:105.

77 Dietrich Bonhoeffer, *Meditating on the Word*, Nashville: Cowley Publications, 1986, pp. 127–8.

78 Peter Block, *The Answer to How is Yes: Acting on What Matters*, San Francisco: Berrett-Koehler, 2003, p. ix.

79 Peter Block, *The Answer to How is Yes: Acting on What Matters*, pp. 38–9.

80 Erik Johnson, www.christianitytoday.com/biblestudies/areas/biblestudies/articles/le-2000-002-5.36.html, accessed 30 May 2008.

81 Neil Cole, *Cultivating a Life for God*, St Charles: ChurchSmart, 1999, pp. 123–31.

82 Richard Neuhaus, *Freedom for Ministry*, Grand Rapids: Eerdmans, 1992, p. 92.

83 Laurent A. Daloz, *Effective Teaching and Mentoring*, San Francisco: Jossey Bass, 1986, p. 215.

84 Ken Gire, *The Reflective Life*, Colorado Springs: Cook Communications, 1998, p. 27.

85 See Robert J. Clinton and Richard Clinton, *The Mentor Handbook: Detailed Guidelines and Helps for Christian Mentors and Mentorees*, Altadena: Barnabas Resources, 1991.

86 See Edward de Bono, *How to Have a Beautiful Mind*, London: Vermilion, 2004 for an introduction to these techniques.

87 Some websites worth investigating are: www.christianmentoring.com.au; www.mentoringgroup.com; www.andrewgibbons.co.uk; www.mentorsforum. co.uk; www.peer.ca/mentor.html; www.mentoring-resources.com; www. enneagraminstitute.com; www.mentoringcentre.org; www.trainingzone.co.uk; and www.oscm.co.uk

88 Stephen R. Covey, *The Seven Habits of Highly Effective People: Restoring the Character Ethic*, New York: Simon & Schuster, 1989.

89 See John Whitmore, *Coaching for Performance* (3rd edn), London: Nicholas Brealey Publishing, 2002.

90 Bobb Biehl, *Mentoring: Confidence in Finding a Mentor and Becoming One*, Nashville: Broadman & Holman, 1996, pp. 64–6.

91 Vickie Kraft, *Women Mentoring Women*, Chicago: Moody Press, 1992, p. 21.

92 Margo Murray with Marna A. Owen, *Beyond the Myths and Magic of Mentoring: How to Facilitate an Effective Mentoring Program*, San Francisco: Jossey-Bass, 1991, pp. 173–7.

93 John Mallison, *Mentoring: To Develop Disciples and Leaders*, Adelaide: Openbook/Lidcombe: Scripture Union, 1998, p. 16.

94 Ruth Prescott and Peter Marshall (eds), *Relating Faith in Public Life: Australian Mentoring Stories*, Adelaide: OpenBook Publishers, 2002, *passim*.

95 Gordon F. Shea, *Mentoring: How to Develop Successful Mentor Behaviour*, Menlo Park: Crisp, 1998, p. 83; Carson Pue, *Mentoring Leaders: Wisdom for Developing Character, Calling and Competency*, Grand Rapids: Baker, 2005, p. 12.

96 Luke 10:38–42.

97 Edward C. Sellner, *Wisdom of the Celtic Saints*, Notre Dame: Ave Maria, 1993, pp. 137–45.

98 John Telford (ed.), *The Letters of the Reverend John Wesley*, 8 vols., London: Epworth Press, 1960.

99 Lois J. Zachary, *The Mentor's Guide*, San Francisco: Jossey-Bass, 2000, p. 41.

100 Phillipe Rosinski, *Coaching Across Cultures*, Boston: Nicholas Brealey Publishing, 2003.